The Impact of Ageing

STRATEGIES FOR CARE

Edited by DAVID HOBMAN

ST. MARTIN'S PRESS NEW YORK

St. Martin's Press, Inc., 175 Fifth Avenue, New York, N.Y. 10010
Printed in Great Britain
First published in the United States of America in 1981

Library of Congress Cataloging in Publication Data

Main entry under title:
The Impact of ageing.
Includes index.
1. Aging–Social aspects–United States–Addresses, essays, lectures. 2. Aged–Services for–United States–Addresses, essays, lectures.
I. Hobman, David

HQ1064.U.5154 362.6'0973 80-24988

ISBN 0-312-40965-6

CONTENTS

PREFACE

What an extraordinary century! On the one hand an age of totalitarian aggression and destruction, on the other hand a time of growth of science, technology and an enhanced quality of life. This century has been characterised also by the extraordinary triumph of survivorship, with increasing absolute numbers and relative proportions of older people in the developing as well as developed world. *The Impact of Ageing: Strategies for Care* is an important volume oriented toward the necessity for a multi-disciplinary, multi-agency, multi-national approach to both public policy making and practice. Growing older is complex. From human nature to economics, the issues are multiple, requiring multiple responses and solutions. It is commendable that this volume takes the broad perspective, emphasising a worldwide context in which we find both an increasingly vital, robust and healthy population of older persons and a still older (close to 80) population of potentially vulnerable and dependent older persons.

What are some of the issues and what are some of the likely responses of policy and practice that we are apt to see throughout the world in the next decades and which are considered in this book?

We see the replacement of the social science notion of 'disengagement' (translation: be a good old person and disappear quietly) by the evolution of the politics of ageing, self-help movements, consumerism and family concern.

The politics of ageing addresses the issue of equity across the life cycle with the necessary balancing of needs and resources amongst the generations. It includes ballot box enthusiasm, grass roots activism and nursing home advocacy. The principal concern centres on the sovereign pact that must operate between the government and its people as they grow old.

How do we develop the knowledge base necessary for the development of geriatrics (medicine, nursing, medical social work) in its broadest sense with the incorporation of social, economic, cultural and personal issues into health care of older people? How do we broaden the importance of such a developing medicine to include improvements in the everyday care of the ordinary ailments of age, in addition to the necessary preoccupation with socially expensive long term care in institutions?

How do we overcome ageism – the pervasive discrimination against older persons – consequent to fundamental dread that we all experience by growing old?

How do we 'loosen up' our lives – add flexibility to the rites of passage – in order to secure the full potential of the middle and later years, not only to be able to cope with old age, but to enjoy what advantages there are to old age and to see that society benefits from the contributions of older people. Could universal portable pension programmes (coupled with lifelong continuing education) reduce inefficiency and prove liberating to peoples lives, allowing them to move from field to field, job to job?

Why haven't tax revolts and tax evasion in various nations gone as much against defence expenditures as against social expenditures? Contemporary worldwide spending on defence is in excess of $450 billion! Are health and social expenditures of the same order?

Is the twentieth century development of biological, medical and social gerontology – the discovery and application of new knowledge – likely to lead to a healthier and more vital old age, and to greater and greater survivorship up to the genetically-programmed age 'ceiling', or will there be the breakthrough in the extension of the inherent life span *per se*?

These are just a few of the disparate issues that are given attention or come to mind in reading this volume. All societies must meet the challenge of the vicisitudes of the life cycle. Societies also vary in their reaction to ageing from natural acceptance to frank denial. Most commonly there is unease about growing older. There is a tendency to lose sight of the connection between our present and our future selves.

By the year 2000, it is projected that 60 per cent of people over 60 will be living in the developing nations. The average life expectancy will have increased by an extraordinary 13 years, from an average life expectancy of 52 to 65. How will societies cope with the claims and needs of its older citizens? How will the old people, disabled children and other vulnerable groups fare in a world that is projected to struggle over increasingly constricted resources? Will a rationale for euthanasia be advanced? Can an alliance of advocacy and science help prevent or ameliorate the problems of age? We must look seriously at important recent reports by former Chancellor, Willy Brandt, on 'North-South relations' and the 'Global 2000' report created by components of the United States government. By responsively confronting (and not avoiding) the concerns so graphically described, we can help support the world's older citizens in the years ahead.

Robert N. Butler, MD
Director
National Institute of Aging
Washington DC

1 INTRODUCTION

David Hobman

The impact of ageing, or the phenomenon which has been described as the greying of nations, makes its mark on each society in response to different local circumstances. Nevertheless, in spite of social or economic features which make one culture distinct from another, there are sufficient common characteristics to confirm that responding to the needs of ageing communities may well represent one of the greatest universal social challenges of the remaining decades of the twentieth century. In its way, its impact will be as great as the application of the silicon chip on mass employment: both will result in unprecedented leisure; both will lead to radical changes in our lives. Either can provide the means of fulfilment or the seeds of destruction. It depends on whether we learn to use them well. If they are encountered with courage, resourcefulness and vision, they can add life to years for those of all ages. They can make it possible for the young to prepare for old age and for those who are old to relish it.

However, although there is abundant evidence about the needs of the elderly, politicians and those responsible for the formulation of policies still seem strangely reluctant to face the facts even though, as Mark Abrams confirms (see Chapter 2), the statistics are clear enough and the self-evident consequences of past neglect cloud the lives of too many older people.

In spite of the absolute and relative numbers of elderly people to be found in every community, in both the industrialised and developing nations of the world, and the influences they should be having upon resource allocation, the budgets devoted towards their particular welfare needs are small in both relative and absolute terms and the senior staff in both national and world-wide bureaucracies with designated posts related to ageing are few and far between.

For example, in the United Nations itself there were no more than two or three middle grade officers before a slightly larger team was recruited for the World Assembly on the Elderly to be staged in 1982. Much the same applies in the World Health Organisation where specialist staff with knowledge of ageing can be counted on the fingers of a single hand. In the European Economic Community (the EEC) questions of social welfare are interpreted to mean those relating to children or migrant workers rather than to those who are older – whether they travel with the young or remain behind.

Much the same applies to domestic governments. There are few designated staff and relatively little concern, so that even when, for example, mobility or handicap are under discussion the debate will almost always centre on those of working age, with little regard for older people. Whilst it would be wrong to set the elderly as a race apart, or to set the claims of one sector against another, it could well be argued that items in short supply might logically be made available first to those with least time left to enjoy their benefits. However, in a recent programme in the United Kingdom to provide behind-the-ear hearing aids the last group to be given the opportunity of benefiting from the new technology were the retired.

The argument for the elderly may be powerful and their cause may be just but, unfortunately, without sanctions their advocacy lacks potency and, with few exceptions, workers in the industrial brotherhood of man tend to press their own claims rather than those of their parents or former colleagues. Although, as it has been stated elsewhere in the *Liberation of the Elders* (Hobman, 1977), their impact as voters will increasingly be felt.

Nevertheless, in some countries, and perhaps most noticeably in the United States of America, where the President himself has a special adviser on ageing on his White House staff, administrations on ageing are beginning to emerge with a clearly defined public presence. However, in the United Kingdom there is still little more than a single Assistant Secretary's desk marked 'ageing' in Whitehall, backed by a small supporting team in the massive Department of Health and Social Security, even though the major consumers under many of its operational headings are over retirement age. They represent at least half the occupants of National Health Service beds. They reflect about the same proportion of those receiving psychiatric treatment and probably three quarters of those who are, or who should be registered under the terms of the Chronically Sick and Disabled Persons Act of 1970.

In local government too, whilst it is true that the elderly may consume a major share of the budgets of the Personal Social Services, they are normally allocated the least amount of time and personal care by the professionally trained members of staff who hold key positions. Their welfare needs are more likely to be in the hands of untrained and lower paid staff.

There are a number of possible explanations for this miss-match of resources to needs. One may well reflect the feelings of those responsible for service provision about ageing in others in relation to the denial of the process within themselves. As Kathleen Gibberd, an 80-year old retired journalist, puts it 'those who plan for our future walk with their backs to the light. They do not see their own shadows are in the way' (Gibberd, 1977). However, it no doubt also results from very limited teaching of the subject on courses for the caring professions, where it is still quite normal for the subject of human growth and development to involve extended studies covering from conception to the end of puberty, with little or no attention to the development which takes place in the seventy or so years which are likely to follow. There is still widespread failure to recognise that the period of retirement may well be longer than either childhood or a working life, and that it will be characterised by a number of major functional ability changes.

Even when limited training is available, it is unlikely to be offered on a multi-disciplinary basis or to filter through the entire academic institution as it does so effectively in those where serious attempts have been made to change attitudes amongst student populations as a whole.

Another cause for apparent rejection, or neglect, of the elderly in relation to other groups which command attention may well reflect the mores of a society in which the work ethic still predominates. As a result, the retired are devalued in common with the unemployed because of a failure to recognise the intrinsic qualities of individuals as such. Their creativity and sense of self-worth may have been seriously eroded in cultures which set greater store by the jobs which people do, by how much they earn, and what they have to show for it rather than on who they are.

But, in spite of what still appears to be an ostrich-like tendency to bury heads in the sand, there are some signs which suggest that quite dramatic changes will follow, as those who are responsible for shaping services begin to see themselves as potential consumers and recognise that enlightened self-interest (that most powerful of motivating forces) (Age Concern, 1977) will lead to the search for creative solutions to many of the difficulties elderly people have to encounter as the authors of this volume so clearly illustrate.

It was suggested at the beginning of this chapter that recognition of the phenomenon of ageing stems from different flashpoints in different cultures and as a result of particular political or economic circumstances. It should also be understood that views can be both widely negative and positive within the same communities as circumstances change. For example, an area to which large numbers of the retired migrate can bring economic prosperity and employment to one sector whilst creating headaches for another. But even within those two groups attitudes may change if a private health care and leisure industry has developed in response to disposable personal incomes which then disappear as a result of inflation.

In some countries, and here again most markedly in the United States of America, increasing consciousness about the needs of the elderly are associated with a flexing of political muscle by the retired themselves, as William Oriol, a former Director of the Senate Committee on Aging, clearly describes (see Chapter 3). But if it is in relation to politics that ageing first made its mark in the United States, it was medicine in the United Kingdom which probably led the way. Social work has lagged behind; although of course the traditional welfare services, from which modern social work practice has evolved, and the long tradition of philanthropy were always much concerned with the old and poor.

Sociologists are now beginning to pay some attention to the ageing process and to comment on the consequences of the removal of older generations from the context of the extended family, but demographers appear to have been slow in impressing this critical dimension of knowledge on policy formulators in their forward planning so that in spite of the known facts, the phenomenon still seems to come as a surprise to those who should know better.

However, once understanding about ageing begins to spread through the many spheres of influence which bear upon our lives, it soon becomes clear that whatever the starting point may have been, and whatever the local circumstances, there are a number of universal features from which shared knowledge and common experiences can lead to acceptable solutions.

These are, first, that effective responses to the needs of ageing demand interdisciplinary, interagency and, where there is a mixed economy, intersectoral approaches. No single group has the monopoly of the problem-solving process in relation to the elderly at its disposal. From this it follows that the personal fulfilment of the individual old person will depend upon a range of factors, from housing described by Derek Fox (see Chapter 5) and transport by Alison Norman (see Chapter 6) to the personal attitudes of those who deliver care services of one sort and another. *All our Futures*, Hobman (1977), attempts to put them into a perspective. This then indicates how adequacy of provisions or absence of any one element in the life of an elderly person will have profound bearing upon the quality of that person's life as a whole.

In a growing number of countries, and again perhaps chiefly in the United States of America, it is possible that the output of academic centres of gerontology have outrun the capacity of practitioners and policy-makers to absorb and interpret much of the research material now being produced. In the United Kingdom, on the other hand, there has been, traditionally, a preference for pragmatic responses and the charming belief in the infinite supremacy of improvisation, which has often led to the right solutions for the wrong reasons, or for no apparent reason at all. Consequently, there are still little more than a handful of serious researchers and scholars in ageing, although in recent years the literature has started to develop, as the bibliography by Brearley (1979) illustrates.

In the United Kingdom too, movements of the elderly have not yet achieved the powerful position they command in relation to decision-making in the United States of America. After forty years of existence, the National Federation of Old Age Pensions Associations has some useful achievements to its credit; but neither it, nor the other very small middle-class orientated British Association of Retired Persons, nor the more recently established trade union backed movements of the retired have begun to make anything like the impact of the American counterparts with their membership rolls which can be counted in terms of millions against the thousands in the United Kingdom. This may be partly because a society with its roots in consumerism is itself better able to develop dynamic consumer movements. On the other hand, the voluntary sector may have been a more effective advocate, innovator, and service provider in the United Kingdom than in most other countries stemming as it does from the long tradition of middle class philanthropy. This has characterised so much social welfare and so many reform movements until the advent of the industrial revolution when working men and women began to assert themselves politically and socially.

In the United Kingdom the major initial thrust in relation to the care of the elderly has been more closely associated with the development of socialised medicine. This is probably because of the existence of the National Health Service. As a result, the practice of geriatric medicine has grown quite rapidly leading to a number of university chairs in this new discipline being established within the schools of medicine. At only one, Southampton, has a senior lectureship bridging medicine with sociology been established. Whilst the current list of fourteen Chairs compares badly with those in other more fashionable disciplines, the growing number of consultancies established in this field is, at least, an indicator of the increasing impact which older patients are having on the health care system in what Bernard Isaacs (see Chapter 8) has described as 'the survival of the unfittest'. However inadequate the British response in relation to the size of the demand may be, and although many uncomfortable, old-fashioned wards in badly placed, isolated and outmoded hospitals still exist, nevertheless the development of geriatric medicine in Britain has attracted widespread attention from abroad.

Yet unless those responsible for resource allocation can be persuaded to divert their attention from élitist forms of medicine, high technology surgery and intensive care on which fashionable reputations are built, in the pursuit of extended life for a selected few, the lives of vast number of elderly people will continue to be associated with unnecessary discomfort, pain and anxiety.

Until there is a major shift in resource allocation, they will continue to be denied treatment and cures which could be more universally available. This would benefit the elderly as well as those who are charged with the responsibility of caring for them. In many cases the intervention through both the health and social services comes too late to change the course of events for the elderly, for their families and for the wider community in which they live.

Whilst gerontology and consumer movements are to be widely found in the United States, and the first thrust in Britain was medically orientated, it is interesting to find that it was in France with the Gallic respect for intellectualism that a movement known as the *troisième âge* has developed very rapidly from the universities and the wider field of adult education, where learning for and about ageing has rapidly gained momentum. In countries within the Eastern European bloc, on the other hand, the main developments have been connected with Institutes concerned with biological gerontology and the prolongation of life within régimes which would, by definition, probably find it more difficult to acknowledge individual difficulties stemming from flaws in the administrative, political and economic systems in which their population live.

However, wherever movements for the elderly have found their inspiration, the routes they take soon begin to converge upon common issues, as Charlotte Nusberg describes in Chapter 11. There are many common causes related to ageing being taken up in a number of countries. For example, the attempts to erode fiscal measures designed to discourage older workers from continuing in employment, such as the ill-conceived 'Earnings Rule' in the United Kingdom or in the wider debate about flexible retirement which can be heard in some form or other in almost every industrialised society.

I have already suggested in the *Social Challenge of Ageing* (1978) that ageing is not a disease, nor are the elderly in some way socially incompetent. Nevertheless these damaging views have gained widespread credence so that services which are available to the elderly are still largely influenced by the values of medicine and social work, but with insufficient scholarship to provide a basis for growth in understanding to match the technological growth which practitioners can now command in almost all fields – antibiotics for the doctors, emergency call-systems for the social workers. For this reason Olive Stevenson's presentation (see Chapter 7) provides a significant contribution, emphasising the urgent need for a coherent social philosophy and a knowledge-base from which skills can be developed, which recognises the intrinsic value of life at all ages, and which can attract professionals to see that there are as interesting prospects in working with older people as there are with the young.

Cherry Rowlings (see Chapter 9) develops this theme in terms of the day-to-day application of social work and allied services, whilst Sally Greengross (see Chapter 10) describes ways in which the retired themselves can play an active part in mutual care systems, using and sharing accumulated experience, linked with sensitive training, to emerge as counsellors and care-givers rather than simply as the recipients of professional services which are themselves in short supply.

Important though it is to build up a store of knowledge about the ageing process, and of developing skills within the caring professions based upon clearer insights free of many of the present distortions, there is still another critical area to explore. This, in its simplest terms, recognises the fact that the continued social well-being of older people, as with those of any other generation, largely depends upon the degree to which they can continue to function as autonomous personalities able to control events rather than having to submit to external circumstances which restrict the lives of far too many old people. They are frequently denied the exercise of even limited choice at the most basic levels of existence, sometimes because there are few, if any, available options, but sometimes because of lack of imagination or fear of risk-taking by those who are responsible, or who feel they should in some way be responsible for their care. However, too often, it is simply because of the old people's poverty.

In this quest for a full life, it is clear that a key factor is the amount of available income which the older person has at his disposal, as well as the distribution of financial resources which can be said to be 'allocated' towards meeting his various needs. However, any system which replaces real choice with concessions to a selected group, for example through vouchers of one sort or another, is in fact playing a part in eroding choice for those who are given these symbols of purchasing power as an alternative to or in compensation for insufficient real income.

This should not be interpreted as an argument against the development of cheap rates on public transport systems for all the community at off-peak hours, or as part of deliberate marketing policy to increase traffic, against availability of civic amenities or cheap seats at cinemas when they are otherwise empty, or for acts of positive discrimination in favour of certain groups who are self-evidently disadvantaged. It is merely intended to restate the importance of developing systems of income maintenance which give the retired the sense of paying their way so that, in the words of a factory manager who allows his retired employees to come back to the canteen for lunch, 'if they pay something, they can grumble!' This means that the income of the retired sector of the population which comes from state pension systems must be administered on the same basis as the income support systems being applied to the working population as a whole. Michael Fogarty (Chapter 4) examines the crucial principles which should underlie the income maintenance system in his contribution.

However, in considering the disposable income of the very old who may well be substantially housebound and dependent, it is still necessary to consider the range of services which may need to be delivered to them if they are to be enabled to function even within the limited environment of their home. In such circumstances, the availability of services as such will assume as great an importance as the availability of income to purchase them.

The argument here begins to focus upon what has been crudely termed *cash or care*. They are far from being mutually exclusive and both are required if the individual is to exercise choice and influence events. This is certainly true within the mixed economy of a pluralist society, but it also applies within the corporate state, because whoever they are and wherever they end their days, the elderly of the future who are the young and middle aged of today, have the right to play an active part in shaping their own lives. Then perhaps the mistaken belief that children have needs whilst the old reflect problems will give place to a more universal recognition that it is not age, but circumstances and attitudes which have the capacity both to create the difficulties we encounter and to resolve them.

References

Age Concern. *Manifesto on the Place of the Retired and Elderly in Modern Society* (Age Concern, England, 1974)

Brearley, C. (ed.), *A Bibliography on Social Work and Ageing* (Age Concern, England, 1979)

Gibberd, K. *Home for Life: Residential Care, What Alternatives?* (Age Concern, England, 1977) p. 15.

Hobman, D. *Liberation of the Elders* (Beth Johnson Foundation and University of Keele, 1976) p. 101

Hobman, D. *All Our Futures* (Liverpool Institute of Socio-Religious Studies (LISS), 1977)

Hobman, D. *The Social Challenge of Ageing* (Croom Helm, London, 1978) p.11.

2 DEMOGRAPHIC TRENDS

Mark Abrams

In the field of demography, as in many others, it is necessary to consider the world not as a single homogeneous entity but, instead, as two very different parts – the more developed regions, and the less developed regions. The former, as defined in various UN publications comprise North America, Japan, Europe, Australia, New Zealand and the USSR; the rest of the world – Africa, Latin America, most of Asia, etc. – constitutes the less developed regions. The former regions are heavily industrialised and urbanised; their inhabitants enjoy relatively very high standards of living; their dwellings and public buildings are, for the most part, constructed to provide hygenic and sanitary services of a high standard; and in relation to population size, the numbers of doctors, nurses, hospital beds, etc. are substantial.

In the less developed regions these are absent. For most of their inhabitants, standards of living are low and dependent upon the outcome of uncertain agricultural crops farmed by methods that are simple and labour-intensive; sanitary conditions for the majority are primitive, and medical manpower and supplies are scarce and usually available only in a few large towns. It is these differences which generate demographic contrasts that are so violent that one is compelled to consider not one but two international contexts when presenting and discussing demographic facts.

2.1 Differences in Total Populations

At mid-1975 the total world population was slightly in excess of 4,000 millions and almost 3,000 millions of these lived in the less developed areas (73 per cent). Over the preceding 25 years (i.e. between 1950 and 1975) total world population had risen from 2,500 millions and 83 per cent of this expansion had taken place in the less developed regions. Moreover, this shift in the balance of population between the two sub-worlds is expected to continue well into the future. According to the demographic statisticians of the UN, 'reasonable' projections of present conditions and trends indicate that by the end of this century total world population will have risen by a little over 2,000 millions between

1977 and 2000 and well over 90 per cent of this addition will be due to population growth in the less developed regions. By the year 2000 these regions will contain 80 per cent of the world's population.

Table 2.1: Total Populations (millions)

Year	World (millions)	Index %	More developed (millions)	Index %	Less developed (millions)	Index %	LD as % of World Pop.
1950	2,513	100	832	100	1,681	100	66.9
1960	3,027	120	945	114	2,082	124	68.8
1970	3,678	146	1,050	126	2,628	156	71.5
1975	4,033	160	1,093	131	2,940	175	72.9
1980*	4,415	176	1,131	136	3,284	195	74.4
1990*	5,275	210	1,206	145	4,069	242	77.1
2000*	6,199	247	1,272	153	4,926	293	79.5

*These projections are based on data available in 1978 and are 'medium variants'. In the words of the UN: 'In general, the medium variant represents future demographic trends which seem more likely to occur in view of past demographic trends, expected social and economic progress, ongoing governmental policies and prevailing public attitudes towards population issues.' The main difference between medium variants and high and low variants is that different assumptions are made about fertility rates; assumptions of higher fertility rates increase the projected population estimates.
Source: 'UN World Population Trends and Prospects by Country', New York, November, 1979.

Changes over time in total population are, of course, the outcome of fertility rates, mortality rates and migration. The last of these plays a very minor part in population changes in either of the two sub-worlds, since the great majority of migrants move within the sub-world to which they originally belonged: emigrating Europeans for the most part move to North America, to other parts of Europe and to Australia; migrants from countries in SE Asia usually seek a new life either in other SE Asian countries or else in other parts of Asia. The overriding determinants of population change arise from differences in the annual number of births and deaths. For example, in Turkey throughout the 1970s there were approximately 1,340,000 live births each year and 440,000 deaths; therefore in the absence of any migration the total population would have grown by 900,000 annually. In the Federal Republic of Germany, in contrast, over the same decade there were 600,000 births in the average year and 725,000 deaths, so that here, again disregarding migration, the natural decrease in total population each year was on average 125,000. The United Kingdom is in this respect almost unique – in each of the two years 1976-7 and 1977-8 the number of deaths equalled the number of births (since then the volume of natural increase in population has recovered and is likely to remain positive, at least until the end of this century, as the babies born in the baby-boom of the 1960s in turn become parents).

In the least developed countries (and these tend to be the ones with the highest fertility rates) most deaths are those of infants and young children. In the most developed countries (and these tend to be those with the lowest fertility rates) most deaths are those of elderly people; for example, in the United Kingdom nowadays three-quarters of all deaths are those of people aged 65 or more. In the LDRs 40 per cent of all deaths occur to children under 5 years of age.

The outcome of these diverse movements in births and deaths show themselves in two summarising series of statistics – life expectation rates and the incidence of different age groups in the population.

2.2 Differences in the Life Expectation Rates

In the more developed areas the average male baby can expect to live approximately 70 years and the female baby to approximately 75 years. In the countries of the less developed areas the comparable figures are much lower for both sexes with the average male baby having a life expectation of little more than 40 years and for the average female baby the figure is rarely more than 45 years. Table 2.2 gives life expectation rates for various countries selected at random from the two sub-worlds. They are calculated at mortality rates that prevailed over the years 1970 to 1975. It will be seen that in all eleven countries the average woman outlives the average man; this consistency suggests that in longevity there is a biological factor related to sex.

2.3 Differences in Age Composition

The very high fertility rates in the less developed countries ensure that, in spite of high mortality rates among infants and children, in the overall population in these regions in 1975 the ratio of children aged 14 or less to adults aged 65 or over was over 10 to 1; while in the more developed regions the ratio of children to elderly people was little more than 2 to 1. These, of course, are averages for very large areas. Even more striking contrasts are found if we consider smaller entities. Thus, in South East Asia (Indonesia, Burma, etc.) the ratio of children to elderly adults was 15 to 1, and those under 15 years of age were well over 40 per cent of the total population. The contrasting situation is found in northern and western Europe where the comparable ratio was little more than 1½ to 1, and where those aged 65 or more constituted one-seventh of the total population.

Table 2.2: Years of Life Expectation at Birth (1970-5)

More developed		Males	Females
N. America:	Canada	69.3	76.4
	USA	68.7	76.5
Europe:	Bulgaria	68.7	73.9
	Netherlands	72.0	78.4
Oceania:	New Zealand	68.6	74.6
USSR		64.0	74.0
Less developed			
Africa:	Ivory Coast	41.9	45.1
	Senegal	39.4	42.5
S. America:	Paraguay	60.3	63.6
Asia:	Afghanistan	39.9	40.7
	Saudi Arabia	44.2	46.5

Source: *UN Demographic Year Book for 1978*, New York, 1979.

In many northern and western European countries currently (1980) the proportion of the populated aged 65 or more is around 14½ per cent and this is five times greater than the 2.9 per cent that is found in most African and Arab countries.

Using the assumptions of its 'medium variant' calculations the UN statisticians have provided population projections for the years 1985 and 2000. Since a country where in 1975 40 per cent of all people were under 15 years of age is bound to produce a great many young capable of being parents in the final quarter of this century, it is not surprising that even by the end of this century the number of children in the less developed regions will still greatly outnumber those aged 65 or more. What is perhaps surprising is that over the same 25 years the proportion of elderly people in the populations of the more developed regions are not expected to increase by much; presumably this is because, as we shall show later, over the past 20 years life expectation for people aged 65 or more has not shown any appreciable increase and there are at the moment no grounds for believing that medical science is about to achieve any advances which will, on a mass scale, fend off the main 'killers' of the elderly – heart disease, cancers and strokes.

Table 2.3: Percentage Distribution of Population, by Age Group, 1975

	0-14 %	15-64 %	65+ %		Ratio children to each old person
More developed regions	24.8	64.6	10.6	= 100%	2.3
Less developed regions	40.6	55.6	3.8		10.7
World	36.4	58.0	5.6		6.5
Less developed sub-regions	0-14 %	15-65 %	65+ %		Ratio children to each old person
Arab countries (e.g. Iraq, Jordan)	46.0	50.9	3.1	= 100%	14.8
Africa	44.7	52.3	3.0		14.9
Western South Asia	43.6	52.6	3.7		11.8
SE Asia (e.g. Indonesia, Burma)	43.4	53.7	2.9		15.0
South Asia	43.1	53.9	3.0		14.4
Middle S Asia (e.g. India, Pakistan)	42.8	54.2	2.9		14.8
Latin America	41.8	54.3	3.9		10.7
China	34.9	59.8	5.3		6.6
More developed sub-regions	%	%	%		
Oceania (Australia, NZ, etc.)	28.0	63.3	8.7	= 100%	3.2
USSR	26.1	65.0	8.9		2.9
Southern Europe (Spain, Italy, etc.)	25.8	63.5	10.7		2.4
N America	25.2	64.5	10.3		2.4
Japan	24.3	67.8	7.9		3.1
Eastern Europe	23.3	65.3	11.4		2.0
Northern Europe (inc. UK)	23.3	63.0	13.7		1.7
Western Europe (France, Germany, etc.)	22.9	63.4	13.6		1.7

Source: 'UN World Population Trends and Prospects', New York November, 1979.

Table 2.4: Percentages of Total Population in Certain Age Groups 1975-2000

	Age 0-14			Age 65+			Ratio children to each elderly person		
	1975 %	1984 %	2000 %	1975 %	1985 %	2000 %	1975 %	1985 %	2000 %
More developed	24.8	22.3	21.5	10.6	11.2	13.2	2.3	2.0	1.6
Less developed	40.6	38.2	34.4	3.8	4.0	4.6	10.7	9.6	7.5
World	36.4	34.4	31.8	5.6	5.7	6.3	6.5	6.0	5.0

Source: 'UN World Population Trends 1950-2000', New York, November, 1979.

On these projections (see Table 2.4) for the year 2000 there will be some parts of the less developed regions where the proportion of elderly people in the total population will still be less than 4 per cent (Africa, South Asia, India, Pakistan and the Arab countries of the Middle East) and correspondingly these areas will still contain very high proportions (approximately 40 per cent) of infants and young children. In the same year even in the more developed regions there will be few countries where the proportion of the population aged 65 or more will have passed the 14 per cent mark – the exceptions will be Japan and the non-communist countries of Europe, and even here the ratio will usually fail to reach 15 per cent. In part this will be due to the fact that even in many of the most developed countries life expectation rates for men who have reached the age of 60 seem to have reached a peak in 1950 and stayed there and only for women have there been significant increases. Some examples of these trends are shown in Table 2.5.

Table 2.5: Years of Life Expectancy at Age 60 in 1950, 1960 and 1970

	Males			Females		
	1950	1960	1970	1950	1960	1970
Denmark	17.1	17.3	17.1	17.9	19.0	20.6
England and Wales	14.8	15.1	15.3	18.1	19.0	19.9
Sweden	17.4	17.3	17.7	18.6	19.6	21.1
Netherlands	17.5	17.7	16.7	18.2	19.5	20.7
Fed. Rep. Germany	16.2	15.5	15.0	17.5	18.5	18.8
Switzerland	15.7	17.1	16.3	17.8	19.8	19.6
Italy	16.0	16.2	16.4	17.5	18.2	19.6

Source: Pierre Guilmot and Monique Renaerts: Demographic Introduction to Council of Europe Seminar on Implications of a Stationary Population, 1976.

One consequence of these sex differences in life expectations is that in almost every country – less developed as well as more developed – elderly women outnumber elderly men. Some examples taken from various less-developed and more-developed regions are given in Table 2.6. In this table the elderly are regarded as people aged 60 or more. For this large age group, in twelve of the thirteen countries studied, the number of women exceeded the number of men (the one exception was Malaysia). The highest ratio of women to men was found in the USSR and this presumably reflects the very large number of male casualties in World War II. The same explanation accounts for the very high proportion of elderly women to men in West Germany (165 to 100). A more typical picture of the position in the more developed regions was given for the four next areas – England and Wales, Italy, the Netherlands and the United States where, broadly, the number of elderly women exceeded the number of elderly men by 33 per cent.

In the remaining countries – mainly less-developed areas – the excess of elderly women over elderly men was of the order of 15 per cent.

For the old elderly (i.e. those aged 75 or more) there was with one exception (Israel) an even greater gap between the number of men and of women, with the latter in some cases exceeding the former by 2 to 1 or nearly 2 to 1 – the USSR, England and Wales, West Germany, the USA and Italy. Even where the numerical gap was smaller it was often such that the number of old elderly women exceeded the number of old elderly men by between 20 and 35 per cent.

One abrupt way of summarising the differences in age composition between the two sub-worlds is as follows. In 1980 the more-developed regions contained one-quarter of the world's total population, but they accounted for half the world's 250 million men and women aged 65 or more and for three-quarters of the 85 million aged 75 or more.

2.4 Some Consequences

2.4.1 Economic

One hundred years ago (in 1881) the German Emperor, guided by Bismarck in an address to the Reichstag declared that 'those who are disabled from work by age . . . have a well-grounded claim to greater care from the state than has hitherto been their share'; and in 1889 Germany pioneered state old-age pensions. The funds were provided by compulsory levies on workers, employers, and the state, and the pensions became due at the age of 70. Fifteen years later the German example was followed by New Zealand, and stimulated in part by this colonial initiative, Britain introduced legislation along similar lines.

Table 2.6: Ratios of Women to Men Among the Elderly (thousands)

	Year	Total population	All aged 60 or more as % of pop.	Among 60+ Ratio women to men	Among 75+ Ratio women to men
USSR	1973	249,747	12.7	213	246*
W Germany	1977	61,400	19.7	165	204
England and Wales	1976	49,184	20.0	143	219
Italy	1977	56,323	17.5	132	171
Netherlands	1977	13,856	15.4	131	157
USA	1977	216,332	14.8	130	175
Paraguay	1975	2,647	5.2	117	132
Zambia	1977	5,302	4.1	116	129
Bulgaria	1976	8,759	16.0	114	136
Morocco	1973	16,165	4.2	111	123
Iraq	1973	10,473	5.3	110	114*
Israel	1977	3,613	11.7	109	100
Malaysia	1976	10,242	5.6	99	113

*Men and women aged 70 or more.
Source: *UN Demographic Year Book for 1978*, New York, 1979.

By now pensions for the elderly – usually available at ages between 60 and 65 – are part of the fiscal and welfare system throughout the more developed regions. Their generosity varies from country to country but the British situation can be regarded as a reasonable average. In 1978 almost 8½ million British people (out of a total population of 56 million) were receiving, from the state, retirement or old persons' pensions. In that year, according to the official Family Expenditure Survey, weekly expenditure of the average household consisting of a retired man and his wife, and where at least three-quarters of the total income of the household was derived from national insurance retirement and similar pensions,[1] amounted to slightly under £38; and this was less than half (45 per cent) of the weekly expenditure of the average non-retired household consisting of a man and his wife.

The same survey provides a detailed account of how people adjust to the poverty that even in a relatively affluent welfare state is usually the consequence of reaching the 'official' retirement age (see Table 2.7).

Table 2.7: Weekly Expenditure by Households of one Man and one Woman, 1978

	(a) Retired and mainly dependent on state pension	(b) Not retired	(a) as % of (b)	Absolute 'saving'
Average age head of household	72	48		
Commodity or service	£	£	%	£
Housing	5.84	12.87	45	7.03
Fuel, light, power	4.23	4.67	91	0.44
Food	13.23	18.01	73	4.78
Alcohol	1.29	4.49	29	3.20
Tobacco	1.70	2.80	61	1.10
Clothing, footwear	2.70	6.68	40	3.98
Durable household goods	1.22	6.67	18	5.45
Other goods	2.70	6.25	43	3.55
Transport, vehicles	2.30	13.33	17	11.03
Services	2.60	8.93	29	6.33
Miscellaneous	0.03	0.46	7	0.43
Total	£37.83	£85.17	45	£47.34

The very large difference between the two households in expenditure on housing is in part due to the fact that over half (57 per cent) the poor elderly live in subsidised municipal dwellings, while half the non-retired are owner-occupiers and two-thirds of these are still repaying their mortgages. A second reason springs from the fact that many of the poor elderly occupy dwellings which are old, in poor condition, and often small.

But the biggest 'saving' achieved by the poor elderly is their very limited expenditure on transport – both public and private. It is true that they do not have to spend money on travelling to and from work, but the bulk of their transport economy arises from their limited use of trains, buses and aeroplanes for leisure and social purposes; and only one-third have a car.

Apart from the £10 a week 'saved' by the elderly poor household on transport a further £10.65 'saving' is achieved by cutting back ruthlessly on the discretionary expenditure that the average household takes for granted – an occasional meal in a restaurant, a holiday away from home, a visit to a cinema or theatre, a colour television set, etc.

In addition to their other losses the elderly poor, at least in Great Britain, lose much of their significance and status as consumers and thus lose the raw material on which a good deal of everyday conversation and discussion is based in an affluent society (see Table 2.8).

Table 2.8: Weekly Leisure Spending by Households of 1 Man and 1 Woman

	Elderly poor £	Not retired £
Meals out	0.32	3.01
TV, radio, musical goods	0.15	0.81
Sports and travel goods, etc.	0.08	1.03
Books, magazines, etc.	0.85	1.39
Photographic and optical goods	0.02	0.35
Seeds, plants, etc.	0.21	0.43
Animal and pets	0.20	0.64
Cinema, theatre, etc.	0.08	0.72
TV licence and rentals	0.75	1.06
Hotel and holidays, etc.	0.61	4.02
Betting losses	0.23	0.69
Total	£3.50	£14.15

From time to time it is claimed that even the present modest economic circumstances of the elderly in the more developed countries is threatened by demographic changes making for a decline in the proportion of the total population that constitutes the working population – broadly, those aged 15 to 64. On this definition of the working population these fears are groundless. Current and expected trends in birth-rates indicate that any increase in the proportion of elderly people will be offset by the decline in the proportion of children in the population; and this is true for both more-developed and less-developed regions. The necessary economic adjustments may be slow, since schools cannot be transformed into day centres for the elderly overnight nor can primary school teachers be easily persuaded to retrain as nurses in geriatric wards. Occupational shifts of this kind are most likely to come about through the natural wastage of manpower in some jobs and differences in rates of recruitment to them; but, whatever the means, all the projections indicated that in 1975 in the more-developed regions those aged 15 to 64 outnumbered the rest by 1.82 to 1; in the year

2000 the comparable ratio will be slightly higher at 1.88 to 1. In the less-developed regions the improvement will be even greater: the ratio of economically active to dependants will have grown from 1.28 to 1 in 1975 to 1.56 to 1 in the year 2000. If in either sub-world the economic condition of the elderly fails to improve over the next twenty years it will not be because of any deterioration in the demographic composition of the population.

2.4.2 Health, Mobility and Self-care

The widespread use of the age of 65 as the point when people normally qualify for both state and private pensions has had one regrettable consequence: the great majority of age-related statistics lump all those aged 65 or more into a single age-band and they are commonly regarded as 'old people'. This is particularly unfortunate where health statistics are concerned, since even casual observation suggests that in health, mobility and self-care ability there are considerable differences between a person aged 65 and one aged 80. In an attempt to break away from unrealistic and fixed chronological definitions of old people, it has been suggested that they should be defined as those who have reached or passed the age when average life expectation is approximately 10 years. Currently this is 70 for men and 75 for women in Great Britain and probably the same is true for most parts of the more-developed world. We would therefore in the light of these figures expect to find throughout the more-developed regions that most men and women in their late sixties are generally in good health, are able to get out and about without any help and are fully capable of looking after themselves. We would expect to find small but significant decrements in these conditions among those in their early- and mid-seventies and only among those over the age of 75 would there be widespread ill-health, immobility and the need for regular and frequent support in even the simplest processes of self-care. Certainly this is the picture that emerges from the survey carried out in 1976 in England on behalf of the Department of Health and Social Security,[2] among a sample of 2,622 people aged 65 or more who were not either permanently or temporarily institutionalised.

In terms of mobility the survey found that at the time of the interviews at least 90 per cent of those under 75 years of age had no difficulty in getting out and about without any assistance, but that this ability then declined steadily with increasing age so that among those aged 80 or more less than two-thirds were able to get out without any assistance; over 15 per cent were permanently either bedfast or housebound (see Table 2.9).

Table 2.9: Personal mobility, by Age, England, 1976

	Age				
Mobility	65-69	70-74	75-79	80-84	85 & over
	%	%	%	%	%
Bedfast or housebound permanently	1.1	2.5	5.9	11.5	20.6
Bedfast or housebound temporarily	1.5	2.0	4.6	4.8	6.7
Goes out, with assistance	3.2	6.6	9.6	12.5	26.8
Goes out, without assistance	94.2	88.9	79.9	71.2	45.9
Total	100.0	100.0	100.0	100.0	100.0

When respondents were asked 'Would you say in general you enjoy good health or not' the same age-related decline emerged: as many as 83 per cent of all those aged 65 to 69 described their 'health in general' as good; beyond that age this proportion fell steadily so that among those aged 80 or more only two-thirds expressed this attitude. And it would appear that many in this latter age group were taking an optimistic view of their health: nearly 40 per cent said they could not take a bath on their own; and in addition to those bedfast and housebound almost 30 per cent said they could not use public transport without physical help from someone, and 15 per cent could not cope with steps and stairs without help. Indeed, when asked about specific ailments and disabilities (e.g. arthritis, rheumatism, strokes, blindness, etc.), then apart from the bedfast and housebound, only 32 per cent of the women aged 75 or more said they did not suffer from any of them.[3]

Throughout the more developed regions it is the number of those aged 80 or more who, over the next 20 years, will be growing most rapidly; in the UK, for example, it is expected their numbers will increase by almost 25 per cent between 1980 and the end of the century to reach a total of well-over 3½ million; over the same period the total population of the country will probably increase by no more than 4 per cent.

In its recent publication 'A Happier Old Age', p. 36, the English Department of Health and Social Security reported that already those over 75 years of age occupy nearly a third of all hospital beds in the country and that in hospitals specifically concerned with mental illness at all ages, over a quarter of all beds are occupied by patients over 75.

Clearly the ageing of the elderly population in the more developed countries will from now on demand a considerable increase in the human and material resources devoted both to their care in hospitals and in other institutions for the elderly and to their non-institutional care undertaken by doctors, statutory social workers, voluntary social workers, relatives and friends. There is no satisfactory method of measuring in monetary terms the contribution made by voluntary workers, relatives and friends but, according to the Department of Health and Social Security, within the government-provided 'health and personal social services the average cost of care and treatment of a person aged over 75 is seven times that of a person of working age'.

Notes

1. These constituted nearly two-thirds (64 per cent) of all retired households consisting of one man and one woman.
2. 'The Elderly at Home' by Audrey Hunt, HMSO, London, 1978. The sample excluded all those in institutional care; among those aged 80 or more this is about 15 per cent at any point of time.
3. In addition, over 20 per cent of all those aged 80 or more are affected by dementia and at least two-thirds of these have serious symptoms; a minority – possibly no more than one-third of the seriously demented are in long-term institutional care; the rest are cared for at home – usually by an elderly spouse or by elderly offspring.

3 AGEING AS A POLITICAL FORCE

William E. Oriol

Older persons tend to regard political systems and politicians very much as other age groups do. Some eschew a direct role in the governmental process, the better to condemn decisions made by 'those in power'. Others may be so pervasively involved in political action that it becomes the most absorbing interest in their lives. Others may maintain a polite interest in a few issues of general interest, and a fierce interest in those matters which have pocketbook or personal importance.

At the same time, however, relationships among governments and older persons in any nation take on a special characteristic because of the fact that public policy impinges, for better or for worse, on life's essentials in the later years: the level and certainty of retirement income, the availability of appropriate living and care arrangements in the event of long-term disability or illness, even the esteem in which the elderly are held.

Much therefore depends on the mutual understanding of government and the increasingly large number of persons in advanced years who in most of the nations of the world are increasing proportionately as well as numerically.

Ageing as a political force is a highly visible feature of the governmental scene in the Unites States. Once the primary purpose of advocates there for the elderly was simply to depict the elderly as a problem group requiring widespread attention and direct government intervention of almost an emergency nature. As the 1980s began, however, the need is for sustained commitment to face the challenge of grand designs said to be in the best interest of older persons. The suitability of such designs needs to be approved by the older persons themselves.

The potential balking by the so called beneficiaries of public policy need not, however, be negative. In fact it is essential for the healthy growth and channelling of interest by government into the well-being of persons considered to be old.

3.1 A Brief History: US Public Response to Ageing

What are the problems with which the government has struggled in the United States and what are the political realities which have already caused alterations in the patterns of political response within recent years? Answers are to be found in the historical origins of national policy development related generally to ageing since 1930 and specifically to several issues undergoing rapid change nearly a half-century later.

3.1.1 Early Action: The Social Security Breakthrough

One of the most striking facts about social security in the United States is that it took a depression to end the long struggle for its enactment. And even then the resentment of its critics was deepfelt and often harsh. The common warning was that regimentation was not far away if millions of working people were to be given numbers in a plan *compelling* them to give up part of their pay over a period of years. As finally enacted in 1935, the Social Security Act was about 50 years later than the social insurance programme established in Germany, and about three decades later than in the United Kingdom and other European states.

Historian W. Andrew Achenbaum has traced the growing perception of old age in the United States as a 'national problem'.[1] He shows that researchers early in this century tended to accept negative notions about loss of ability among older persons to keep up with the rest of society. The job market reflected this bias; earnings declined after the age of 55 during the first few decades of this century. For women, 'older worker' status was conferred unofficially but extensively at a comparatively young 35. Widely varying estimates as to the number of older Americans in the 1920s who could not support themselves ranged from 40 per cent to 67 per cent. But the difficulties of early advocates for economic security in the later years of life proved fruitless until their goal became a rather modest provision in a legislative package dominated by the launching of an unemployment compensation system. The significance of Social Security far transcended the dollar amounts and sparse coverage of the first enactment, which Achenbaum regards as a crucial watershed:

> It opened a new chapter in the history of old age in the US by establishing the first nationwide institutional structure to assist older Americans. Large-scale organizations henceforth played an independent and significant role in transforming popular

attitudes about the elderly's status and in generating new ideas about the physical, mental, psychological, and behavioral aspects of senescence. They also provided or led to the establishment of unprecedented options for those who were old as well as for those preparing for their old age, and thereby affected the aged's actual status in society. The creation and subsequent expansion of governmental bureaucracies, private agencies, and professional bodies to deal with the elderly's problems at the national level, in fact, have been instrumental in shaping many of the distinctive features of growing old in America today.

But as former US Social Security Commissioner Robert Ball has written, it took a long time for most people in the United States to receive effective retirement protection under Social Security.[2] Only 6 million persons, less than 15 per cent of the work-force, were covered at first. By 1950 only about a quarter of all older people were protected; and by 1960, only 70 per cent had protection. Benefits were not lavish; the United States Senate reported in that same year that the average monthly payment was $74. It further stated that almost three-fifths of the nation's older citizens had less than $1,000 annual income.

Yet in a report which for the first time documented the statement that the elderly of the nation were 'disadvantaged to an almost unique degree', a Senate study group posed as its primary legislative goal not the raising of social security benefits, but the financing of the provision of health services including hospitalisation, outpatient laboratory diagnosis, skilled nursing home care, home health sevices, and essential medications.[3] The means to finance such protection would be the social insurance principle established in 1935. The Senate report was based not only on the advice of experts but also in 'on-the-spot' testimony taken in many parts of the nation. It evoked the recurring fear of elderly witnesses that catastrophic or chronic illness would wipe out their savings and drain the resources of younger family members.

3.1.2 The Struggle for Medicare

The legislation which was to establish a social insurance base for many of the health costs facing older Americans became known as Medicare. It was enacted in 1965 only after often bitter debate similar in tone to that which 30 years before had condemned social security. Warnings against regimented health care were common; physicians foresaw the end of the private practice of medicine.

A number of events and trends helped to overcome such opposition.

John F. Kennedy, in his uphill election campaign of 1960, pledged his support for a Bill encompassing Medicare principles at a dramatic rally in New York City's Madison Square Garden attended by large numbers proudly calling themselves 'Seniors for Kennedy'. The official Democratic recognition of this activist group, incidentally, was delayed at first by sceptical Democratic political experts who had little faith in the liberalism of older voters. After the election, organised labour was instrumental in the organisation of the forceful National Council of Senior Citizens.

In addition, a 1961 White House Conference on Aging provided another focal point for the rallying of support for Medicare. And what had been the small study subcommittee in Congress on the problems of the ageing and the aged was transformed into a large fact-finding Special Committee on Aging (cq) which became increasingly potent in the many skirmishes and near-victories preceding the final Medicare approval.

But this did not occur until 1965, when President Lyndon Johnson exerted priority attention to it as a centre-piece of his social legislation.

One astute observer and moulder of the political power of older persons believes that large numbers of the elderly were unmoved and even uninterested in the struggle for Medicare. Charles Odell, who had a leading role in the organisation of retiree units of the United Automobile Workers labour union, said in 1961 that polls clearly indicated that the cutting edge of the movement for Medicare was among the middle-aged who apparently had a clear understanding of the difficult choices between the medical bills of their aged parents and the educational, food and shelter bills of their teenage children.[4]

Yet in the same speech, Mr. Odell also saw a need to maintain and broaden the fledgling effort to enlist older voters in causes of direct importance to them:

> There cannot be adequate social progress made in behalf of the aged unless they themselves are actively enlisted in the cause. Those of us who represent what (have been called) 'respectable organizations' therefore have a responsibility not only to maintain our respectability but to become ever more respectful of the innate good sense and responsiveness of an educated, politically alert, and informed senior citizenry.

3.1.3 A Federal Agency on Ageing

The involvement factor of which Odell spoke became more pronounced as the 1960s advanced. Not as noticeable as Medicare, but more directly representative of an issue springing directly from spokespersons for the elderly, was the enactment of the Older Americans Act, also in 1965. The need to establish a special unit in the Federal Government had been sought for some years by members of the House of Representatives. But equally important was support by major organisations. The chief actors were:

(1) The National Council of Senior Citizens (NCSC) which by 1965 had become a fast-growing organisation appealing in particular to labour union retiree groups and social clubs.

(2) American Association of Retired Persons (AARP) which had differed significantly on Medicare from the NCSC position, but which was a staunch advocate of a strong unit on ageing in the Federal Government. AARP had begun to build its huge membership in the late 1950s in what was originally a subsidiary relationship to a retired teachers organisation having its roots in California. But soon the AARP was outstripping its parent organisation.

(3) The National Council on the Aging which began its work in 1950 under a different name, but picked up sharply in public policy impact soon after the 1961 White House Conference on Aging. Unlike NCSC and AARP, with their large memberships drawing directly from the older population, NCOA was an advocacy, research and technical assistance organisation which enlisted organisations and professionals in the field.

These organisations became increasingly effective not only in providing advocates to testify in the Congress and to approach members of the Congress as constituents in their own Districts of States, but in developing concepts which were to broaden the base of public policy affecting the well-being of older Americans. The NCSC, for example, became an authoritative source of information about community employment service programmes designed to channel the experience and talents of persons 55 and over into part-time work with strong public goals. The NCOA, concerned about under-representation of the elderly among those served by the 'War on Poverty' in the final years of the 1960s, developed action models which have since had growing application. AARP paid early attention to the need for State, as well as Federal action; and has conducted forums directed at members of State legislatures. The Senate Special Committee on Aging often heard from representatives of these organisations and others on such matters as nursing home betterment, shortcomings of Medicare, and the need for improved housing programmes specifically designed to serve the elderly.

3.1.4 The 'New' Social Security System

Despite the often similar positions taken by the national organisations on these and other issues, however, no single dramatic issue such as Medicare emerged until the early-1970s. Senator Frank Church, who became Chairman of the Senate Committee on Aging in 1971, made an early announcement about his long-range goal of ending poverty once and for all among older Americans. His means to achieve this was to be the Social Security system. Church was not a member of the powerful committee which considers Social Security legislation in the Senate. But his evident determination and his timing led to a leadership role. One powerful advantage was the White House Conference on Aging which had been held in 1971, and was again called by the Congress. As in 1961, the actual convergence of thousands of delegates in Washington was merely the culmination of a process. It had been preceeded by numerous community forums and state-level conferences; it had produced technical studies which marshalled facts needed to make the case for action on a wide range of issues, one of the most widely recognised of which was the need for greater economic security in retirement years.

The campaign for improved social security, in which NCSC took an active part and conspicuous role, reached a dramatic conclusion in 1972. Senator Church and the Chairman of the crucial House Ways and Means Committee, Wilbur Mills, were successful in winning approval of legislation which provided a 20 per cent benefit increase. At least equally as important was the decision to authorise automatic cost-of-living adjustments on social security retirement benefits. Additional improvements followed, including a Supplemental Security Income (SSI) programme which began operations in 1974. It was designed to help, among others, older persons whose social security coverage was either non-existent of far below poverty levels. In some States, SSI has become the means, through State supplementation, of ending poverty for the elderly within their borders. In others, however, the SSI payments are unsupplemented and below the official, rockbottom poverty levels.

One detailed study of the 1972 amendments pays special attention to the NCSC role, which extended far beyond the usual testimony and visits and telephone calls to wavering legislators. An example given by the author of the analysis, political scientist Henry Pratt, is indicative of the very direct pressure exerted by NCSC:

> The NCSC monthly house organ, *Senior Citizen News*, with an estimated readership of 4 million, appears to have been an effective means of mobilizing rank-and-file support. In addition to containing articles and commentary on all national legislation concerning the elderly, *Senior Citizen News*, often prints list of proponents and opponents to major age-related proposals. According to NCSC leaders, expressions of support for the Mill-Church Amendments increased markedly just before the *Senior Citizen News* went to press, a not-untypical development when a major floor fight impends on which the organization has taken a strong stand.[5]

3.1.5 A Triangular Subgovernment?

Pratt, writing in 1976, saw evidence that an 'old age policy system' had come into existence within the national government:

> The participants in this triangular alliance – appointive officials in the executive branch, committee and subcommittee leaders in Congress, and leaders of the major clientele groups in the aging field – deals with one another not only through formal structured channels but also on a regular and informal basis. These ongoing relationships are significant at all stages of the policy process – formulation, initiation, decision-making, and legitimation. The system, of course, is not wholly self-contained and autonomous, since from time to time key decisions affecting it are made by 'outside' actors, such as the president or presidential aides. But on all matters of routine importance – and this includes a broad range of issues – the system functions relatively autonomously as a 'sub-government', having broad powers within its domain.

Pratt's later conclusion that the alliance 'contributes decidedly more to the public interest than it threatens that interest' is welcome. And it seems sustained by later events. In 1977, for example, a genuinely emotional and far-reaching effort was made to save the Senate Committee on Aging when it was threatened by a Senate reorganisation plan. As a participant in that effort, the author was astonished and deeply moved by the outpouring of support, not only by organisations, but by affronted individual older persons who seemed to regard the Committee as their personal representative in Washington.

So overwhelming was the support for the Committee that it was not only continued, but for the first time given permanent status. It was no longer necessary to win yearly extensions of its authority.

Senator Church saw the outcome as having significance far beyond immediate Senate reorganisation issues:

> It recognised the growing need for special attention to aging in both Houses of Congress. That need is caused partially by the increase in the number of aged Americans, with even more extreme changes in proportion of young and older populations expected in the not-too-distant future. It is also caused by the need to take stock of existing Federal programs and agencies for adequacy and effectiveness, all the more so since the new administration (that of President Jimmy Carter) has a clear commitment to reorganization of the executive branch as one step toward responsive and efficient government.[6]

3.1.6 The Mandatory Retirement Opposition

Another outstanding example of joint action (not only by the three major national organisations mentioned earlier, but by many others) occurred in 1977 and 1978 in a broad based challenge to mandatory retirement at fixed ages. A House Committee on Aging, established in 1974 to fulfil functions similar to those performed by its Senate counterpart committee, took up the cause with zest and flair. The House Committee Chairman, septuagenarian Claude Pepper of Florida, seemed to be a living example of the folly of cutting off employment at a given age, such as 65. As Representative Pepper himself observed:

> This issue is filled with dilemmas and ironies. On the one hand Congress sets individual competence – not sex, race, or age – as the test of employability. On the other hand, Congress refuses to protect those over 65 from age discrimination. Yet, ironically, Members of Congress insist that they be judged by perfomance, not age; consequently, this 76-year-old Chairman of the House Committee on Aging was re-elected to Congress by many persons who themselves face forced retirement at 65 years of age.[7]

In a protracted battle which took on civil rights overtones, the House and Senate finally agreed in 1978 to a Bill which attacked forced retirement by raising the age limit in a law designed to protect older persons against age discrimination in employment. It allowed a few exemptions and was disappointing in other ways to Pepper and his supporters, but it was one of the most significant victories in ageing during the 1970s.

3.2 Diversity, Yet Common Goals

A full listing of organisations concerned about ageing at the national level, with descriptions, would be lengthy. One of the concrete results of the 1971 White House Conference on Aging was the establishment of centres or coalitions representing minority group concerns of Blacks, Hispanics, Native Americans, and others. Urban interests related to ageing are the specialised concerns of two study and action groups based in Washington. A nationwide Gerontological Society serves as as organisation for professionals and scientists concerned primarily about Federal support for research and training. Its public policy committee and individual members have taken an active interest in other issues related to the place of ageing in society. In addition, the Society has twice conducted briefing sessions for Congressional staff in order to provide current informaion about research findings and their significance. A National Interfaith Council on Aging flourishes.

Seeing a need for a means of speaking with one voice on certain broad areas of agreement, large and smaller organisations in 1977 established what was to become an apparently ongoing Ad Hoc Coalition of Leadership Organizations in Aging. The first chairperson was the executive director of an organisation concerned primarily about long-term care and housing, the American Association of Homes for the Aged. A plan for rotating chairperson assignments among the three major organisations was successfully advanced in 1980. At that time, the list of member organisations numbered two dozen. Leaders of the coalition have become accustomed to attending White House briefings and an occasional meeting with the President or his chief advisors on ageing. At one point they were assembled for what became a stern lecture on the compelling reasons for their support of a treaty to return the Panama Canal to that nation, and several registered their disappointment at the apparent unwillingness of the President to listen at that point to their concerns.

The Coalition does not send representatives to testify at Congressional hearings; each member organisation maintains its own freedom to choose its own testimony on its own subjects. But the advantages of searching out common areas of agreement on broad issues have become more apparent. And in case of what are regarded as emergency situations, coalition members may choose to join other temporary groupings. In 1979, for example, when the Carter administration proposed actions, regarded by individual coalition members as potentially damaging to the Social Security system, many joined a new alliance representative not only of ageing organisations but of labour, social action units, professional organisations and voluntary service agencies.

3.3 The Shape of Ageing Advocacy to Come

Signs of continuing growth in age-related organisations continue to abound in Washington and elsewhere. AARP has a membership approaching 12 million persons of age 55 and over; its public policy staff is large and growing; a recent listing of its legislative priorities put general economic issues as its foremost concern, primarily double-digit inflation.[8] Long-standing AARP concern about consumer economics have produced substantial studies showing the special impact of continually rising prices upon retirement budgets, particularly in the necessities – food, housing, fuel, and medical care – which demand the bulk of the elderly's resources. The AARP statement also deals with income and tax policy, the need for alternative models to institutions in the delivery of health care, and AARP's own guidelines for State advocacy activities by their own Joint State Legislative Committees. An AARP listing of State laws originating from or actively endorsed by their state committees shows that more than 270 were enacted in 1979.

The National Council of Senior Citizens makes a national health insurance plan, as advocated by Senator Edward Kennedy, its major goal. Its position is that the health care protection which would thus be advanced for all age groups in the nation could benefit older Americans as well, through improvements to Medicare and other health-related programmes. Its list of high priority issues for attention in 1980s included a number of issues related to all age groups, such as its determination to protect a consumer-orientated Federal agency – the Federal Trade Commission. It also included many directly related to its senior constituency, including higher funding for the Older Americans Act and tighter control of often misleading health insurance policies said to provide coverage not afforded by Medicare.[9] Another sign of NCSC vitality was an announcement that it was to move into its own downtown Washington headquarters in mid-1981.

The same is true of the National Council on the Aging, which provides special service to practitioners in the many fields grouped under the heading of ageing. Some idea of its diversity as a central national resource for planning, consultation and training can be gathered from an official listing (NCOA Publication list, Spring 1979) of nineteen major programmes, programme units and services gathered under the NCOA umbrella. Among them are a National Institute on Age, Work, and Retirement; a Senior Community Service Project; a National Institute of Senior Centers; and a National Center on Arts and the Aging. The NCOA public policy agenda for 1979-80 is a 26-page document. NCOA also has impact through its often seminal publications and studies. In 1975 its *The Myth and Reality of Aging in America* released findings of a survey conducted by an eminent analyst who had probed deeply into the public's attitudes toward ageing, its perception of what it is like to be old and the often negative attitudes older Americans have about themselves.

An entire chapter in this book could be devoted to State and regional ageing organisations at the State and regional level in the United States. The Western Gerontological Society, for example, attracts 3,000 to 4,000 participants at its annual conferences and is more attuned to practitioner issues than the national society. As we will see later, action groups formed by older persons themselves are becoming increasingly active at the State level.

Challenges to advocates, scientists and policy-makers related in one way or another to ageing inside and outside of government are now beginning to take shape.

One such challenge is the complexity of issues standing in need not only of attention, but patient persistence.

Another, closely related challenge is what has been described as a 'New Age-ism', caused largely by inflation, a growing conservatism and questioning of public programmes and demographic changes which are already causing intergenerational strains and concern about the future financing of retirement incomes programmes.

A third factor may be the changing expectations of older persons themselves as to their perceptions of the role of government in matters related to an 'ageing' population.

3.3.1 The Complexity of It All

Dramatic victories on the scale of Medicare enactment and sharp

ard revision of social security coverage are likely to be infrequent in
e future. Instead, the breakthroughs are likely to be subtle and in many cases technical. A few examples can help make this point.

Economic Security. The United States has not yet arrived at a clear-cut national goal for retirement income adequacy, together with a proposed timetable flexible enough to sustain progress throughout shifting economic and social circumstances. Instead, policy changes related to retirement income take place on a contingency basis, directed only to the next problem or crisis, rather than to a measurement point along a route toward an agreed upon goal.

And yet under the dire impact of inflation, a large number of older persons find life increasingly difficult, even with the cost-of-living adjustment enacted in 1972. The single most compelling fact is that older persons continue to have half the income of their younger counterparts. Half of the 8.5 million families headed by an older person had incomes of about $159 a week in 1978; as compared to $371 for familes under the age 65.[10] For unrelated individuals of age 65 or above, the median income in 1978 was $83 a week, as compared to $165 a week for those under 65. Official poverty definitions provide a controversial and perhaps misleading basis for the measurement of problems and progress but they do provide some perspective. In 1970, 4.7 million, or a quarter of the elderly lived in 'poor households'. Largely with the help of social security increase and – in some States – supplements to below-poverty SSI levels, that number stood at the beginning of this decade at 3.2 million older persons, or one seventh of the 65-plus population.

Improvement is still acutely needed, but the tendency among national budget-makers in the United States is inclined to a contrary course: cut-backs in coverage. Part of the concern is caused by warnings that a social security system beset by lower income because of widespread unemployment and larger outgoings because of more beneficiaries and the cost-of-living adjustment will eventually require more and more financing through payroll taxes or other means.

Such decisions cannot be made lightly, and Washington DC, late in the 1970s, had more that a dozen groups at work on issues related to retirement income. The most expensive mandate was to the President's Commission on Pension Policy. Its responsibilities included:

1. providing an overview of all existing retirement, survivor and disability payments;

2. assessing the ability of existing programmes, and systems – encompassing the Federal, State, local, and private sectors – to meet future commitments and future needs;
3. devising a national policy on retirement that can be used as a guide by all programmes, and
4. proposing reforms that are needed to meet national policy goals, now and in the future.

All of this was to be accomplished by May 1981, culminating an effort which began in July 1978. Clearly, the Commission's report and recommendations will require exhaustive analysis and reasoned response by 'The Gray Lobby' over a period of years, and close communication with other sectors of society if there is to be fruitful intergenerational understanding of the high stakes involved in successful resolution of the problems with which the Commission is grappling. Once again, a White House Conference on Aging may be helpful. The next such assembly was to take place in late 1981.

Long-term Care. Impatient at what is usually called a 'non-system' of long-term care and help for persons with chronic diseases is expressed with growing intensity in the United States by government, gerontologists, care providers and the press.

One dramatic summary of the problem is the declaration that the ratio of medically-orientated service expenditures (including doctor's bills, hospitalisation and nursing home treatment) to health-social services expenditures for the long-term support of the health of the elderly may be placed at 30 to 1.[11]

That declaration was accompanied by the observation that nursing home costs rose from $1.2 billion in 1965 to $10.6 billion in 1976, an increase of 310 per cent, while total health expenditures increased by almost 270 per cent. Nursing home beds, at the 1.3 million level, exceeded acute care beds; the Congressional Budget Office has predicted that the number of skilled nursing beds will rise to 2.5 million by 1984 unless current trends are altered.

Strategically-placed Members of the Congress have bitterly expressed impatience about the imbalance in expenditures for institutional care and the relative pittance spent for help and professional attention in day centres or within living quarters of the homebound or temporarily disabled. After prodding a Federal agency for a definitive status report on steps needed to make home health care more generally available than had been the case, Congressional units in both Houses angrily rejected the long-delayed report as unresponsive and demanded another, which they in turn received late in 1979. At the end of the same year, the only outright response to the Congressional concern was a $20 million demonstration grant programme related to development of long-term care delivery systems. It was slow in developing, as two Federal agencies discussed terms of their shared responsibilities and jurisdictions.

Older persons may share Congressional irritation about the slow progress in the development of genuine long-term care systems. A more immediate concern, however, might be related to personal economics. A government report shows that during the calendar year 1978, direct out-of-pocket payments by the elderly came to $608, an increase of 15 per cent over 1977, and $371 more than in the prior fiscal year.[12] In addition, the shortcomings in Medicare coverage are so pronounced that it has been described as an excellent programme for young people, but not very satisfactory for older persons. It is at its most effective in dealing with acute health problems, particularly those requiring hospitalisation. But it falls short in dealing with chronic conditions of crucial importance for many elderly individuals and their families or friends. For those who finally need nursing home care, another programme called Medicaid may be helpful if the potential patient's income falls below eligibility lines. The common complaints are, however, that Medicaid varies widely from State to State; and it is weighted heavily to institutional care at a time of growing demand for community-based health care/support systems providing in-home, outpatient and health maintenance services, along with short-term institutional stays, *when needed*.

Social Services. Closely related to the long-delayed but much-discussed development of 'spectrums' of long-term care are community-based systems for the delivery of other services. The Older Americans Act, which as late as 1971 had a budget upwards of $30 million, was at the $500 million level in 1979. Its Federal hub, the Administration on Aging, was working closely with a nationwide 'network' of state ageing agencies and almost 600 area agencies and close to 12,000 nutrition sites. The range of services authorised under 1978 amendments includes such items as health, continuing education, welfare, information and referral, transportation to nutrition sites or social and health services, health screening, and legal and counselling services, and more than 20 others.

A persistent critic of the Older Americans Act, however, has accused it of promising too much without having the means really to deliver. Dr. Robert Binstock identified the following deficiencies in a 1978 testimony before a Congressional Committee.[13]

1. The funding distribution is so thin as to have little impact on any given problem.
2. The illusion that a variety of problems can eventually be solved through funding and implementation under the Older Americans Act.
3. The bureaucratic components of the network – the public and voluntary agencies and the universities and the colleges – have quite understandably become preoccupied with sustaining and expanding the different, thinly-funded programme elements with which they are directly involved.

Another concern about the Older Americans Act and a 'services strategy' in general has been voiced by Carroll Estes, a professor of sociology who as a member of the California Commission on Aging and as a researcher has had extensive acquaintance with state and local operations authorised under that act:

> It created dependency on two levels: first, for the aged themselves and second, for the society as a whole. First the aged who are economically prohibited from creating their own choices and options and depend upon service providers for minimal assistance quickly learn that they must be cooperative (perhaps even submissive) to receive services. Publicly funded social services are more than systems for distributing services; they are systems of *social relationships* that reflect and bolster power inequities between experts and lay persons, as well as between providers and recipients of service. An increased emphasis on the services solution also means a greater degree of bureaucratization. This is likely to increase the alienation and isolation of the elderly client population, since they must negotiate their way through complex organisations in order to receive services. Further, services that might contribute to the independence of the old (for example, home health care) are given low priority.
>
> Second, policies that provide for the jurisdictional expansion of service providers and middle-level bureaucrats are likely to increase the general public's dependency on services. Thus, social services previously rendered by other institutions (for example,

> family or church) now come to be performed by paid providers. This leads to further atrophy of traditional support systems, and a vicious circle is thus created that allows the expansionary tendencies of human services professions and industries free rein.[14]

A similarly sceptical viewpoint is advanced by an authoritative researcher who has contributed considerably to an understanding of the differences among generations in the last third of life:

> A Society in which age is becoming increasingly irrelevant as a predictor of lifestyle or as a predictor of need, policies and programs formulated on the basis of age are falling increasingly wide of the mark; income and health care and housing and other goods and services should be provided, not according to age, but according to need.[15]

Thus, despite glowing success stories heard regularly from programme directors in the Older Americans Act network, criticisms about the fundamental future were being heard with increasing frequency in the late-1970s. Furthermore, in 1978 amendments to the Act, the Congress ordered a thorough evaluation and study of its programme and analysis of the means to identify accurately the elderly population in the greatest need of such programmes.

Here, again, advocates were to be presented with new issues requiring fresh thinking and perhaps new directions.

3.3.2 A New Age-ism?

This term was coined by Harold Sheppard in 1980 soon after he became Special Counselor on Aging to the President of the United States. As originally conceived a decade or so before, 'age-ism' was said to be any of the irrational but deep-rooted negative responses to the process of ageing and to the elderly which were, and are, so common in the United States. Sheppard was concerned in 1980 with what he perceived to be a growing irritation at governmental action to improve the well-being of older Americans.[16] He referred to a book which had set out to 'prove' that a majority of older Americans were so well off that governmental concern was displaced. He said further that 'neo-conservatives' seem to begrudge the fact that poverty among the elderly is diminishing. Similarly, other advocates for the ageing population have responded to press accounts which make it appear that unconscionable amounts of the Federal budget are committed to income maintenance programmes and others of direct importance to the elderly.

Robert Butler, Director of the US National Institute on Aging (a research centre), acknowledged in late 1979 that the politics of austerity, as he called it are becoming more ingrained in most industrialised nations of the world.[17] This tendency, he said, is 'affecting mostly those whose positions are weakest – children, older people, minorities, the poor, the handicapped, the mentally ill – all of those who are disadvantaged, either through unequal starts in this vast marketplace of American aspirations or who through no fault of their own, become adversely affected over the course of their lives through disability, disease, or structural unemployment – in other words victims of individual life experiences or socioeconomic contingencies'. He warned that science, as well, suffers from the politics of austerity. He called for alliance, not antagonism.

3.3.3 Resistance by the Retired

Another factor which could lead to more difficult times for progammes devised by government is what appears to be a deepening feeling among many retired people that the system is far from perfect. An article in a widely distributed weekly supplement to Sunday newspapers in the United States dealt with what was called 'The Old Age Trap'.[18] One of its interviewees said: 'Uncle Sam has kicked me in the teeth. I've worked hard all my life; I've earned a good retirement. Instead, every day's a struggle.'

This particular complaint was prompted by inflation's inroad into retirement income. Another bitter outburst, by the leader of an activist group, was directed as a different target:

> We are powerless, and victims of a paternalistic system. We get many calls from distressed old people who have been given the runaround. It may take a dozen calls to get the things they need. They have to stand in long lines to be hassled by competing systems . . . fill out endless forms. The services they offer are often unreachable.

Estes and others have speculated about the positive effect that greater citizen participation could have in programmes for the elderly or self-help efforts devised by the elderly.

There is little prospect that greater control by the elderly will occur overnight. But particularly at a State level, interesting developments are occurring with increasing frequency. Two examples may be forerunners of new approaches useful elsewhere.

The Colorado Collaboration. Independent-minded from its very beginnings less that 10 years ago, the Colorado Congress of Senior Organisations is a private non-profit organisation which accepts support from three public agencies. The latest evidence of constructive collaboration occurred in 1979, when CCSO was joined by the State Division of Services for the ageing in publishing a newsletter. CCSO now speaks of enlisting 10,000 persons within three years, each volunteer capable of being called within 24 hours for whatever advocacy action is needed. CCSO is also advising its members to join 70 State boards or other State decision-making units on which vacancies were to occur within the following year.[19]

The Washington State Senior Lobby. A detailed account of the steps leading to enactment of the Senior Citizen Services Act in 1979 tells how the lobbyists went about their work:

> During November and December 1978, a series of local 'legislative conferences' had been held throughout the state. Subsequent meetings offered the Senior Citizens Lobby the opportunity to examine those legislative issues most needed by the elderly in Washington State. The three issues demanding the largest share of the Senior Lobby's time and efforts were property tax relief, permanent reenactment of the Senior Citizens Services Act and nursing home staffing legislation. The lobby has a coordinator in each of the state's 49 legislative districts and lobby captains under each coordinator to contact other senior citizens. In all, about 3,000 persons made up a legislative communications network around the state to help lobby for the needed legislation. These people, in turn, are today connected to their individual senior citizen organizations whose total state memberships reach into hundreds of thousands, making the Senior Citizens Lobby a far-reaching network blanketing the entire state.[19]

The fruit of their labour was the allocation of $13.6 million in general revenue funds for services to older Washington state residents within the next two years. The covered services include information and assistance, transportation, health screening, education, home repaid, day health centres, mental health counselling and much more. The programme does not supersede Older American Act support in the

State, but complements it. It also raises the State to a leadership position in the development, not only of a service network, but in the enthusiastic acceptance of older persons who regard it as their own.

Whatever the future of government and ageing is in the United States, the lessons learned from years of advocacy and activism deserve close attention and adaptation on changing times. Complicated and frustrating as governmental structures sometimes become, the driving force for resolution of the problems is powerful but simple.

Intelligent concern about ageing is based on the realisation that today's progress for and by today's older persons becomes tomorrow's victory for those now middle-aged and younger.

Notes

1. W. Andrew Achenbaum, *Old Age in the New Land: The American Experience Since 1790* (The John Hopkins University Press, Baltimore and London, 1978).
2. Robert M. Ball, *Social Security: Today and Tomorrow* (Columbia University Press, New York, 1978).
3. US Senate Subcommittee on Problems of the Aged and Aging, *Action for the Aged and Aging* US Government Printing Office, March, 1961).
4. Charles E. Odell, 'Attitudes Toward Political Activities Among the Aging', in *Politics of Age*, Wilma Donahue and Clark Tibbitts (eds.) (University of Michigan Division of Gerontology, Ann Arbor, 1962).
5. Henry J. Pratt, *The Gray Lobby* (The University of Chicago Press, Chicago and London, 1976).
6. Frank Church, US Senator, Preface, *Developments in Aging* (1976,Annual Report of the US Senator Special Committee on Aging, 7, April, 1977).
7. Claude Pepper, US Representative, at a hearing on 'Retirement Age Policies' US House Select Committee on Aging, Washington, DC, 16 March, 1977).
8. *AARP New Bulletin* (American Association of Retired Persons, Washington, DC, March, 1980).
9. *Senior Citizen News* (National Council of Senior Citizens, Inc., Washington, DC, March, 1980).
10. Herman Brotman, 'Every Ninth American', in *Developments in Aging:* (1979 Annual Report of the US Senate Committee on Aging, Washington, DC, 27 February, 1980).
11. S. J. Brody, 'The Thirty-to-One Paradox: Health Needs and Medical Solutions', in *Aging: Agenda for the Eighties: A National Journal Issues Book* (Washington, DC, 1979).
12. US Health Care Financing Administration, 'Age Differentials in Health Care Spending', in *Health Care Financing Review*, (Washington, DC, to be published in Spring 1980).
13. Robert H. Binstock, Testimony, House Select Committee on Aging, 1 February, 1978, Washington, DC, as summarised in *Developments in Aging: 1977* (Annual Report of the Senate Special Committee on Aging, Washington, DC, 24 April, 1978).
14. Carroll L. Estes, *The Aging Enterprise* (Jossey-Bass Publishers, San

Francisco, 1979).

15. Bernice Neugarten, 'Policy for the 1980s: Age or Need Entitlement?, in *Aging: Agenda for the Eighties: A National Journal Issues Book* (Washington, DC, 1979).

16. Harold L. Sheppard, in interview, 'Carter Advisor Warns of New Ageism', with J. Sam Ray, *Weekly Review* (Chicago, 3 May, 1980).

17. Robert N. Butler, 'The Alliance of Advocacy with Science: Kent Lecture – 1979', in *The Gerontologist*, Vol 20, No. 2 (Washington, DC, April, 1980).

18. Michael Satchell, 'Tragedy for Millions – The Old Age Trap', in *Parade* (6 April, 1980).

19. *CCSO Alliance for Statewide Advocacy*, Monthly Publication of the Colorado Congress of Senior Organizations, vol 1, No 2 (Denver, Colorado, February, 1980).

20. Pat Rowe, 'Washington State Senior Lobby Sparks Passage of Landmark Legislation', in *Human Development News* (US Human Development Services, Washington, DC, April, 1980).

4 REMOVING POVERTY

Michael P. Fogarty

Poverty is a remarkably elusive concept, about whose difinition volumes can be and have been written.[1] For practical purposes, however, removing poverty among the elderly means solving problems of three main kinds. None of these is special to the elderly – the elderly are not a class apart – but all three take on special aspects because of the point which the elderly have reached in their life-cycle and the way in which they accordingly live.

4.1 'Maintaining Status': Stabilising the Balance between Income and Commitments

The first issue is about relative poverty and prosperity at different stages of people's life-cycle. Typically, in industrial countries, young adults begin with modest income but still fewer commitments, a time of relative prosperity. They marry, start a family, and move into a stage where income per head and the margin of free income, after meeting essential commitments drop rapidly. There are new costs for children and for acquiring and installing a home, but while there are young or very young children only one partner may be working, or at least working full time, and in no country do families' tax and social security benefits fully fill this gap. An intermediate stage follows: commitments for children are still rising, but husbands reach their peak earnings and wives are likely to return to work. Then, however, as parents move into the second half of their working life, though earnings may pass their peak, particularly in the case of men in blue-collar work, commitments fall in a way which more than compensates this. Children leave home, house purchase and other installation costs have been paid off, free income per head rises, and there is a new phase of prosperity. But, finally, at and after retirement, income falls very sharply indeed, while commitments fall only in the sense that, if there is less to spend, ways of living must be adjusted to match this; relative poverty takes over again.

Removing poverty among the elderly thus means, in the first place, ensuring that resources are spread over the life-cycle, in the case of the elderly as of groups such as families with young children, so as to avoid the alternation of periods of prosperity and deprivation and to permit reasonable stability in the standard of living. There used to be a classic distinction in French and Belgian discussions of pay and social security between 'equal pay for equal work' and 'equal standard of living for equal work'. Parents with children, it was argued, should be helped to maintain the same standard of living as colleagues in jobs at the same level who had none. The corresponding argument in the case of pensioners is that they should be able to maintain into old age the standard of living earned through their working life. The guiding light of pension reform in Germany after the second world war was 'to preserve the individual's social status' in this way.[2]

4.2 The Social Minimum

Secondly, there is the concept of the social minimum, which again applies not only to the elderly but to groups such as the sick, the unemployed, or families with children. The social minimum is a political concept, reflecting what a society is willing to tolerate in the way of inequality, having regard both to what is seen as the urgency of personal and family needs – minimum standards of nutrition, of housing, of heating, and so on – and to the acceptable degree of contrast between the more well off and the relatively poor. The right to a social minimum applies to all, but the elderly are one of the groups for which it has special significance because of the typically large proportion of them whose incomes are low compared to the general standard in the societies in which they live.

4.3 The Elderly as Consumers

Thirdly, in acting to remove poverty in either of the two previous senses it is necessary to take account not only of money income and wealth but of the availability, or otherwise, of means of converting these into an actual standard of living. Money by itself is no guarantee against deprivation if the services which people need are not available and accessible, or if there are difficulties in the way of using and supplementing them to the best advantage. The elderly are consumers as well as receiving an income. Putting money into their hands is one problem; effectiveness in the supply and use of the things that they need is another.

What, in the first place, can the money of the elderly buy, directly out of a current disposable income, through insurance rights, or in return for past and present taxes and social contributions? What, for example, is the quality and availability (and on what financial terms?) of health and social support services, including such things as medical care, sheltered housing or residential homes, and meals on wheels? What arrangements are available for mobility and physical access, both for day-to-day needs such as shopping and for special occasions such as holidays: or for ease of social communication, for instance the availability of telephone service or the practical possibility of members of an extended family finding housing and work in the same neighbourhood as an elderly relative? Have resources been committed to ensuring a high general quality in the environments in which people live, as affected by such things as noise, air pollution, crime, or vandalism, or on the positive side by the availability of shopping and leisure facilities or of parks and open spaces? In all these respects, is the pattern not only of markets but of insurance services and public expenditure geared to the needs of the elderly?

What, again, is available from non-monetary sources either to supplement financial entitlements or to help in using them to the best advantage: opportunities for self-help, for mutual aid and voluntary service in the family and the community, and for friendship and informal social relationships?

Last, but not least, what efforts have been made, and with what success, to develop people's own capacity to make the best use of the resources available to them, of whatever kind, and to extract from them the most satisfactory quality of living which these resources permit?

Once again, considerations like these do not only apply to the elderly, but do apply to them in a special way and with special force. The services needed by the elderly have a different balance from those needed by younger people. The elderly are particularly likely to need health and social support services or support from other members of their family, or through voluntary services. They are particularly likely to be restricted in their physical mobility and to depend for their personal, social, and economic needs and the enjoyment of their environment on what is available in their own locality, through their families, and with the help of special facilities in transport and communication: all the more so because they eventually lose the opportunities of mobility and social contact associated with work. These things incidentally imply a different balance in their case between services obtained directly from the market, through social and insurance provision (public or private), and through mutual or family aid. And in all these cases money income and entitlements do not necessarily lead directly to freedom from deprivation; the availability and terms of supply of services, and the possibility of supplementing them from non-monetary sources, are problems in their own right.[3]

The question of personal capacity to make the best of the resources available also takes its own special form in the case of the elderly. They move on retirement into a new way of life and, as in the case of other major life transitions, such as from childhood to adulthood or from a single life to marriage and the family, have to learn to cope with a new pattern of living and to use it to the best advantage. One implication of this is the need for pre- and post-retirement counselling. In a remarkable piece of research on the patterns of living of retired members of a French pension fund, Anne-Marie Guillemard brings out another.[4] Success in developing a positive and satisfying style of life in retirement, she found, correlates to only a limited extent with resources in the sense of money, health, an established family network, housing, or access to town facilities. A very important factor turns out to be the way in which people's capacity to cope and adapt (their 'potential' for using their resources) has been developed, or stunted, through their experience in work and the family and their general pattern of living in earlier years. The extent and dangers of the 'flat tyre' phenomenon in middle age – the tendency for many people in the second half of their life to slip into a rut in their work and a devitalised style in their family and leisure life – is well documented in American and to a less extent in British studies.[5] Guillemard brings out the devastating effect which loss of vitality and capacity to develop during middle age can have on people's capacity to cope with the transition to retirement, and underlines the importance of 'upstream' measures to stop these losses.

Factors like these on the side of the supply and utilisation of the services needed by the elderly are vital to any policy for removing real deprivation among the elderly. In a chapter with the title 'Removing Poverty' it is right to begin by emphasising them. They are considered in detail, however, in the chapters which follow. The remainder of this chapter turns back to finance: the income and assets of older people, the problems of stabilising the balance between income and commitments through the life-cycle, of the social minimum, and generally of the mobilisation and allocation of resources for the budget for the elderly.

4.4 A New Ice Age for the Elderly?

It is right to begin with a warning. Financial support for the elderly is a matter not only of what they want or need but of what it is practicable to obtain, and in this respect the climate in Western industrial countries in the next decades is likely to be chillier than in the twenty or twenty-five years after the second World War. The period after the second World War was a time of remarkable progress for the elderly, particularly in north-western Europe. In one country after another the coverage of social security or occupational pension plans was extended, pension systems were reformed and made more coherent, levels of pension were raised both by general comparison with the earnings of people in employment and at the level of the social minimum, and direct services to the elderly were expanded.

There were difficulties enough even then, as anyone who lived through that period will remember. Progress was uneven and imperfect, and in the seventies there was still a long agenda for the elderly to be worked through. Progress itself often meant that some were left behind, particularly the oldest. In a number of countries new benefits had to be earned by long periods of service: middle-aged and younger people gained from them, older workers and existing pensioners did not. Countries varied in their success in ensuring the effective replacement of earnings and 'preservation of the individual's social status'. Not many could match the claim in a study of the Swedish pension system that 'the "poor pensioner" is largely a problem of the past'.[6] Within countries, benefits often remained unevenly spread between occupations, sectors, and social groups. Pension plans were slow to come to terms with a number of problems specially affecting women: even, sometimes, the classic problem of widowhood, and certainly those of the changed economic position of women and the effects of the rising tide of divorce. The implications of flexible retirement, for example, the effects in advanced old age of early retirement on a low pension, were only beginning to be explored.

Nevertheless, progress was made, but by the mid-seventies the party was over, particularly as regards social security and other public expenditure. The official figures and forecasts in the European Commission's Second European Social Budget show that in the first half of the seventies public expenditure for old age, death, and survivors' benefits in the European Community was still rising faster, as a percentage of gross domestic product, than the proportion of the elderly in the total population; but between 1975 and 1980 it was expected that this relationship would be reversed, and public expenditure for the elderly, as a percentage of average income per head of the active population, would fall.[7] In the words of Stanford G. Ross, Commissioner for Social Security in the USA, summing up his impressions from a number of countries in 1979:

> The new economic and social forces at work today clearly have brought to an end the long period of expansion of social security programs. Social security systems are now entering a period of painful adjustments in which finances and benefits will have to be closely scrutinised and carefully balanced. The optimistic expansionist philosophy that underlay social security planning ever since World War II has now changed to one of guarded hope that the best of the past can be preserved while the considerable needs of the future are addressed.[8]

There are three connected reasons for thinking that this situation is more than a temporary reaction to the economic crisis of the seventies. The first is the long-term prospects for employment and growth. The optimum assumption is that the industrial economies may in the long run find their way back towards full employment through a combination of work-sharing with meeting the need still widely felt for more employment in under-manned public services and in small-scale and service enterprises. Growth, however, as conventionally measured by gross domestic product, is likely for ecological reasons, and because of the changing world balance of economic power to remain lower than it was in the decades between the second World War and 1973. If these guesses at the future prove correct, there will continue even in the long run to be greater difficulty than in the 1950s or 1960s in obtaining new resources for the inactive elderly: though there is also the positive implication that the active elderly, the young-old, would have opportunities as good or better than in recent years to support themselves by their own work.

Secondly, in the sixties and early seventies there was a rapid rise in taxation and public expenditure, across the industrial countries, at a time when growth was slowing down, and this led to taxpayers' revolts and what could prove to be a permanently more critical attitude to social expenditure.[9] In France, for example, these developments led by the early seventies to a new interest in means-tested rather than universal social security benefits. In Britain there was until the sixties no significant 'welfare backlash', by contrast, for example, with the

United States. From then onwards, however, it is easy to trace the growth in Britain both of a taxpayers' revolt and of a welfare backlash which were sometimes, as in changing attitudes to poverty, in particularly unattractive forms.[10] By 1979 the elderly as well other groups felt the effect of this. British social security pensions, for example, were henceforward to be guaranteed revaluation only in terms of prices and not, as previously, of earnings, and cuts began to be made in locally-financed direct services, such as residential homes.

Thirdly, within the field of public social expenditure, there has been increasing competition by other groups in need of funds, which might otherwise have been available for supporting the elderly. This competition, of course, cuts both ways. In France, one of its most notable forms has been a battle to maintain the traditional French policy of high family benefits in the face of increased pressure for funds for the elderly as well as for health services.[11] But the elderly too have felt its effects. In Britain, one of the most significant shifts in social policy in recent years has been recognition of the need to give a new priority to benefits for the family and the disabled, and so less priority to the elderly than they had traditionally enjoyed.

These last two tendencies do not imply that it is useless to hope and work for further benefit for the elderly from public expenditure. Minor if not major advances can often be slipped through even at a time of stringency. Backlashes have a way of producing their own counter-backlash as their consequences strike home. If that happens, and as and when growth is resumed, the prospects for public expenditure may be better than they appear at the start of the eighties. It would be unwise, however, to assume that attitudes to increasing public expenditure and taxation will again be as easy as they were in the 1950s or early 1960s. And, in the face of increasing competition for funds for other social purposes, pensions and related provisions for the elderly have one very awkward characteristic. Because of the numbers and levels of support involved, they are relatively very expensive. When, in 1977, the British Department of Health and Social Security published the costs of potential advances over the whole range of social security and related benefits, one fact which stood out was that for the cost of any one of two or three major pension reforms then in discussion it would be possible to finance significant new programmes in half a dozen other directions, all with their own substantial body of political and pressure-group support.[12]

One implication is that even in the longer run it will be sound strategy to look for as much support for the elderly as possible from sources other than public expenditure, and also to ring the changes skilfully within the various categories of public expenditure itself according to where advances are currently possible; for 'public expenditure', as is shown below in relation to pensions, is itself an elastic term covering a variety of channels for expenditure and sources of finance.

Another implication is that it will be advisable to differentiate more carefully than sometimes in the past between priorities for the various categories of the elderly, since advances may still be made for high priority groups at times when advances all along the line are impracticable. One obvious distinction is between the able-bodied young-old and the very elderly. The number of the very elderly, as was shown in Chapter 2, is everywhere increasing rapidly. They have particularly clear and strong needs for geriatric and other health services, residential homes, and social services support in the community, and these services are expensive. British figures for 1976/7 show that public expenditure for health and personal social services for the over-75s averaged £555 a head – and, even then, with serious deficiencies in geriatric services – compared to £220 for people aged 65-74 and £80 for those aged 5-64.[13] The very elderly also have a particular case for support for their cash incomes. They depend on them more heavily than younger pensioners, because they are less likely to be able to earn through work or to provide for themselves through do-it-yourself. They have a high need for spending in areas such as heating, transport and domestic help. They may well, because of the times in which they lived, have had less opportunity than younger pensioners to build up modern domestic equipment – washing machines, refrigerators, etc. – or to own their own homes free of rent and mortgage payments. They are particularly likely to have been left behind by pension reforms of the type under which full benefit can be earned only by years of service after the date of this reform, and to have had their private pensions and initial savings eaten away by inflation. Where there are deficiencies in survivors' benefits, it is the high proportion of widows among the very elderly, who are likely to feel them most.[14]

Other special cases can be made for groups such as miners who have worked in severe or damaging conditions, and for younger disabled pensioners. American statistics are particularly clear on the extent of poverty among workers who accept early retirement on health grounds, on a minimum social security pension and often from occupations where no second pension is available.[15] Groups like these have, like the very elderly, cases which can stand up well in competition with the needs of people in other groups when the funds available are short, and their cases need to be highlighted on their own. It will not help to bracket them with claims on behalf of younger able-bodied people of pension age whose priority is less obvious.

4.5 The Incomes of the Elderly – Pensions and Social Assistance

Granted, then, that securing adequate support for the elderly is likely in future, even more than in the past, to require skilful manoeuvring between a variety of possible channels of progress, what, so far as the money incomes of the elderly are concerned, are the channels open?

Table 4.1: Incomes of Elderly Pensioners: Netherlands, 1970*

	Age		
	65-69	70-79	80+
Social security pension and social assistance	40	50	58
Occupational ('private') pensions	20	22	21
Earnings, including self-employment	31	13	5
Others	10	15	17
Total	100	100	100

* The table excludes 25-30 per cent of wage-earners over 65 who had only social security and social security benefits.

Source: *Socio-Economic Policies for the Elderly – Netherlands*, OECD paper SME/SAIR/E/79.5, Paris 1979.

Table 4.2: Incomes of the Elderly: France, 1970

	Age		
	61-65	66-70	Over 70
Pensions, annuities, etc.	35	75	88
Wages and salaries	49	13	5
Commercial profits (crafts, shops, etc), partnership income	13	9	5
Other dividends, interest, etc.	4	3	2
Total	100	100	100

Source: Institut National de la Statistique et des Etudes Economiques (INSEE), *Données Sociales 1978*, INSEE, Paris, 1978.

Table 4.3: Household Incomes of the Elderly, UK, 1977

	Single adult, 65 or over	Married couple, head aged 65 or over	All households with a retired head	
			Per cent of: Cash income	Income in cash and kind
	Per cent of cash income			
Social security including supplementary pension[b]	63	48	51	40
Occupational pension and annuities	12	16	13	10
Investments:				
Home-ownership (including imputed income from owner-occupation and rent from sub-letting)	8	7	6	5
Other	13	11	10	8
Work (including self-employment)	4	18	19	15
Miscellaneous	1	a	1	a
Total	100	100	100	
Health and personal social services				18
Housing subsidies[c]				4
Total				100

(a) Less than 0.5 per cent.
(b) 7½ per cent of this income was from supplementary benefits, for pensioners as a whole.
(c) This might alternatively be grouped with income from home-ownership as 'income from home occupation'.

Source: *Family Expenditure Survey*, 1977, and Cmnd 7439, 1979, p. 143.

The incomes of the elderly come from a number of sources: Tables 4.1-4.3 give some illustrations. Earnings from employment and self-employment are important for younger pensioners. Investment income is likely to be dominant for only a very small minority (3 per cent of elderly married couples in Britain in 1975), but income from more modest savings, plus for example the imputed value of an owner-occupied house, is significant across a wide band of pensioners. The value of a capital asset such as a house lies not only in the current income (real or imputed) which it yields but in the fact that its capital value can, given the right facilities, be converted into an annuity without the owners losing possession of their home; an interesting possibility to which we return below, along with the possibilities of increasing personal saving for retirement and of better opportunities for pensioners to earn. The main source of elderly people's incomes, however, is pensions, together with social assistance programmes designed to guarantee the social minimum.

Looking across countries, pension and related income has a remarkable variety of sources. In all countries some part of it, and in many a significant part, is private and non-statutory. In the private business sector individual firms' pension plans are important in Britain and the USA, firms' and industry-wide plans in the Netherlands, and nation-wide 'complementary' plans in France and Sweden; whereas in Germany no less than 97 per cent of pension expenditure in 1975, other than from personal savings, was under statutory schemes.[16] These 'private' schemes are initiated and financed independently of the state. The state is however, likely to regulate them, may give them administrative support – for instance, in France and the Netherlands, by requiring firms to join an industry or nation-wide scheme once it has been set up – and may also subsidise them. Tax concessions on contributions to British pension schemes were officially estimated in 1978/9 at £520 million. British legislation allows occupational pension schemes to 'contract out' of the part of social security which provides earnings-related pensions and to provide a corresponding pension themselves: they cannot contract out of provision for the flat-rate basic social security pension. In the case of contracted-out schemes, the British government accepts responsibility for inflation-proofing, once it is in payment, that part of a private pension which corresponds to the guaranteed minimum earnings-related pension otherwise payable under social security.

Private schemes thus in practice shade over, through varying degrees of state intervention, into a variety of special statutory schemes for public servants and, often, for special categories such as mineworkers, farmers, or independents. In countries such as Britain, the Netherlands, and the USA they are commonly grouped together with these as 'occupational', 'private', or 'second' pensions. But special statutory schemes in turn shade over into and are often integrated with a country's general system of social security pensions, usually financed for the most part from special payroll or social security taxes, though sometimes, as in Denmark and Sweden, mainly from general state revenue; either way, through what is usually defined as public expenditure. Finally, the ultimate safety net of social assistance or supplementary pension is always publicly financed as well as publicly administered. But even here there is a degree of shading, for countries vary in the extent to which they build a minimum income into their general social security pension systems; in Germany, for instance, in principle not at all.

In principle it may not matter from which source a pensioner gets his or her pension and related income, but in practice it matters a great deal. When a Louis Harris poll in 1978 asked American employees and pensioners what they saw as the characteristics of a good pension plan, the answer came through loud and clear, in terms which would be echoed in other countries: it is a plan which gives the advantages to be expected in America as in other countries by members of pension schemes for the public services.[17] Civil service and related public service plans may or may not have advantages over others in detailed respects such as benefits on death in service, but tend to have three characteristics which together add up to a general advantage of a very substantial kind. One is a high ratio of replacement of earned income. German civil servants can expect a pension of around 75 per cent of their final salary, Swedish civil servants 65 per cent, and British civil servants 1/60 of final salary for each year of service: or, more precisely, 1/80 plus a capital sum equivalent to the difference. Secondly, public service pensions in payment are likely to be inflation-proofed by reference to current salaries, as in Sweden or Germany, or to prices as in Britain, and with a guarantee from the state. And, thirdly, pension entitlements are likely to be either – or both – freely transferable within the public sector, or a reflection of the fact that public service careers often involve a lifetime of service with a single employer or (as in local government) in a single related employer group. Either way, public service careers tend to be relatively free from losses of pension rights on changing jobs.

These characteristics may also extend in practice, when not strictly by law, to special schemes within the public sector. In Britain, for example, public service organisations such as the nationalised industries finance their pension schemes in a variety of ways, and often have no formal guarantee from the State, but all are within a public sector transfer club and offer in practice the same standards of pension and inflation-proofing.

By the 1970s the idea that income replacement through pensions, from one source or another, should reach 'public service' standards had become widespread in Europe.[18] In Germany an average earner with the qualifying length of service might in theory expect about 60 per cent replacement of his revalued lifetime earnings through social security, and perhaps 75 per cent where special scheme benefits or private occupational pensions were added. A moderate earner in Sweden – an industrial supervisor, for example – might expect on retiring in 1980 about 75 per cent replacement of revalued lifetime earnings through social security, and 85 per cent or more if he also had an occupational pension.[19] The ultimate target for average earners in France, from social security plus private sector 'complementary' pensions, was by the 1970s 65-70 per cent. In the Netherlands it was hoped that replacement for average wage-earners from social security plus occupational pensions would come to be around 70 per cent. British occupational pension plans were moving steadily towards a standard of 1/60 of final salary for each year of service: total pension would depend on the degree of integration of occupational pensions with social security.

Pension contracts, however, are a case where it is important to read the small print. Even public service provision is not always as good as it seems, and, in the case of other types of pensions, theory and reality continue to diverge. To take first social security, pension provision under general social security does to some extent have the same characteristics as public service schemes, including free transferability and a more or less formal (according to the country) state guarantee of solvency and inflation-proofing. Social security payments and their adjustment to rising prices and earnings are a matter of political debate, but in Europe at least there is a basic confidence that they will be forthcoming in something not too far distant from their promised form. It is startling to European observers when the Louis Harris poll just quoted records that half of all younger social security contributors in the USA had in 1978 'hardly any confidence' that retirement benefits promised would actually be paid, or that future generations would be willing to pay the necessary social security taxes.

In principle and as a matter of technique, there is no reason why general social security should not also guarantee from its own resources – irrespective of supplementation from any other source – a 'public service' standard of replacement. The Swedish and German social security systems do in principle aim for this at least in the case of the main band of earners. It is at this point, however, that the difficulties already described over increasing public expenditure and taxation become of key importance. Civil servants, or even public servants generally, are a limited part of the work force. General social security beneficiaries are the whole or at least the major part of it. To provide for their pensions fully through social security is expensive and politically difficult. Some countries stop at providing a minimum flat-rate benefit, as Britain did till 1978 and the Netherlands and Ireland still do. That position may be taken as a matter of principle: that the state should provide a basic minimum, while the rest is left to occupational pensions. But public expenditure considerations have been relevant both in these cases and in those where social security provides earnings-related pensions. There have been limitations even in the cases of Sweden and Germany: ceilings for the incomes against which benefits are calculated, long periods of build-up to full entitlement (the Swedish earnings related scheme was introduced in 1960 and matures only in 1980), and limits to revaluation. In Germany there is a power, which has been used, to delay the revaluation of pensions in payment. In Sweden lifetime earnings and pensions in payment are revalued only by reference to prices, not to increases in real incomes. The actual replacement rate for average earners in Sweden at the beginning of the seventies, half way through the maturing of the earnings-related social security scheme, was about 40 per cent (single pensioner) and 55 per cent (married couples) in the case of the less than one-third of pensioners who at that time received earnings-related pension, and 30 per cent and 45 per cent in the case of the majority who did not: and these figures include certain non-pension benefits, notably housing allowance.[20]

Other countries do not attempt to provide a 'public service' standard of replacement through social security. The target for British earnings-related social security pensions, when fully in payment in 1998 – as in Sweden, there is a twenty-year build-up period – is to replace 50·5 per cent of the earnings of an average married male wage-earner (40 per cent if single), tapering to 40·5 per cent if earnings are 1½ times the national average: and there is as mentioned earlier the British government decision to relate the growth of social security pensions in future only to prices and not to earnings. American men who retired in 1973/4 had a median of 35 per cent of their earnings replaced by social security, with a range from 56 per cent in the case of the lowest earners to 23 per cent in that of those earning over $12,500 a year.[21]

Figures like these do, of course, look higher if account is taken of the higher incidence of direct taxation on people still in employment. On that basis, the Swedish replacement rate for an average pensioner couple with earnings-related as well as basic pension was estimated in the early seventies to be as high as 75 per cent. Replacement for an average British wage-earner (married) in 1977 was 35 per cent in terms of gross income, but 46 per cent if account was taken of the different incidence of tax. Account has also to be taken of the different number of people to be maintained by pensioner and employee households. In Britain in 1977 households with their heads still in employment contained an average of 2.6 'equivalent adults', but pensioner households only 1.6. In terms of maintaining real standards of disposable income per head, social security systems often perform better than appears on the surface.

The fact still remains that in few cases do they in practice come near by themselves to matching the 'public service' standard, and in current economic and political conditions progress towards that standard is likely to be slow and difficult. How much, in that case, can be expected from the private or, more generally, the occupational pensions sector?

In some respects, a good deal can be expected already. In some countries at least it appears to be much easier to obtain additional contributions directly for occupational pensions than for general social security. Britain in recent years has been a case in point.[22] There is also in many countries a large foundation of occupational provision on which to build. Just what occupational pensions are designed to achieve depends on local circumstances, in particular on what is already available from social security and how far occupational pensions are integrated with it. Swedish or German occupational pensions add only a small margin to the total pension of even moderately high earners, but this is on top of an already high social security pension. In other countries the share of occupational pensions in total pension income can be large. American married men retiring in 1968-74 had a median of 31 per cent of their earnings replaced through social security, but for those who had occupational pensions the combined replacement rate was 50 per cent.[23] French 'complementary' schemes in the mid-seventies were designed to add from a third to 100 per cent to the general social security pensions of moderate to low earners.[24] The share of occupational or 'private' pensions in British and Dutch pensioners' salaries is shown in Tables 4.2 and 4.3. For the 35 per cent of elderly British families who had a second pension in 1975, that pension commonly meant the difference between poverty and modest comfort. Of families with only a social security pension, 49 per cent had incomes at or below the defined social minimum level – the level qualifying for supplementary pension – but of those with a second pension only 7 per cent were at this level.[25]

'In principle' is the catch, for the reality is often different. A series of large questions hangs over the future of occupational pensions in countries such as Britain, Ireland, the United States, or Germany where private sector pensions still depend essentially on initiative and financing by individual firms – through employer action or collective bargaining – or by individuals themselves. Coverage, in these conditions, tends to be uneven. There can at one end be 'over-pensioning' in cases where occupational pensions are high and not adjusted for social security, but at the other end many, particularly of manual workers and women, tend to be left out. There are liable to be severe losses of entitlement on changing jobs. The British Institute of Management's *So you Thought you were Earning a Two-third Pension?* provides one disturbing analysis of companies' practice on this: what companies are willing to transfer out when an employee leaves is usually well below what they would expect to have transferred in if his replacement was to enjoy the same pension rights as he has done.[26] Because the future of individual firms is uncertain, single-firm pension schemes have to rely on investment to provide security for pensions. This may have valuable results for the economy. In 1977 net investment by pension funds and by life assurance companies (including pension schemes insured through them) accounted for 25 per cent of savings in the personal sector of the British economy, and at the end of 1978 the capital assets of pension schemes of all kinds were about £40 billion. From the point of view of the pensioner, however, funding plus such amount as individual firms can provide by way of top-up has proved an unreliable means of keeping pace with inflation, the rise of real incomes, and the relatively high administrative costs – by comparison with social security pensions or pay as you go public service plans – of operating funded schemes. Worry over the inadequacy of pension plans in relation to inflation comes through as a major factor among pensioners and current employees even in a country with, taking one year with another, a relatively modest degree of inflation such as the United States.[27]

A good deal can be and in some countries has been done to mitigate these problems of occupational pension schemes by State regulation, as by the Employee Retirement Income Security Act (ERISA) of 1974 in the USA or the British Social Security Act of 1973 and Social Security Pensions Act of 1975. The most basic issue, however, is raised by the success of the private sectors in Sweden and France in overcoming problems of these kinds by creating new national frameworks of their own through national collective agreement.[28] The French private sector's 'complementary' pension plans for managers and white-collar and manual employees were established after the second

World War by national agreement between the main trade union and employers' organisations, and are financed by employers' and members contributions. Their essence is that they constitute a nation-wide superstructure, on top of firms' and other smaller pension schemes, for pooling risks, levelling out differences in resources (for example, the effects of changes in the ratio of employees to pensioners within individual schemes), pooling start-up costs, such as those of creating in new members to benefit or existing members to new benefits, and ensuring full transferability of pension rights. Contributions are raised nation-wide, on the security of the whole of French business and industry: funding is thus not needed for security, and these plans are financed through pay as you go. Pension rights are both fully transferable and inflation-proofed. Coverage within each category of employer is comprehensive, and crediting-in has been possible on a massive scale. The managers' scheme, for example, gives pension points for service back to 1918, thirty years before the scheme began. And contributions have been modest.

The precise technique used in France may not suit all countries. Some may for instance prefer to retain funding as the first tier of resources for pensions: the Swedish national plans for salaried and manual employees do in fact do this. Whether, however, the French approach is used as the basic means of providing pensions or simply as a means of re-insurance and extra provision on top of funded plans, what French (and Swedish) experience shows is that an occupational pension system which gives itself an appropriate superstructure can successfully overcome the classic deficiencies of fragmented enterprise-centred, occupational schemes in countries such as Britain, Ireland or the USA. In so far as that is done, occupational pensions can become for pensioners a generally available and primary source of income, capable in terms of benefits provided of competing on equal terms with general social security and even with public service pensions; in which case their advantage as a channel through which additional resources for pensions may be obtained more easily than through public expenditure comes into full play.

Pensions of course support not only individuals but families. Traditionally, pension plans were geared to the concept of lifelong marriage with the husband earning and the wife keeping the home – one pension replacing one wage or salary, and a survivor's pension for the widow as a dependant. In some countries the method of providing for the presumed dependant wife under social security has worked to the serious disadvantage of single pensioners as distinct from intact married couples. It does not do so in, for example, West Germany, where social security pensions simply replace a (relatively high) percentage of previous earnings, and no special provision is made for a wife unless and until she becomes a widow.

In countries such as Britain, Ireland, and the Netherlands, however, a significant part of the pension for a married couple consists of an allowance for a dependent wife, and the part of the pension which directly replaces previous earnings is kept correspondingly low. So, therefore, is the pension of the single former earner, who receives only this latter part; and this includes not only those who never married but those who become single through death or divorce.

A former British wage earner (male and married) whose basic pension at the end of 1979 replaced around 38 per cent of average wages was not particularly well provided for, but still considerably better than the single man whose pension replaced 23 per cent; and a widow's basic pension in Britain is identical with that of a single man. The cost of providing basic necessities such as a home, heating and food for one person rather than two does not fall in the same proportion as this, and it is not surprising that British surveys find a particularly high proportion of pensioners who live alone to be at or below the official social minimum.

In recent years the change in sex roles, and particularly in the position of married women in work and the family, has given the question of pensions and the family a new dimension. This has led to claims of several kinds with which both social security and occupational systems are still wrestling.[29]

One claim is for equal access to and protection of pension rights, and elimination of the treatment of wives as dependants. The question of equal access and protection may arise even in social security. In Britain, until the Social Security Pensions Act of 1975, it was open to wives not to contribute for a social security pension, but to rely instead on a dependant's allowance, and ultimately a widow's pension, paid on their husbands' contributions. Most did in fact do this. There was also a rule that they could not in any case receive a social security pension in their own right – irrespective of their total number of years' contribution – unless they had been in employment for half of the years since their marriage. In the case of occupational pensions there may be both discrimination against women as regards the age and other conditions for entering schemes, and special problems over preserving their entitlements because women are more likely to experience breaks in employment.

A further claim is for equality of men's and women's pension ages and for equal pensions – basic or in relation to earnings – at any given age or length of service, irrespective of the difference between men's and women's expectation of life. Another is for clearer recognition in pension plans that wives and husbands share responsibilities in marriage, and, whatever their particular division of activities between home and employment, are equally entitled to share in any pension entitlements which result. Practically, this has two implications. In the case of a divorce, it implies that social security or occupational pension entitlements earned up to the time of divorce should be shared equally. In that of the death of one partner, it implies that a survivor's benefit should be payable to husbands on their wives' contributions as well as, on the traditional pattern, to wives on those of their husbands.

There is also a claim for recognition of the fact that the care of children and the disabled now normally involves, in the case of a wife as well as of a husband, an interruption in earnings which needs to be compensated if families with young children are not to be put at an undue disadvantage compared to the rest of the population. In part this is a claim for payment to replace the lost wage or salary at the time when young children are present, on the lines of Swedish 'parenthood insurance' or the French *complément familial*. It is also, however, a claim for pension credits for periods of essential duties at home.

Elements of policy for meeting these claims are already written into a number of countries' practice. Britain and Quebec provide pension credits for home duties. West Germany and Canada provide for splitting pension credits (occupational as well as social security, in the case of West Germany) in the case of divorce. Britain provides that a male survivor may benefit from his former wife's social security pension contributions as well as vice versa. Equal access and equal pension ages are spreading, and West Germany is a case where the idea of a dependant's allowance for married men has been abandoned.

The problem which has still to be solved is to assemble these elements into a fully coherent package. This is partly a matter of debate and understanding, but in some areas there is also, as always, a question of costs. It is expensive to change from low replacement of earnings, plus a dependent wife's allowance for married male pensioners whose wives are still living, to high replacement of earnings, and no wife's allowance, for all former earners including those who are living alone. In Britain where the minimum social security pension age is 60 for women and 65 for men, a main factor in the debate on equal pension ages in recent years has been the massive cost of bringing the men's age down to the women's, combined with resistance to raising the women's age to the men's.

There remains the question of the relation between mainstream pensions, whether occupational or under social security, and schemes for guaranteeing the social minimum. This minimum is as has been said a political concept, whose interpretation will depend on circumstances in each country. In practice, however, as a survey at the beginning of the seventies noted, interpretations in Europe have tended to converge on figures for a married couple, and including any separate provision for housing costs, around 40 per cent to 50 per cent of average wage earnings. The problem is how best to guarantee this.[30]

In principle the ideal is to build the minimum into the main pension structure itself. There is no technical difficulty about providing a guaranteed minimum through general social security. There is more difficulty in doing so in fragmented occupational pension systems, where pensions may ultimately have to be assembled from a number of previous employers: but that difficulty need not apply in more comprehensive nation-wide occupational schemes such as the French 'complementary' plans. The basic problem, here again, is cost. Given the inherited deficiencies of both social security and occupational pension systems, the cost of moving at once to guaranteeing within a country's main pension systems an outcome matching the social minimum may be politically unacceptable: still more, of course, if there is a question of raising the level of the social minimum itself.

In Britain the trade union movement and pressure groups for the elderly such as Age Concern have pressed for some years for a minimum social security pension of 50 per cent of average men's wage earnings in the case of a married couple and one-third in that of a single pensioner. In 1975, the cost of awarding to all British pensioners a minimum social security pension at this level was estimated as equivalent to adding 25 per cent to the total social security budget (not only the budget for pensions) in that year: and around 45 per cent if the same minimum standard had overflowed from pensions into other types of social security benefit.

The alternative is means-tested support for those elderly people who do actually fall below the social minimum: in the UK about 30 per cent of pensioners in 1978, of whom 22.3 per cent actually received supplementary pension.[31] There is no simple formula for support of this kind, but experience suggests three main guidelines.

The first is clear and definite entitlements, with minimum scope for local and subjective discrimination and the resulting anomalies and inequities. Some scope for discretion is always necessary, for example in the case of catastrophies through fire and flood. But there is a wide difference between the chaos of local support systems in, for instance, the United States before (and even after) the introduction of federal Supplementary Security Income in 1974 and the more coherent pattern of the supplementary benefit system in a country such as the UK: though there are disputes about discretion even in the latter.[32]

The second guideline is to minimise use of special allowances, or provisions in kind, which restrict old people's own discretion in the use of their resources. The balance here is a difficult one. The cost of important elements in the standard of living varies considerably from one individual or family to another, and movement from high-cost to low-cost situations may not be easy, for example in the case of housing or exceptional heating costs. It may be necessary to allow directly for these differences, and also for cases where costs differentially affect the elderly as compared to the active population. Special concessions on public transport, for instance, may be justified because the elderly must rely more on it. In other cases there may be reasons for special allowances which have little directly to do with the elderly, but from which the elderly might as well benefit as anyone else. If there are farm surpluses to be disposed of outside normal markets, then why should not the elderly be the ones to benefit from food stamps in the USA or from cut-price butter (or some bottles from the wine lake: an attractive thought) in the European Community? But it is easy to enmesh the elderly in a bewildering network of public and private concessions on anything from telephone service to cinema seats and dry cleaning which they may or may not manage or wish to take up, and to forget that a first principle of provision for the elderly is to enable them to 'preserve their status' and to choose their own pattern of expenditure as they did when they were economically active.

The third guideline is that there should be an effective system of delivery: guaranteed minimum incomes must actually reach those for whom they are intended. The two previous points are of course relevant to this. The greater the variety of special provisions and the scope for discretion in awarding allowances, the greater is the chance of unequal treatment and of failure by intended beneficiaries to take up their benefits. Even the more coherent systems, however, have a high degree of slippage. Some 27 per cent of British pensioners entitled to supplementary benefit failed to claim it in 1977, at a cost to them of about £100 million.[33]

In principle, in a country such as the UK where income tax is payable on incomes even below the official 'social minimum' level, the most effective answer might seem to be to link the social security and assistance and the fiscal systems into a tax credit or negative income tax plan, which could be relied on more fully than any of these systems on their own to deliver benefits where they are required. The UK's experience suggests, however, a rather large question about this. The possibilities of tax credit plans have been examined in detail by the British Conservative and Liberal parties. A Conservative government at the beginning of the seventies set out actually to legislate for one, but left office before a bill could be introduced.[34] The Conservative party maintained its commitment to tax credits while in opposition, but backed off on returning to office in 1979. Some of the reasons for this are special to the Conservatives, in particular a strong reluctance in current economic conditions to undertake any plan which might involve increased public expenditure. There are however other reasons which have always deterred the Labour party, and which the writer has found increasingly convincing after several years of association with Liberal plans.[35]

The net additional cost of the plans which have been seriously considered in Britain is less, certainly, than of simply increasing pensions or other social security benefits across the board within their existing pattern, but is still very substantial: it is not of a different order of magnitude. A tax credit plan would also take some years to install, and could have some unwanted by-products; for example, in the Liberal plans, a high rate of taxation on marginal additions to social security income from sources such as occupational pensions or part-time earnings. The question is whether the money and effort involved could not be used to better advantage in other ways. Even if there are no new departures in British social security, the maturing of earnings-related pensions under the Social Security Pensions Act of 1975 will lift increasing numbers of pensioners above the minimum.

Equipping the occupational pensions system with a new superstructure on the lines suggested above would make it possible to give occupational pensions something like the universal coverage of social security and to reduce the number of pensioners close to the minimum still further. In these ways the numbers to whom the minimum is relevant will or could fall, and, if the new public money which would be needed for tax credits were used instead to raise the minimum social security pension for those still close to the edge, it could be expected to stretch correspondingly further and to make a significant improvement possible. If so much time, legislative and administrative effort, and money would in any case be needed to bring in tax credits, might they not be better used to promote changes like these?

That question must remain an open one, for the advantages of a tax credit plan as seen through British eyes could still be considerable, in terms not only of effective delivery of the social minimum but of clearing up a wide range of anomalies in the social security system generally. Some of these, such as the effect of means-tested benefits in creating a poverty trap for low-paid earners with families, are even more important for people in the active age groups than for pensioners. But it is fair at least to say that the verdict on tax credit plans in one country where they have been seriously considered remains a matter of dispute.

4.6 Home-Ownership and Investment

Pensions and means-tested guarantees of the social minimum are the main resources of the elderly, but, as Tables 4.1-4.3 illustrate, 'own resources' in the shape of home-ownership and investment also make a significant contribution. Approaching half of all households, with the head aged over 65, are owner-occupiers in Britain, over half in France, and still higher proportions in Canada or the USA. Pensioners at any income level may also have minor assets in cash and savings. Only a very small proportion of elderly families in Britain had, in the seventies, enough income-yielding assets to provide an income of the same order of magnitude as their pensions. Excluding the capital value of pension rights, the distribution of personal wealth remained much more unequal than that of incomes, and this inequality was as marked among the elderly as among the middle-aged.[36] But, though the financial assets of most of the elderly were small, a high proportion had at least some. Even of those actually receiving supplementary pension in 1978, and so by definition living on the edge of the social minimum, nearly half had assets of this kind.[37] Most had fairly small amounts, equivalent to less than six months' basic social security pension for a married couple, but a few had capital equivalent to a year's pension or more.

Could this situation be improved? How far is it practicable to increase the accumulation of 'own resources' in the hands of the wide bands of the population, and to provide facilities for converting these into income, on a scale large enough to make these assets not merely a reserve for a rainy day or, like an owned home, the means of making a useful but marginal saving on expenditure, but the source of a substantial and regular addition to their pension income? The self-employed, such as farmers and small business owners, already often have assets on the scale required for this. In the case of farmers, the problem with which many countries have wrestled is how to enable them to convert these assets into retirement income without in the process either losing their own social status or compromising their children's inheritance of the farm. But what of the general employed population?

One very interesting possibility is to apply to home-ownership a technique not unlike that which is beginning to be used in retirement plans for farmers, i.e. to make it possible for home-owners to convert their asset into retirement income without losing their title to it or the other advantages which it brings. The ownership of a home, normally by this time of life free from mortgage charges, is in any case a useful addition to real income, as well as widespread. What is new is appreciation of how this asset can be reconverted into pension income, particularly in the case of the oldest pensioners, without losing control of it. The Home Income Plan, pioneered in Britain by a small group of insurance companies and brokers, enables an elderly owner-occupier to remortgage his home and buy with the proceeds an annuity.[38] From the annuity he pays the mortgage interest, less income tax relief if he is eligible, but not capital repayments: the capital is repayable only at the death of the pensioner or of both members of a pensioner couple. This type of scheme is of benefit chiefly to pensioners in and beyond their middle seventies, but it is precisely these who tend in any case to be in the greatest need. In their case the net annuity from a mortgage on a typical owner-occupied property, at current British values, can (depending on age, tax position, and whether annuities are single or joint) double or more than double the minimum social security pension.

Expansion of personal and family savings is another possibility. Employers and pensioners themselves may not be particularly enthusiastic about this. Among current and retired employees in the USA in 1978, 43 per cent thought that more income should be provided from social security and 16 per cent from occupational pensions, but only 9 per cent saw a need to increase personal savings.[39] There are however, a number of recent social changes which could facilitate saving in mid-life with an eye to retirement. Middle-aged married women have moved into employment, there are fewer late births, which brings down the age at which children's dependency ends: and, as the movement towards owner-occupation develops, the proportion of families in later middle age who are free of both rent and mortgage payments rises. The problem is how to exploit the possibilities opened up in this way. The European Commission's report on *Asset Formation and Employee Participation* reviews the remarkable variety of arrangements developed or proposed in European countries in recent years to encourage asset formation by families at ordinary earnings levels.[40]

Many of these, and of others outside the scope of the Commission's report – stock options for executives, for example – are likely in practice to benefit only limited categories or to produce only modest amounts of additional saving, an improved version of the traditional reserve for a rainy day. But what European discussion and experience has also shown is that it is technically possible, though often politically controversial, to develop schemes which will place really substantial amounts of capital in the hands of ordinary families and strongly encourage their retention for long-term purposes such as retirement. This could in particular be true of schemes for capital sharing, including the 'investment wage', the payment of part of wages or salaries in capital. France, in 1967, was the first country to impose compulsory capital sharing on all companies above a limited size, with a five-year freeze on liquidation of the assets acquired in this way. A variety of comprehensive plans for capital-sharing have since been proposed in countries such as Denmark, Germany, the Netherlands and Britain, and in several cases have been brought close to the point of legislation.

The point of political controversy about these plans is also one highly relevant to policy for the elderly. The target of plans proposed by employers' groups and the political Right is to put freely disposable capital (though perhaps, as in France, with an initial freeze) in the hands of individuals and families, accepting the risk that it will in fact be disposed of. A common feature of plans proposed by trade union movements and the Left, on the other hand, is that redistributed assets should be retained in a trust fund or funds, usually under trade union control. This would guarantee that the beneficiaries retained a permanent asset, but the form of control usually proposed raises objections from the political centre and Right. These objections would be much weaker if it were a case of redistributing capital in marginal amounts. Their force comes precisely from the fact that over a period of years the amounts redistributed could be large in relation not only to individuals' and families' resources – which is the point of special importance for pensioners – but to the balance of ownership and control in industry.

From the point of view of the elderly, the question is whether it is possible to reach generally acceptable formulas which combine large-scale redistribution with the guarantees of retention and accumulation offered (but in a form unlikely to achieve political consensus) by the proposals of trade unions and the Left. In principle it should be possible to do so, for the problem of guarantees in this case is no different from that of ensuring that contributions to pension schemes shall remain committed to that purpose, though with freedom to administer and invest the committed funds in different ways. As in the case of pensions, nation-wide measures, by law or collective bargaining, are likely to be needed to ensure that all are covered. The institutions for administering committed funds, however, do not – any more than in the case of funded pensions – have to be on a national scale. Small decentralised trust funds or registered investment accounts for individuals may serve as well, and need not run the same risk of political backlash.

Exploitation of the possibilities of increasing the accumulation of personal and family assets for old age, and of making it easier and less damaging to convert some of them, such as homes or farms, into income when the time comes, is still only in a primitive stage. It is not surprising that American respondents in 1978 put so little emphasis on it. But it has substantial possibilities even in the short run and for the benefit of existing pensioners, particularly in the case of income from home-ownership. Its potential is still greater if schemes for capital accumulation and redistribution can be developed over a period of years.

4.7 Work: The Future of the Age of Retirement

The other main resource of the elderly, particularly of the young-old, is employment or self-employment. It is an important source of income to those who have it. Among elderly families in Britain in 1975, only 7 per cent of those with a head still in paid work (the great majority part-time) had incomes at or below the social minimum level, compared to 40 per cent of families whose head was no longer working: though even among young-old pensioners, in families where the husband was aged between 65 and 69, only one family in three did have a working head.[41] But there are contradictory trends on work for the elderly, and these point to a major question about the future of retirement age.

On the one hand, there is a widespread trend towards earlier retirement and the reduction of minimum pension ages. This trend is clear in the case of men and single women. In that of married women, the proportion who remain in employment after minimum pension age has increased in a number of countries. This, however, reflects the increase in the proportion of married women who are in employment in middle age rather than any new tendency for women, once they are in employment, to work longer. There is a mixture of reasons behind the general trend. One is the general shift in preference between work and family and leisure interests, which shows itself also in younger age groups. Others are more selective, for example, recognition of the case for early retirement for workers who have health problems or are employed in severe conditions or in posts of high executive responsibility. In recent years the trend to earlier retirement has been accelerated by unemployment, and one country after another has introduced plans to encourage older workers to leave the labour market.

There are also, however, pressures the other way. One is for flexibility of retirement ages upwards as well as downwards. Evidence from a number of countries shows that a significant proportion of people who are compulsorily retired (under the 'retirement guillotine', in the well-chosen French phrase) would have wished to work longer if they had had the chance; according to one British survey, perhaps 35-40 per cent of them.[42] They tend to be in white collar or service rather than industrial jobs, and more in self-employment than among employees, and their reasons vary. A factor in some countries, including Britain and the USA, is inadequate coverage or benefits under occupational pension schemes or the erosion of benefits by inflation and transfer losses. British executives with good pensions after long service with a single employer tend to retire early, others work on.[43] This reason for continuing work would presumably fade away if pension standards were improved, but others would remain. It is significant that the self-employed, who can choose their own moment at which to retire and often also have substantial assets on which to support themselves, tend everywhere to phase themselves more gradually into retirement than employees. More of them withdraw at least partially from work before the normal retirement ages for employees, but more, also, continue in at least part-time work afterwards.

National policies have increasingly responded to this wish for flexibility of retirement age upwards. The American case is particularly striking. The federal Age Discrimination in Employment Act of 1967, as amended in 1978, prohibits compulsory retirement at any age for federal employees, and compulsory retirement before age 70 in all establishments employing 20 or more. How older Americans will respond to this opportunity remains to be seen, but the fact that there was enough political pressure to generate the 1978 amendments is significant in itself. American social security still retains a retirement rule, in the form of an earnings limit for pensioners aged less than 72. A number of other countries, however, for instance Denmark, the Netherlands, and France, already have no earnings or retirement rule, and in Britain the earnings rule is being phased out.

Another reason for pressure towards later rather than earlier retirement is, again, the question of pension costs and public expenditure.[44] Some countries face a continuing rise in the proportion of the elderly – or, more significantly, of the combined total of the elderly, children, and other dependents – to the active population. The expectation of life of the elderly has risen, and bio-medical developments could increase it further to an extent not easy to foresee. When a forecast of the American population aged 65 and over in the year 2000 was made in 1977, the expected number turned out to be three million greater than had been anticipated in a similar forecast in 1971.[45] A French study by Bourgeois-Pichat shows how, on some admittedly well-stretched assumptions about fertility and longevity, the proportion of the population of Europe aged over 65 could by 2050 reach 43 per cent.[46] Britain happens not at the moment to have the prospect of an increase in the numbers of the elderly to the active population, but has also by European standards a particularly low expectation of life for elderly men. Simply catching up with other countries' standards could thus make a substantial difference to the size of its elderly population.

Besides demography, there is the question of rising support costs for the inactive elderly. Though the position differs from country to country, pensions systems in general still fall short, and often well short, of the 'public service' standard. If existing commitments to advance towards this standard are combined with possible new claims on behalf of pensioners, including better benefits, earlier retirement, and the effects of earlier retirement in reducing the active population and the base for taxes and contributions, the resulting bills can look very formidable indeed.

Detailed examination of the case of British social security (even on fairly optimistic assumptions about future employment and growth) shows reason to doubt whether existing (and rising) commitments to raise social security pension expenditure, plus claims – likely to have substantial political and industrial support – for such things as a higher basic pension or its equivalent through a tax credit scheme, crediting in existing pensioners and older workers to earnings-related social security pension, and earlier retirement will be met in full as they mature towards 1990 or 2000. It would be easier to meet these claims and commitments if it were possible to cut back on expenditure for other groups in need, such as single-earner families, and there are some short-term tendencies in that direction. As was said above, however, the needs of some of these groups have in recent years attracted increased priority. In the long run, it is not necessarily pensioners who will win in a competition for scarce funds.

On the other hand, examination of the British case also leads to two conclusions about how work for the young-old could help to relieve the situation. One is that, given world economic conditions, there is more chance that full employment will be recovered than that there will be a high rate of economic growth. It could be easier to ensure employment for the young-old than to secure large increases of funds to support the elderly outside employment. Secondly, if it became the norm for the able-bodied young-old – this argument, clearly, does not apply to the disabled – to work at least part-time up to, say, age 70, the release of funds through saving on pension costs, plus the increased yield from taxes and social security contributions, would be on a scale substantial enough to allow at least the most urgent of the claims and commitments likely to arise on behalf of the very elderly and disabled, for whom support through pensions and direct services is essential, to be met without any net increase in pension contributions or taxes.

The writer happens to be particularly familiar with the British case, but as Stanford Ross' report on *Social Security: a World-Wide Issue* shows, Britain is simply one illustration of an issue now raising its head right across the industrial world. So far as pensions technique is concerned, there is no special difficulty about enabling the young-old to continue part-time work with part-pension. Sweden, for example, had built a plan of this kind into its social security system since 1976. In other respects, however, work for the able-bodied young-old is not only a very big issue but one which is only now beginning to be explored. It would involve a large change in the attitudes and expectations of young-old people themselves. Can it be brought home to them that their own chances of fully adequate support in disability and advanced old age may depend on their willingness to forgo part of their present pension rights, and to continue to earn at least part of their living through work up to later ages than at present? Discrimination would be needed not only between the able-bodied and the disabled but, probably to a greater extent than at present, between the pensionable ages of those working in more and less severe conditions. Large changes would be needed in employment practices, including more openings for part-time work and greater willingness to accept the elderly as new recruits, given that older workers often need to change occupation if they are to continue to work, and that this will often involve a change of employer. A policy of work for the young-old is likely also to be practicable only as and when full employment is recovered. Married women got their footing in the labour market in the last generation largely because, at the time, the demand was there; that will also be a condition for the young-old in the next.

No country is likely to embark easily on a policy which reverses the trend towards earlier retirement. A first step might be to recognise that this trend could in the long run be counter-productive and that measures to encourage it should be discontinued. That, however, would be a minimum: the question which is becoming pressing is whether these measures ought to be put into reverse. If the arithmetic of demography and support costs is as has been suggested, work for the young-old is a key issue for social security policy as a whole as well as for policy for the elderly. Ensuring adequate support for all those who *must* depend on income transfers from the active population, whether the very elderly, the disabled of pension age, or people in need in younger age groups is likely to depend on willingness of people of all ages, while they have health and opportunity, to minimise their own claims on the money available for transfers and to continue to provide their share of taxes and contributions as active workers.

4.8 Conclusion

This chapter has discussed the four main sources of income from the elderly: social security, including supplementation to guarantee the social minimum; occupational pensions; alternative 'own resources'; and work for the young-old. It has one essential theme. The going in the years to the end of the century is likely to be hard. If the bill for what has come to be seen as the desirable standard of income for the elderly is set alongside the prospects for additional resources from public or industrial expenditure, it is clear that all four sources will need to be used wherever and so far as is practicable. Advances will have to be looked for where they can be found. The keyboard will need to be played with more flexibility than has sometimes been the case in the past, according to where the best prospects in each country appear.

The least easy area in which to find additional resources seems likely in many countries to be taxation (including social security contributions) and public expenditure. Possibilities in the other three resource areas will therefore need to be particularly carefully examined, and one thing which even a preliminary examination shows is that the policies required in them are likely in many countries to have a different quality from those usual in the past. Piecemeal advances are useful, and worth having where they can be obtained. A common thread running through the last three sections of this chapter is, however, the need to systematise, generalise, and where necessary develop new institutions, so as to convert what have hitherto been sporadic, unevenly spread, and often minor and unreliable sources of income into substantial and reliable resources available to all or at least (as in the case of income from owner-occupation) large sections of the elderly. Occupational pensions need a superstructure to enable them to become a primary, reliable, and generally available source of pensioners' income. Policies for converting home-ownership into income, and for savings, capital sharing, and the 'investment wage' need to (and can) be developed on a scale big enough to make them a substantial source of income for the general body of the elderly, but only if a number of large and potentially controversial policy decisions are faced and the necessary new institutions and legal frameworks are created. The question of work for the young-old calls both for major decisions of principle and for a comprehensive and systematic approach to the wide range of problems which it raises.

Ensuring adequate income for the elderly in the coming years is likely to require thinking sideways (exploration of the possibilities of under-exploited sources) and thinking big. A touch of acid drips from the writer's pen when he reflects that in France the class of private sector employee to which he belongs has, for thirty years, enjoyed transferable and index-linked occupational pensions, related to their whole number of working years, because the French national employers' and trade union confederations had the vision to see, as their British opposite numbers had not, what could be achieved by agreeing to equip their pension schemes with a nation-wide superstructure.

Lastly, it is worth adding a reminder about the point emphasised at the start of this chapter. Income provision by itself does not remove poverty. To guarantee a standard of living free from deprivation, it is also necessary to consider what money can buy, i.e. to consider the elderly as consumers, not only as receivers of income. The final link between income and standard of living is made by factors such as are considered in other chapters: the availability and accessibility of services, including financial accessibility to insurable services, e.g. health; mutual aid and voluntary supplementation of services; and, last but not least, the development of individuals' and families' own 'capacity to cope'.

Notes

1. E.g. P. Townsend, *Poverty in the United Kingdom* (Penguin, Harmondsworth, 1979).
2. Quoted in T. Wilson (ed.), *Pensions, Inflation and Growth* (Heinemass, Sweden, 1974), p. 54.
3. See, e.g. the assessment of their own deprivations by British pensioners in M. Abrams, *Beyond Three-Score and Ten* (Age Concern, 1978).
4. A. Guillemard, *La Retraite – une Mort Sociale* (Mouton La Haye, Paris, 1972).
5. Summary in M.P. Fogarty, *40 to 60 – How we Waste the Middle Aged* (Beford Square Press, London, 1975).
6. T. Wilson (ed.), *Pensions, Inflation and Growth* (Heinemass, Sweden), p. 199.
7. *European Commission, Second European Social Budget 1976-80* (1979), and underlying Tables in Commission paper COM (78) 318 final/A.
8. Stanford G. Ross, *Social Security – a World Wide Issue*, typescript, July, 1979.
9. See figures quoted in M.P. Fogarty, *The Future of Pensions and Retirement Age in Britain* (publication by Policy Studies Institute in 1980), Table 27.
10. Commission of the European Communities, *The Perception of Poverty in Europe* (Brussels, 1977); and Table 28 and text, Fogarty, M.P. *The Future of Pensions and Retirement* (1980).
11. See the discu ssion by N. Questiaux and J. Fournier in S.B. Kamerman and C.J. Kahn (eds.) *Family Policy* (Columbia, New York, 1978).
12. M.P. Fogarty (1980), Table 29.
13. *The Government's Expenditure Plans 1979/80 – 1982/3*, Cmnd. 7439, 1979, p. 143.
14. M. Abrams, *Profiles of the Elderly – Their Standards of Living* (revised edn.) (Age Concern, 1979).
15. E.g. summary in M.P. Fogarty, *40 to 60 – How we Waste the Middle Aged*, p. 115.
16. T. Wilson (ed.), *Pensions: Inflation and Growth.*
17. *American Attitudes Towards Pensions and Retirement*. Hearing before the Select Committee on Aging, US House of Representatives, 28 February, 1979.
18. Data from T. Wilson (ed.), *Pensions, Inflation and Growth*, and Government Actuary, *Occupational Pension Schemes 1975* (HMSO, 1978).
19. Example from T. Thunberg, *The Swedish Pension Scheme*, in J.A. Fry (ed.), Social Policy and Practice in Sweden, mimeo, 1976.
20. T. Wilson (ed.), *Pensions, Inflation and Growth*, p. 194.
21. *Socio-Economic Policies for the Elderly – Contribution from the United States*, OECD, paper SME/SAIR/E/79.07, 1979, p. 68.
22. See the rapid increase in contributions shown in National Association of Pension Funds, *Survey of Occupational Pension Schemes 1978*.
23. *Socio-Economic Policies for the Elderly*, OECD.
24. T. Wilson, (ed.), *Pensions, Inflation and Growth*, pp. 274, 277.
25. R. Layard *et al.*, *The Causes of Poverty*, Background Paper 5 for the Royal Commission on the Distribution of Income and Wealth, HMSO 1978, Table 10.12.

26. British Institute of Management, *So You Thought you Were Earning a Two-thirds Pension! – Well, Think Again*, Mimeo, December, 1978.
27. *American Attitudes Towards Pensions and Retirement*, (1979).
28. Details in T. Wilson (ed.), *Pensions, Inflation and Growth*.
29. E.g. the summary of the American debate in *Aging and Work*, Fall, 1979.
30. T. Wilson (ed.), *Pensions, Inflation and Retirement*, p. 363.
31. Supplementary Benefits Commission, *Annual Report 1978*, Cmnd. 7725, 1979, ch. 12.
32. Department of Health and Social Security, *Social Assistance – A Review of the Supplementary Benefits Scheme in Great Britain*, DHSS, 1978.
33. Supplementary Benefits Commission, Cmnd. 7725.
34. See the Green Paper on *Proposals for a Tax-Credit System*, Cmnd. 5116, 1972.
35. For Liberal proposals see P. Vince, *To Each According* . . . Liberal Publications Department, 1979.
36. Royal Commission on the Distribution of Income and Wealth, Reports 1 and 7, Cmnd. 6171 and 7595, 1975 and 1979.
37. Supplementary Benefits Commission, Cmnd. 7725, Table 12.16.
38. Summary in 'Capital Gains – With Great Relief', *New Age*, Winter, 1978-9.
39. *American Attitudes Towards Pensions and Retirement* (1979).
40. *Asset Formation and Employee Participation*, European Commission, 1979.
41. R. Layard *et al.*, *The Causes of Poverty*.
42. Age Concern, *The Attitudes of the Retired and the Elderly*, 1974. For the USA see *American Attitudes Towards Pensions and Retirement* (1979), Ch. 2.
43. R. Berthoud, *Unemployed Professionals and Executives*, PSI, 1979, Ch. 9.
44. Data in M.P. Fogarty, *The Future of Pensions and Retirement Age in Britain* (1980), one of six national reports (UK, USA, Sweden, Denmark, France, Germany) for a series of policy seminars in 1980 organised by H. Sheppard (American Institutes for Research in the Behavioural Sciences). See also H. Sheppard, *The Graying of Working America* (Free Press, New York, 1977).
45. *Socio-Economic Policies for the Elderly* (OECD), pp. 109-111.
46. J. Bourgeois-Pichat, *Le Dilemme de la Révolution Démographique, Croître ou Vieillir*, paper to World Conference of Institut de la Vie, Vichy, April, 1977.

5 HOUSING AND THE ELDERLY

Derek Fox

5.1 The British Housing System

In Britain, housing problems and policies have been prime issues at most national and local elections, ever since the returning soldiers in 1919 were promised 'homes fit for heroes'. Consequently all political parties have treated the subject positively, and although policies and programmes have been adopted with varying emphases, there has been little dispute on the current gravity of the housing situation at any time.

Much housing was built for Britain's working classes during its Industrial Revolution to very poor standards. A great deal of the better housing built in inner cities for Edwardian gentry has since drifted into multi-occupation and considerable over-use. To this inheritance has been wedded a policy of rent control, which has applied to much of the privately rented housing stock since 1914. Thus a large proportion of houses owned by private landlords has been slum-cleared or bought by owner occupiers or public housing agencies, and the majority of the remainder is becoming obsolescent.

Table 5.1: Tenure Patterns of Households in Great Britain

1945	Type of Tenure	1978	
%		%	% over 65
25	owner-occupier	55	48
15	public housing	32	36.5
60	privately rented	13	15.5

The rent control policy has also had a side effect of leading to an expectation of low housing cost levels; this has allowed the British to indulge in high aspirations of housing standards. Tradition has it that 'an Englishman's home is his castle' for more than security reasons. It can be said that good housing is considered a necessity of life for social, economic and climatic reasons, more than in most comparable nations. It is also an indicator of social and economic attainment.

There has been considerable state and individual investment in housing since 1919. There has also been a large shift in tenure pattern since 1945. At 1978 there were some 18.5m houses for 18m households, although these figures conceal regional shortages and include substandard dwellings. Five million of these households contain a person over 65.[1]

5.2 Housing Financial Policies

Government assistance towards the provision of new housing and the improvement of existing dwellings has tended to be blunt and haphazard. A major provision has been in the form of tax relief on interest paid on mortgages by owner-occupiers; but most mortgages are the result of increasingly expensive trading up-market and do not in themselves improve the housing situation; there is also the resultant anomaly that those who can afford high mortgages gain more than poorer mortgagees – or indeed those who have paid off their mortgage.

Generous government subsidies have been made available to local authorities; this has resulted in the growth of an exceptionally large public housing sector, accommodating a third of the population. Only a comparatively minimal amount is provided by voluntary housing associations (250,000); the latent encouragement of this sector is fostered by the public misconception that such 'voluntary' efforts must consume less subsidies than local authorities, who have a large housing income from profit rents of houses built when costs were low.

Capital spending on public housing is determined by an annual review by the Government of the Housing Investment Plans of 459 local housing authorities and of the Housing Corporation (which determines the allocation to some 2,900 housing associations). Revenue subsidies are determined annually, and the Housing Act 1980 provides for an annual calculation of the local contribution from rent and rates (the local property tax).

Separate statistics for expenditure on housing for the elderly are not recorded at central or local level so the actual costs of this service cannot be assessed; however, limited information on the costs of wardens indicate that these vary widely among local authorities, even within the same county area.[2] The markedly different levels of provision also suggests wide variances in loan debt liabilities for housing old people.

5.3 Housing Conditions of the Elderly

It could be assumed that housing conditions of the elderly would tend to compare unfavourably with the remainder of the population because they have lower income, they have less mobility from older housing, and they are often prepared to tolerate substandard housing because they have not experienced anything better. Thus of 1m households lacking at least one basic amenity (inside WC, bath or shower, hot water supply) in 1978, almost half of them contained people over 65.[3]

But comparative housing hardship cannot be conveniently quantified in statistical terms. Many elderly people are more accustomed to outside WCs than younger households; but the journey to it gets progressively more arduous and hazardous with advancing years. Good but inconvenient housing may effectively ruin the quality of life of many elderly persons; steep stair-rising may well virtually imprison some for the remainder of their lives; heating the home adequately may become physically as well as financially impossible to those who need warmth more than most; the proximity of 'family' to assist in some of the every day tasks in life may be crucial; and too much living space can be almost as difficult as too little.

Thus 'housing need', the criterion normally used to judge the allocation of public housing, may have little relevance to the need for more suitable housing. Indeed it could well be that moving an elderly person may well release housing which could be better utilised and maintained by a larger, active family.

Many elderly people have great worries about property maintenance and of keeping a large house clean, the garden tidy and the hedge trimmed. But opportunities are limited to move to more appropriate housing in the owner-occupied sector, and few vendors would wish to restrict their potential market by producing housing solely for the needs of the elderly.

5.4 Public Housing Provision in Britain

Responsibility for providing housing for the elderly – or any other group of need which cannot obtain suitable housing – has been fixed firmly in Britain on the local housing authorities; legislation has been framed deliberately to minimise accountability by the government or the central departments of state. Local authorities, themselves democratically elected, delight in this ability to decide their own policies and priorities, and vehemently defend any attacks on their local autonomy. Indeed an independent local government is jealously regarded as one of the essential checks and balances of the British form of democracy. Paradoxically it has not prevented the massive growth of 'council' housing; this term needs no further adjectives to describe in many people's minds a drab standardised ubiquitous product provided in every locality – wherein live those people who are not responsible enough to obtain their own housing, who appear to enjoy many luxuries of life at other people's expense, and who are the source of vandalism and unruly behaviour, if not potential criminals and opponents of society. In other words, a similar epithet for public housing in most other countries. What is of concern is that in Britain this can be applied to a third of the population, who somehow find themselves looked upon as second class citizens.

Similarly during the decade 1965-75 Britain embarked upon an expensive public housing programme, under varying political powers at central and local levels, which produced much housing which was patently disliked by potential consumers, and which is proving unduly expensive to maintain and manage. It seemed more important to allocate resources into producing a large number of dwellings, rather than securing more effective local policies and the sensitive management of the already huge public housing stock. For example, a much discussed report in 1969 pointed out that the then Ministry of Housing employed over 150 professionals to control the public building programme whilst it had only one professional housing manager to advise the department, the then 1,356 local housing authorities in England and Wales, and a myriad of housing associations.[4] (In 1978, the Department of the Environment appointed 3 housing management advisors, but other building professionals were maintained at the previous level despite a dramatic decline in the programme). Similarly of the 50,000 officers employed by local authority housing departments, less than 4 per cent are professionally qualified for the work they do, and DOE has never taken on any responsibility for training and certification which, for example, the departments of Education and Health accept as part of their similar central/local administrative arrangements.

Consequently although local accountability would appear to be more responsive to democratic control, the absolution of central responsibility in public housing for national policies and practices has effectively blurred fixing liability for egregious errors and omissions. But as control of public sector spending has grown important in successive governments' overall financial policies, so local authorities have effectively found their autonomy emasculated. The Housing Act 1980 will continue this trend.

Public housing also suffers from fragmentation from other allied services in most areas. For example, only 68 of the 402 housing authorities in England and Wales are also responsible for social services; in 333 non-metropolitan authorities a separately elected county council deals with residential care, i.e. communal accommodation provided under Part 3 of the National Assistance Act, and domiciliary services for the elderly. A separate Area Health Authority is a directly appointed body whose areas may well not be coterminous with either housing or social services councils.

5.5 Public Housing for the Elderly

Thus housing for the elderly in Britain tends to lack the central direction of a national policy, and there are considerable variations in local policies, level and type of provision, and who-gets-what. This can take the form of an effective bar on some people in need, e.g. newcomers to a district, owner-occupiers. It has been pointed out that such barriers may be detrimental to the needs of elderly persons more than the general population.[5] Such parochiality of vision is a strong counterbalance to the benefits of local autonomy. Nevertheless the provision of specially designed and managed housing for the elderly has a strong emotive appeal to local housing authorities and voluntary housing associations, and it is true to say that it has generally escaped the criticism mounted at other public housing, or indeed other types of residential care for the elderly.

Like most other public housing provision, the local cost of old persons housing policies is obscured because of the large-scale effects of inflation on historic building costs, variable subsidies from the national exchequer and local rates, altering commercial interest levels, the pooling of all rents for all properties in the local housing revenue account, and side benefits such as freeing existing housing stock. It would seem, however, that whatever form it takes, it has cost advantages over other forms of residential care.

Originally many housing organisations provided old people's dwellings as an accepted method of introducing variation in the public housing stock. These were generally in the form of bungalows spread around a housing estate and examples from the interwar years can be found in many cities. Voluntary bodies also pioneered special housing provision for the elderly, and a noteworthy example is Whiteley Village, Walton on Thames, which was started in 1908. As the provision of flats becomes seemingly more inevitable because of planning considerations on the dwindling supply of building land, so most authorities began to erect a large number of one-bedroomed flats, which could be allocated to elderly people as well as one or two person younger households. However, such provision did not solve the problem of caring for elderly people when they became ill or frail; many have also been caused great worry because of the proximity of noisy neighbours especially children – they prefer to be able to observe everyday life taking place around them, but prefer not to take an active part in it.

5.6 The Growth of Sheltered Housing

Consequently the concept grew of grouping old person's dwellings together, served by a resident warden. This has become known as 'sheltered housing for the elderly', although the term has not yet been used in DOE advice. A plethora of central advisory publications assisted the spread of this practice during the 1960s.[6] Yet in my visits to over 300 housing authorities as DOE's advisor on housing management 1968-73, I encountered many who had not considered the subject, and many others who had had to be spurred on by grants from their county councils (who saw benefits to their other elderly person's social services). This culminated with the publication by DOE of circular 82/69, which not only spelled out a comprehensive policy for housing old people, but included very detailed advice on design. Again, however, there was very limited housing management input: I was preoccupied at the time as secretary to the Cullingworth Committee and with surveys into housing organisation in Northern Ireland, and thus was unable to devote much attention to it. I did, however, voice my concern at the overriding philosophy of the circular, but was assured that it would be reviewed within two years. In fact not only was the 1969 circular not amended during the decade of explosive growth of sheltered housing which followed it, but in contrast with the earlier flurry of activity, the only official advice published by DOE during the 1970s was one design bulletin on the size of schemes.[7]

By the beginning of 1980, it could be estimated that local housing authorities in England and Wales had provided 250,000 dwellings which meets the definition 'grouped housing specifically designed for the elderly and served by a resident warden', and 40,000 have been provided by housing associations (a quarter by three large national ones); this is 5 per cent of the public housing stock then in management. Updated census material suggests that 5 per cent of people over 65 live in such housing, with a further 3 per cent in old person's housing without a warden and 3 per cent in residential care.[8]

5.7 The Design of Sheltered Housing

The introduction to the check list on the special aspects of designing for old people's dwellings which accompanied circular 82/69, outlined the general concept thus:

> The purpose which underlies the design of housing for the elderly is the provision of accommodation which will enable them to maintain an independent way of life for as long as possible. With improved health services more people may be expected to remain in a home of their own for the rest of their lives. If they are to do this in comfort, they will need housing designed with the special requirements of the elderly in mind, coupled with the availability, as far as possible, of a balanced range of different types of accommodation to meet their varying needs and preferences. It has to be remembered too that most old people for whom housing is being provided will eventually be living alone and all housing for old people needs to be planned for sociability so as to avoid loneliness and isolation. This is particularly desirable where rehousing involves moving to a new area and, though the subject is outside the scope of this circular, good housing management practice can assist by keeping together groups of friends and neighbours as far as practicable.
>
> Of the different types of housing which can be provided for the elderly, bungalows – traditionally regarded by old people themselves as the ideal form of housing – are best suited to couples who are able to maintain a greater degree of independence, who can manage rather more housework and who may want a small garden.
>
> Two storey flats are more economical of land than bungalows, can provide a more compact layout, fit in well with family housing and can be used on infill sites. Many people over the age of 64 can still manage one flight of stairs and an upper flat may be preferred by those who dislike sleeping on the ground floor. Taller blocks with lifts can provide acceptable accommodation for old people, if suitably designed and sited, in those places where the density justifies

> their use.
>
> For less active old people, often living alone, who need smaller and labour-saving accommodation, grouped flatlets as described in Circular 36/67 (Welsh Office Circular 28/67) and the two publications 'Flatlets for Old People' and 'More Flatlets for Old People' are the most suitable. The tenants of these flatlets will have the services of a warden and also communal facilities such as a common-room and laundry; and possibly a guest room as well. Bathrooms may be shared for one-person flatlets (in the ratio of one bathroom to four flatlets) or private in the case of two-person flatlets but every flatlet will contain a w.c. and hand basin. Additional facilities such as a call-bell system will also be needed.

Note that two distinct forms of housing are envisaged, outlined in the circular as Category 1 'to accommodate one or two old people of the more active kind', and Category 2 'to meet the needs of less active elderly people'.

Professional housing management opinion over the ten years since 82/69 has hardened against 'flatlets' i.e. bedsitters with shared bathrooms, and most sheltered housing at present being built consists of one-bedroomed dwellings. This obviates the need to transfer a person from Category 1 to 2 on death of a partner. An audio alarm system has also superseded the call bell in most new schemes.

The check list also suggested that a scheme should consist of 30 units maximum; whilst this is still regarded as an optimum number, larger schemes have proved successful and it is possible to recommend making better use of good sites with double that amount, as long as the design and management is sensitive to the problems of an unflattering image of an old people's colony.[9]

5.8 A Policy for Rehousing Elderly People

It seems that for every ten people who begin to thrive and obtain a higher quality of life when allocated sheltered housing, there is one who goes into a decline because he moves at the wrong time of life. I have always been perhaps unduly concerned about this experience, and in 1971 I put forward a suitable policy for housing elderly people thus:

(1) to provide sufficient housing specifically designed and managed for the needs of the elderly people – attractive to active elderly

but adequate for the infirm;

(2) to allocate this to tenants before their need is urgent – an aim could be state retirement age;

(3) to encourage the active elderly to assist in the management of the scheme and in the social well-being of the group;

(4) to encourage independence as much as practicable, but also to provide services, e.g. emergency call, domestic assistance, a luncheon club, and an active social intercourse;

(5) to arrange for the full provision of medical and welfare services for those needing care and attention, with the object of maintaining the tenant in his own home within the community and minimising the admittances to residential care.

This would entail a recognition that sheltered housing has become so successful that its original concept now needs to be replaced by an alternative objective of providing suitable housing for as many old people as possible until the end of their lives.

5.9 The Success of Sheltered Housing

There can be no doubting the success of sheltered housing, both with its tenants and administrators. It passes the acid consumer test; few social workers would want to live in an old person's home, but most housing officers aver (only half in jest) that they have made arrangements to retire into one of their sheltered schemes!

Success can be assessed in the following criteria:

(1) providing old persons with housing specifically designed to take account of their needs, capabilities and limitations, free of the frustrations many experience in normal housing in a non-sheltered environment;

(2) freeing elderly people from worries like 'what's going to happen to me if I'm ill, or fall'?, and giving them greater opportunities to live independently longer in life – often until the end of life itself;

(3) encouraging easy social intercourse with elderly people of similar interests, and generally improving the quality of their life;

(4) assisting social service and area health authorities to plan their resources;

(5) promoting a more rational use of public housing stock by

allowing larger housing vacated by elderly people to be occupied by larger families, who can maintain it better (and it is assumed also in the private sector when owner-occupiers are housed).

I estimate that I have now inspected some 350 sheltered schemes and studied some in considerable depth. I have not found any scheme which I have judged to be a failure and the great majority could be described as very successful. A doubt however persists: could not they provide a better contribution to the whole range of social care policies for the elderly by adopting a revised philosophy based upon experience since 1969, with an added injection of resources?

5.10 Criticism of Sheltered Housing

The major concern of sheltered housing emanates from its very success: people are living in schemes much longer than was ever considered, and they refuse to move on to the next sequence of care, as originally envisaged, i.e. Category 1 to Category 2, thence to residential care under social services and eventually to a geriatric ward of the area health authority. The economies in health and social services have compounded the problem, in that old people's home and hospital places are often not available when required. Thus older schemes tend to become 'silted-up' with old people who require a great deal of supervisory care and domiciliary services to remain within the community. Even if people could be divided into Category 1 or 2, they will not stay that way, and it is wrong to move people at a time they can least adapt to change.

The provision of sheltered housing has not kept pace with the demands now being placed upon it, and in many cases new schemes are being opened with a high potential degree of intensive care to be provided. Although recommendations on the role of the warden have found general approval, there is little standardisation of her duties and emoluments; in any event the increased responsibility resulting from older communities has rarely been recognised by additional staff.[10] Health and Social Services tend to over-rate the warden's services, and economies may well force them to give priorities to other old people with no support, jeopardising confidence in the sheltered scheme and engendering opposition in the housing authority left with the responsibility.

There is no general acceptance of scale of needs; an initial target that

5 per cent of people over 65 should be in sheltered housing recommended by Townsend in 1959[11] as an alternative to further development of residential care has now been achieved nationally, but an analysis of Housing Investment Plans for London Boroughs in 1979 indicated variations between 2.5 per cent and 15 per cent.[12] A study of 12 local authorities in England and Wales in 1978 indicated wide differences in actual provision ranging from 13.2 per cent of sheltered housing per population over pensionable age (i.e. man 65 woman 60) to three with less than 1 per cent (the lowest was 0.3 per cent and a median would be 2.5 per cent).[13]

5.11 Findings of a Sheltered Housing Survey in Essex

In 1979, with the co-operation of the Essex Chief Housing Officers Group, I undertook a survey into 42 sheltered housing schemes – three structured samples chosen by the housing officers in each of the 14 local housing authorities. The principal findings, which did not differ substantially from earlier studies made by the Essex Wardens Association into less representative samples, were as follows.

Table 5.2: Essex Survey (1)

Age Range of all Residents	No	%
Under 70	250	17
70-74	344	24
75-79	435	30
Over 80	423	29
Total Residents	1452	

Table 5.3: Essex Survey (2)

Dependency Rated with Type of Scheme						
Type	Schemes	All Residents	Over 75	%	Infirm	%
Cat 1	18	581	340	59	210	36
Cat 2	19	653	399	61	255	39
Dual	5	218	119	55	81	37
Total	42	1452	858	59	546	38

Note: 'Infirm' was defined as a resident who was likely to be confined within the scheme for long periods.

Table 5.4: Essex Survey (3)

Dependency Rated with Age of Scheme

Date Built	Schemes	All Residents	Over 75	%	Infirm	%
Up to 1969	10	324	229	71	132	41
1970-74	17	559	338	60	217	40
1975-79	15	569	291	51	197	35
Total	42	1452	858	59	546	38

Note: 'Residents' include people living with tenants, but not the warden's family.

The Tenants were Older than Planned. Most schemes had over half their residents over 75, and were accommodating people over 90: in all 50 per cent were over 75 and thus of an age where dependency expectancy could be high (see Table 5.2).

There was Little Difference in the Character of Tenants of Category 1 and Category 2. The age and the warden's rating of infirmity was similar whatever the type of scheme. Indeed it was remarkable how few wardens knew what category of scheme they were managing. Obviously the choice and allocation of tenants depended more on location rather than design and amenities (see Table 5.3).

There was not a Wide Variation in the Needs of Tenants of Older and New Schemes. Housing managers and wardens have only been too aware of the 'silting up' syndrome of schemes which have been accommodating old people for 10 years or so, who cannot or will not move to the next sequence of care. But, although all Essex councils try to follow a policy in allocating a good mix of ability, such are the demands and shortages that new schemes are starting with a high potential (if not actual) dependency ratios (see Table 5.4).

Wardens had an Onerous and Demanding Job. Most wardens were undertaking duties beyond their job description and were obliged to cover long hours of stand-by without adequate recompense: they had had little training to cope with the myriad of responsibilities thrust upon them by the needs of tenants, but in truth few thought they needed it. Many wardens felt isolated, insecure and unhappy with their dealings with other officers concerned with care of the elderly: a quarter were classified as manual workers, which had obvious reflection on their status and attitudes.

The Provision of Domiciliary Assistance was Low. Potentially dependent tenants like those in these 42 schemes should need support from health and social services. But the following incidence was reported; 28 per cent of tenants had home help, 8 per cent regular visits from home nurses, 6 per cent social workers and 12 per cent received cooked meals. Wardens drew the conclusion that they were expected to cope with the remainder.

Few Tenants had Help from Relatives. There were very wide variations in schemes, but only a median of 18 per cent of tenants were reported as receiving regular assistance from relatives. Although this can be taken as a diminution in the acceptance of responsibilities of extended family support, there are other factors, e.g. the more mobile society for young and old, the low interwar birth-rate, fatalities during the last war, and the inescapable fact that many tenants are so old that their children are now elderly too!

5.12 The Future of Sheltered Housing

There is no reason to believe that this snapshot situation report of the sheltered housing in the 14 Essex local authorities is particularly untypical of the national picture in Britain. However, a wider study is now being undertaken in Leeds University, funded by the Joseph Rowntree Memorial Trust and the National Council for the Care of Old People. The study has an objective to examine the role and contribution of sheltered housing and related services for the elderly provided by public and voluntary agencies, and to assess the potential for developing such provisions or altering them. It will assess the situation in England and Wales, and concentrate profiles of 600 tenants, 280 wardens and administrative arrangements in 12 sample local authority districts. It is envisaged to take four years from 1978.

When the study has reported, it will then have to go through the normal processes of discussion among departments of state and with local authority associations and representatives of those interested housing associations. It will therefore be some time before its implications are fully appreciated and these are translated into policy formulation. But I believe that sufficient is now known about the development of sheltered housing since 1965 for reviews to be made at national and local levels to ascertain how this fits in with an overall policy for care of the elderly, and what demands it makes on it.

DOE should now publish its long overdue review of circular 82/69. In particular it should decide whether it wishes to continue the artificial distinction between Category 1 and 2 schemes (already dropped in Scotland) and to give advice on the assessment of need and targets to be adopted (it is an unfortunate consequence that Housing Investment Plans have inevitably become objectives to be cut, rather than a base for growth). Above all, DOE should amend the statement in 82/69 '1 warden = about 30 units' in view of the much higher degree of assistance required from the older case-load of the warden.

5.13 Improving Warden Support

The support required to a sheltered scheme from the warden and other domiciliary services should be decided annually by an on-site meeting between housing, health and social services, and firm arrangements made for their provision.

Compared with the £10,000 million national annual expenditure on elderly,[14] the £30 million p.a. spent on warden service[15] (albeit to only 5 per cent of elderly) is minimal, and any improvement would bring considerable benefits with very little difference to the public expenditure programme. In any event, any additional warden cost could be recovered in a service charge, allowable for rent rebates and supplementary benefits.

The residential warden service could be improved in the following ways:

Making Conditions of Service More Attractive. The Local Authorities Conditions of Service Advisory Board is currently examining the national position, and it is hoped that any recommendations would be firmer and implemented more widely than its previous report in 1975. The opportunity should be taken of creating greater job satisfaction and opening possibilities of some career progression by a greater involvement in other front line management duties.

Giving a Resident Warden more Assistance. Many housing authorities operate a relief warden purely on 1 or 2 days a week to allow the resident warden some time from responsibility. This is an under-use of an expensive provision which should be extended to allow other periods when she could assist the warden directly with her work; the maximum warden service should not be necessarily restricted to only one warden on duty at a time, in view of the increasing demands from ageing tenants.

Better Training. The perceived need for training has been abysmally low throughout the whole public housing service, and this has been a dominant factor in many of its much criticised shortcomings. It is considered that wardens would be eager to co-operate if it could be demonstrated to them how training could help them better understand and cope with the physical, mental and social demands and changes in their tenants.

Utilising Relatives More. There is often misunderstanding of the concept of supported independence of sheltered housing; the necessity for continuing support of those relatives which are available should be emphasised by the compilation of a special leaflet; similar information for health and social workers has also been found of value.

5.14 Very Sheltered Housing Schemes

Some local authorities and housing associations have been encouraged by the success of sheltered housing in keeping old people in the community (albeit a sheltered one), to increase the degree of domiciliary support substantially in order to cater for people who would normally be considered for residential care. Chichester DC, one of the pioneers of what has become known as very sheltered housing or Category 2½, caused great comment in providing 7½ management staff for 100 tenants in a sheltered scheme at Farrsfield in 1972. However, by the standards of a residential home, this provision was considered well worthwhile by the social services authority, West Sussex County Council. A similar partnership between Southampton DC and Hampshire CC provided Kinloss Court in 1977; this project is being monitored by Southampton University to examine whether this allows its tenants to maintain or develop sources of self-esteem (the preliminary results have been encouraging).[16] (See Table 5.5)

The development of such schemes indicate a welcome departure from the widespread belief that one resident warden can be expected to cope with an ever expanding case-load, as the tenants in her care get older and more infirm. Furthermore, by securing the ready co-operation of housing and social services, they have shown that the level of support can be reviewed according to variable needs, and that the resident wardens can be given the task of organising such services. However, the scale of needs at Kinloss Court is not all that higher than shown in the Essex Survey, yet the scale of services provided is much greater.

Table 5.5: Kinloss Court Project

	Essex Survey	Kinloss Court
Residents over 65	59%	72%[b]
Low ability	38%[a]	62%
Cooked meals	12%	67%
Home helps	28%	75%
Community nurse	8%	50%

(a) not identical criteria.
(b) 79 per cent at nearest residential home.

Very sheltered schemes are therefore demonstrably reaching a market a large proportion of which at present would be normally on the waiting list for residential care, and they seem to be stemming and filtering entry into 'the last refuge'. However they have been the source of criticism that there is little difference in public image between the two, and thus the social desirability of sheltered housing will suffer. If they were to develop as part of the normal provision in future years, then this would entail an extension of the 'sequential theory', which involves moving people at the wrong time of life and has encountered consumer resistance.

5.15 Sheltered Housing Linked to a Residential Home

In 1968 I inherited a report from Miss M. Empson, my predecessor at the then Ministry of Housing and Local Government outlining a survey she had made of 12 schemes where sheltered housing had been linked with a residential home. Although this had formed the basis of departmental policy, it was decided not to publish it, I therefore resolved to bring the survey up to date by studying a further 12 schemes. These ranged from old schemes provided by voluntary bodies (such as Whiteley Village and Sevenoaks and District Housing Association) to new schemes provided by district councils in co-operation with county councils (such as at Basingstoke and several districts in Cheshire). My report reached identical views to the previous one, but again it was decided not to publish it (with hindsight I should have modified the comments on residential homes, which had aroused the opposition of the Department of Health and Social Security, but even so the Ministry of Housing preferred not to state its views so plainly so that its policy could be attacked). By coincidence an article was published by Selwyn Goldsmith at this time, which had arrived at the same conclusions from a more detailed study at Norwich of a linked scheme compared with a nearby orthodox sheltered scheme.[17]

The 3 studies had looked at the advantages of the linked concept:

(1) there can be economies in providing shared amenities and services;
(2) a better standard of service can be provided, in particular a 24-hour emergency call and cooked meals;
(3) tenants can move into the home when it becomes necessary, either short term or permanently;
(4) a small residential home can be provided which may otherwise not be economically viable.

The disadvantages were:

(1) the combined scheme may produce too large a colony of old people, segregated and inward looking;
(2) it may be difficult to acquire a suitable site large enough and to co-ordinate the building and staffing of the developments, and even then the layout usually entails either the housing or the home being shielded from the active view of the street;
(3) the association of the two types of consumer do not prove to be cohesive, and in fact produce a 'we and them' division so great that the progression from housing to residential care is seen as a downgrading in status;
(4) the type of service required for the housing is different to the home, and indeed the former may well take second place to the latter.

We all came to the conclusion that the advantages claimed were theoretical, and had not worked out so well in practice. On the other hand, although the disadvantages involved taking value judgements, they all seemed so real to the three of us, all working separately without preconceptions, that we judged them to completely outweigh the advantages of the 25 linked schemes studied.

If a linked scheme is to be successful, then the predominant image must be of orthodox housing, rather than residential care. This was achieved in Cheshire, where the social services authority was able to erect 20 bed homes, generally considered to be not financially viable. But additionally the home needs to develop gradually by accommodating existing tenants, sometimes on a temporary basis. Should the home open with imported residents then opposition will inevitably occur; if it can accommodate existing known tenants when they can no longer look after themselves, then it may become acceptable. Thus the residential home should be built several years after the housing, and should be confined as much as possible to serve those tenants.

5.16 Housing Aid for the Elderly

Almost 90 per cent of elderly people in Britain live in a non-sheltered environment. In many cases they would not want to move – their housing may suit their needs, they may like the area, and they may have friends or relatives living nearby to assist. But many others would like to consider some change, and advice on how to go about it.

Since 1970 there has been a growth of housing aid and advice centres, some attached to local authority housing departments and a similar number of voluntary agencies. This new philosophy of housing aid has grown simultaneously with comprehensive housing departments, that is that housing authorities should be as interested in the private sector, and the problems and opportunities therein, as in building and managing council housing estates.

However, a survey of Housing Aid Centres in London in 1975 showed that they were essentially geared towards assisting families (or exceptionally single people) and they had relatively few elderly clients: whatever advice on housing elderly people were receiving was from non-housing trained counsellors in organisations like Age Concern or Citizen Advice Bureaux, or from non-housing officers such as social workers, health visitors, community nurses, general practitioners or home helps.[18] This led to the recommendation that new skills should be developed by a specialist housing advisor with the following brief:

(1) to centralise procedures around one person – e.g. allocation of

special accommodation for the elderly, consideration of non-routine application forms for elderly clients;

(2) to centralise information about the range of possible housing options and the range of support services, so that the information can then be disseminated as appropriate to those who need it, e.g. housing aid staff, housing visitors, housing welfare officers;

(3) to give a member of staff a watching brief for the elderly person's interests so that housing policy and procedures that tend to be family orientated are just as relevant to the elderly.[19]

5.17 Non-sheltered Housing Options

A specific housing advisor for the elderly was pioneered in London Borough of Hammersmith from 1976,[20] and this has been instrumental in developing a more sensitive and comprehensive approach to elderly people and seeking additional and often preferred options in assisting in their housing problems. For example, a project was developed for the inner-city programme 'to ascertain whether it be possible and appropriate to bring the sheltering, supportive and recreative aspects of sheltered housing to isolated individuals in the community; to enable elderly persons to remain in their homes by the provision of communication, alarm systems and support from an area warden'. This project fits naturally into a crowded inner-city area; it could, however, be extended to all areas surrounding a sheltered housing scheme, so that the warden services and community provision can become the hub of a much larger catchment area, many of whom may eventually become sheltered tenants. Those staying in their own houses can be advised on what adaptation could be effected to make life easier; the transfer of such work to housing departments has led to a great increase – the Chief Housing Officer for Wrekin DC has estimated that this has doubled in two years since he took this responsibility from Shropshire CC.

5.18 Consumer Choice

Many elderly owner-occupiers do not wish to become council tenants, mainly because of the associated stigma, but also because of confusion of the roles of sheltered housing and old people's residential homes.

Many, however, would be happy to rent some housing association sheltered housing if they knew that they existed, where they were, and whether they were eligible; advice would also be relevant as the best means of utilising the windfall from the sale of their house to provide for future income. Alternatively, there are some associations specialising in leasehold retirement schemes of sheltered housing with warden support; this is a method whereby elderly people purchase a lease expiring at death of tenant (and partner if applicable), when it can be sold by the association and the proceeds returned to the next of kin. At Hammersmith it was also proposed that elderly owner-occupiers taking up such a lease could sell their house to the Council at valuation if required; unfortunately the scheme did not materialise.

5.19 Retirement Migration

Public sheltered housing is frequently concerned with the undesirability of forming old people's colonies; they may be insulated but not isolated from the normal community. However, there is evident consumer preference in the private sector to move on retirement to areas which it is known contain a high proportion of elderly people. In Britain migration tends to concentrate in sea-side resorts, as is the case in many other similar democracies. Although this migration is normally confined to owner-occupiers, Bournemouth and Southend have large privately rented sectors attracting the elderly, and the Greater London Council had a successful programme of 'Bungalows-by-the-Sea'.

A study of this phenomenon has recorded that the majority of those migrating on retirement were not disappointed.[21] But problems crop up, usually associated with death of partner or unforeseen ill-health or financial hardship. Thus there is marked opposition in such resorts, particularly because of the extra expenditure required by social services to support twice a normal aged population, few of which have relatives nearby to turn for assistance. It should not be impossible for the government to give more adequate weighting in its Rates Support Grant to assist such areas and allow the free expression of consumer choice.

5.20 Miscellaneous Financial Assistance to Elderly Householders

Although almost half the people over 65 are owner-occupiers (see Table 5.1), the financial benefits of tax relief on mortgage interest to this group is small, as compared to the general population. It has long been a British aspiration to own their own house outright on retirement; thus it can be assumed that a large proportion of those owner-occupiers without a mortgage (some half the total) would be elderly persons.[22] Similarly it can be inferred that most of those elderly people with mortgages will have comparatively small ones, and thus do not qualify for much tax relief, especially as many will be paying tax on a lower scale, if at all. Inflation in house prices has proved a fortuitous friend to most elderly owner-occupiers, most of whom could not otherwise afford to live in their currently priced homes.[23] It is perhaps unfortunate that most elderly people have not been able to cash in on the enhanced value of their houses by annuity linked mortgages determinable on death of householder and spouse.

Many old persons are, by historical accident, tenants of privately rented homes subject to rent control; thus they benefit indirectly by government policies, although this may also cause the private landlord to be reluctant to invest on necessary repairs or improvements. Central and local subsidies are also payable for the Housing Revenue Accounts of public housing authorities, and although these increased to some half of annual income following the Housing Rents and Subsidies Act 1975,[24] there is a definite intention to reduce these under the provisions of the Housing Act 1980.

A more direct form of financial assistance to old people in straitened circumstances may come from national schemes, propounded by the Housing Finance Act 1972, for rent rebates (to local authority tenants), rent allowances (to private and housing association tenants) and rates rebates (to all householders). Those pensioners receiving supplementary benefit may also apply for a special grant calculated on rent payable and also for heating their homes. Working knowledge suggests that the majority of elderly tenants will benefit from one or more of these schemes of assistance towards housing costs, although cases are still frequently encountered where old people's pride has not allowed them to apply for such entitlement.

5.21 Conclusion

The availability of suitable housing in the right area can be crucial to the quality of life of elderly people. This will become more important when the population over 75 rises by 25 per cent during the 1980s.[25]

Sheltered housing for the elderly, provided by local housing authorities and housing associations, has proved to be eminently successful in meeting such needs, and indeed has become a preventive service in many cases.

But it is being jeopardised by its very success. Elderly do not want to move on to the next sequence of care, and places may not be easily available because of economies in public expenditure. The DOE needs to revise its 1969 circular to take account of evident changes in philosophy. Support should be brought to people in need, rather than expect them to move to where this has been planned to be provided. The role of the warden needs to be re-assessed now that she is not only concerned with allowing old people to live independently, but also to die within the community.

Attention should also now be devoted towards sheltering people in their present homes, and more expression of consumer choice allowed. Housing policies for old people must be considered within the whole comprehensive package of care for the elderly, and they should be regularly reviewed at all levels so that they can play their optimum part. The British experience indicates that good and suitable housing can be provided which assists substantially towards a happier old age; but success should not lead to a sanguine inflexibility and indifference to additional forms of housing assistance.

Notes

1. Statistics based upon National Dwelling and Housing Survey, Department of Environment 1979 (with extrapolations for Scotland and Wales).
2. Housing Statistics, Housing Management and Maintenance, 1977-8, published by the Chartered Institute of Public Finance and Accountancy 1978 indicates an average warden cost of £100 p.a. per dwelling involved. In a survey among the 14 local authorities in Essex, I found this to vary from £50 p.a. to £200 p.a.
3. Source: National Dwelling and Housing Survey, Table 10 plus extrapolated census 1971 material for Scotland and Wales.
4. See paras. 64-70 'Council housing: purposes, procedures, priorities' 9th report of the Housing Management Sub-Committee of the Central Housing Advisory Committee, 1969 HMSO, known as the 'Cullingworth Report'. As secretary to this sub-committee, and the sole advisor on housing management, I had some embarrassment in trying to progress its recommendation that the central housing management functions should be strengthened.
5. Paras. 296-304 'Council housing, purposes, procedures, priorities'.
6. For example 'Flatlets for old People' 1958; 'More Flatlets for old People' 1960; 'Some Aspects of Designing for old People' 1962; 'Grouped Flatlets for old People 1964; 'Old People's Flatlets at Stevenage' 1966; all Ministry of Local Government, HMSO. Also 'Housing for old People', 1970; Scottish Development Department, HMSO; 'Grouped Dwellings for the Elderly', 1967, Institute of Housing Managers.
7. 'The size of Grouped Schemes', 1975, DOE, HMSO. The Building Research

Establishment, a semi-autonomous subsidiary of DOE also published a paper on alarm schemes in 1976. 'Housing Needs of the Elderly', 1971, was one of my series of informal housing management papers distributed at DOE advisory stands at the Institute of Housing conferences, 1972-3. 'Housing for old People – a Consultation Paper' had limited circulation in 1976 from DOE, but the resultant review of 82/69 did not appear.

8. Culled from 'A Happier Old Age', 1978, Department of Health and Social Security, HMSO; see also 'The Elderly at Home' 1978, Office of Population and Census Surveys and Survey of Public Housing for the Elderly, DOE, 1980.

9. See 'The Size of Grouped Schemes' 1975, DOE.

10. 'Role of the Warden in Grouped Housing', 1972, Age Concern. The Local Authorities Conditions of Service Advisory Board issued watered down guidance in 1975 based upon this report, but this did not receive total adoption by local authorities.

11. 'The Last Refuge', P. Townsend (Routledge and Kegan Paul, 1960).

12. Report to London Boroughs Association Housing and Works Committee, London Housing Office, Camden Town Hall, London N1.

13. Reported in 'The Development of Sheltered Housing for the Elderly', Alan Butler and Christine Oldman, 'Housing' July, 1979.

14. Source: 'A Happier Old Age', 1978.

1 15. Source 'Housing Management and Maintenance Statistics', 1977-8 indicating average warden costs of £100 p.a. x 300,000 sheltered units.

16. See 'Assessment of Self-esteem and its Sources in Elderly People Living in Kinloss Court', report to Kinloss Court Steering Committee July 1979, G.P. Coleman.

17. 'Accommodation for old People: Two Schemes at Norwich', Selwyn Goldsmith, Architects Journal, 28 January, 1970.

18. See 'Housing Advice for the Elderly' (Age Concern, London, 1977), Ch. 2.

19. 'Housing Advice for the Elderly', Ch. 10.

20. See report in 'International Help Age' July/August, 1977.

21. See 'Retiring to the Sea-side', Valerie Karn (Routledge and Kegan Paul, 1973).

22. For example Table 11 of BSA Bulletin January 1980 (published by Building Societies Association, 34 Park Street, London W1) indicates that new mortgages granted to people over 55 in 1979, including those trading-in existing houses, was only 3 per cent of the total.

23. BSA Bulletin January 1980 indicates average house prices in UK to their mortgagors rose from £4,640 in 1969 to £20,835 in 1979. Working knowledge suggests that many elderly owner-occupiers purchased their houses when average prices were considerably below £1,000.

24. 'Housing Statistics' Part 2 1977-8, CIPFA, indicates that of the income of the agglomerated housing revenue accounts for 324 local housing authorities in England and Wales, 42 per cent come from central exchequer, 9 per cent from rates, and only 41 per cent from rents of the houses concerned.

25. See Population projections of Office of Population Censuses and Surveys.

6 BARRIERS TO MOBILITY

Alison J. Norman

6.1 Introduction

Mobility is a relative term. For a paralysed man it would be a miracle of freedom if he could get up from his chair. The traffic-bound motorist looks at the helicopter overhead and wishes that his car could sprout rotors. Nevertheless, it is true to say that a physically fit person who owns his own car, and can afford to run it, has a greater degree of personal mobility than any individual has enjoyed in human history. And if his use of a car is extended by high-speed trains and world-wide air services, the world is his oyster (except for those parts cut off by war, revolution, iron curtains and the strikes of air-traffic controllers). This may become less true as the energy shortage begins to bite, but it is still true in 1980. Industry, commerce and social custom have all become geared to this ease of transport. Huge lorries carry components from one specialist factory to another, hundreds of miles away. The corner shop loses out to the supermarket and the supermarket to the hypermarket. Young men and women travel thousands of miles to seek employment or adventure, or just to get away from mum. Holidays in another continent have become commonplace.

In this era of constant movement, people who cannot move so easily are increasingly at a disadvantage. Those who cannot drive, or do not have easy access to a car, depend on their feet and public transport to reach essential goods and services or to enjoy any kind of social life. But walking has become difficult and dangerous because vehicles have priority over pedestrians; pavements are crowded, cluttered and uneven; and mugging and bag-snatching is a constant threat. Public transport in rural areas is fast disappearing, and everywhere it is becoming more expensive and more unreliable. It is not only elderly people who are thus 'transport-disadvantaged'. As I have said elsewhere:

> Our concern is with the transport problems of the population as a whole . . . for it cannot be emphasised too strongly that the elderly are *not* in a special category so far as transport is concerned. Most walk some of the time, some drive, some are dependent on public transport, some are disabled and some need specialised services – all

> in exactly the same way as their fellow citizens in any other age group. The mobility problems of the elderly are therefore of general relevance and any improvements in services would be of general benefit.[1]

This chapter therefore focuses on the barriers to mobility encountered by those who have no easy access to a car and who may have long distances to travel in order to get the goods and services which they need.

Much of the evidence cited has been drawn from research done in the UK, but the international conference on Mobility for the Elderly and Handicapped which was held in Cambridge, England, in 1978, clearly showed that the basic facts and figures apply to any industrialised society. Papers given at this conference have also been extensively used as a source of information and I am indebted to the editors of the conference report for permission to make use of their material.[2]

6.2 Access to Private Cars

Everywhere in industrialised societies, elderly people are less likely to own cars than their younger contemporaries. The highest percentage of elderly car-owners is probably in the United States (57 per cent in 1973), but even there nearly half the elderly population are without access to their own car. In the UK, the National Travel Survey 1975-6 indicated that 70 per cent of people aged 65 or more in England and Wales lived in a household without a car and only 15 per cent had both a household car and a driving licence. Averages of this kind are misleading because car-ownership varies a great deal by location and a vehicle which may be a luxury, or even a nuisance, in an inner-city area becomes a necessity in the depths of the country. Nevertheless, even in areas with poor public transport and a high average level of car-ownership, people of pensionable age are much less likely to live in a car-owning household than members of other age groups. This was well-illustrated by a survey carried out in the UK by Political and Economic Planning (see Table 6.1).

Table 6.1: Housing Density in Relation to Access to Cars for Pensioners and Young Housewives

	high density	medium density	low density	rural
	%	%	%	%
In car-owning household				
pensioners	17	30	58	29
housewives	80	83	93	84

Source: Mayer Hillman *et al.*, *Transport Realities and Planning Policy*, (PEP, London) Vol. 42 No. 567, pp. 137-8.

Such percentages do not remain static, however. We know, for example, that in the UK 64 per cent of men in the 60-4 age group and 18 per cent of the women held a full driving licence in 1975-6 compared with 41 per cent and 7 per cent for those aged 65+.[3] Many drivers in their early sixties will undoubtedly struggle to keep a car on the road for as long as possible after they have reached pensionable age. Migration can also have a dramatic effect on levels of car-ownership in a particular location. For example, Martin Wachs in his study 'Lifestyles and Changing Transportation Needs of the Elderly in Los Angeles' found that during 1940-70 the social and demographic patterns of the elderly in Los Angeles County had changed from a predominantly central city population to a predominantly suburban car-owning one. These trends are expected to continue, though the current energy crisis may have some effect on them.[4]

Another factor which is of key importance in determining the level of car-ownership by elderly people is cost. If, as in the UK in 1977, the cost of running a car is half the basic state pension, it is not surprising that a detailed survey of the travel patterns of elderly people in the English country town of Guildford found that expense was the second most important reason for elderly people giving up their cars (22 per cent of respondents). (The most important factor (29 per cent) was that the licence-holder in a marriage partnership had died).[5]

Costs of purchase, fuel, insurance and maintenance are rising inexorably and it seems possible that during the next few years an increasing proportion of elderly people will find that they can no longer continue to afford a car, even though they have been accustomed to running one during their working lives. As Robson points out, people who are forced to give up car-ownership from ill-health or financial pressure or the death of the licence-holder may be in a less fortunate situation than those who have never had one, because they will not have adapted to travelling by bus or on foot. They may not live close to shops or on a bus route and their social contacts may be spread over a wide area and not easily accessible by public transport. So while more of the elderly population are likely to have cars in the future, the problem of adjusting to living without cars will also get worse as widowhood, poor health and high costs force an increased number of car-owners to give them up.[6]

Lack of access to a car thus implies a higher risk of a number of related handicaps which together make up a generally disadvantaged state of life. Robson, quoting unpublished material from the Guildford study, states that those most likely to be without access to a car are the older age groups; women; those living alone; those with poorer health and difficulty with walking; and those with low incomes in retirement or who used to have low-paid jobs before retirement. They are also often disadvantaged in other ways. For instance, they tend not to have telephones and this of course hinders their ability to request domiciliary visits from doctors and other supporters, make enquiries, order goods, ask for help from neighbours, or make use of special transport schemes and taxi services – all of which can be employed as a substitute for lack of personal transport.[7]

It is therefore obvious that in planning to meet the transport needs of those who do not have easy access to a car, we must also take into account the numerous other factors which may affect their life-style and their wish and need for mobility. As Barker and Bury have pointed out 'mobility is more than a purely mechanical function and depends on an enabling environment, the ability to continue to achieve active personal goals and the development of social life in the community'.[8]

6.3 Elderly Pedestrians

The importance of walking as a mode of transport is still a very neglected subject. As David White says 'Walking is a bit like breathing; an activity so natural that we are scarcely conscious of it . . . Far easier to conceive of day-to-day transport as wheels, and a choice of transport as simple a choice of wheeled vehicles – car, bus, train or bike.' Yet, as he points out, the UK 1975-6 National Travel Survey showed that 44 per cent of all journeys were made on foot, slightly more than by car (39 per cent) and considerably more than by public transport (12 per cent).[9] Paradoxically, the more disabled a person is, the more likely he is to walk rather than use public transport because of the physical difficulties of coping with access to buses and trains. The environment for pedestrians is, however, becoming more and more hostile. White describes how:

> Rows of parking meters on the pavement provide a slalom course for the walker, and pavement parking actually pushes the walker off his puny strip of pavement . . . Even if a pavement doesn't actually become narrower, it can seem narrower to walkers if it has to accommodate more of them. Extreme examples are the sidewalks of Manhattan; they have become heavily overcrowded because, while the sidewalks have remained the same width, the density of the buildings leading on to them has increased vastly.[10]

Crossing the road has also become an increasingly hazardous business, even for the young and active. Traffic lights often do not include a pedestrian phase and even when this is provided, it often does not allow enough time for slow walkers. One Swedish study has found that the assumed average walking speed of 1.4 metres per second to which Swedish traffic lights are geared is a 'normal comfortable' speed for only 3 per cent of the people over 70 who were tested, and that only 20 per cent could go as fast as this when asked to hurry. The author concludes that 'traffic signals are definitely not made for slow pedestrians'.[11] A UK study of the use of pelican pedestrian crossings reinforces this view. On this type of crossing the light for the first pedestrian phase is set to require a walking speed of 2.1 metres per second (a third as fast again as the Swedish system). Measurements of the time taken by 179 people to cross a carriageway have shown that such a speed is not attained on average by any age group, least of all the elderly. When the lights go into their next (flashing) phase, pedestrians who are already on the crossing still have priority but vehicles can go through if the road is clear. The study showed that many elderly people do not realise that they can still cross in safety (or should be able to do so) and are very frightened at being still in the roadway, and this fear is often reinforced by aggressive behaviour from waiting drivers. As a result elderly people are often reluctant to use the crossings at all.[12]

It is therefore not surprising that walking is several times more dangerous than travel by motor vehicles, and almost as dangerous as travel by bicycle. Robson states that it has been estimated, using UK National Travel Survey data, that pedestrians have an accident rate of 400 accidents per 100 million miles walked, which is five times the rate for car travellers. Pedestrians account for 37 per cent of fatal road casualties and 25 per cent of serious injuries. These are figures for the population as a whole, but elderly pedestrians are still more seriously at risk. The fatal accident rates for the elderly in the UK are more than two and a half times those for the younger adult pedestrian and pedestrians aged 70 and over have a casualty rate over five times the 25-39 age group.[13]

Greater risk naturally carries greater fear with it and many elderly people are literally afraid to go out. A comprehensive analysis of traffic accidents among the elderly conducted by the University of Bielefeld showed that many older persons, and especially women and those living in institutions, felt insecure and endangered in traffic; 57.3 per cent of those interviewed wanted children and adolescents on bicycles and mopeds banned from pavements and 48.8 per cent felt that traffic lights changed against them too quickly.[14] It is clear that pedestrians in every country need to acquire the organisation and the will to fight the motorist's lobby and other powerful commercial forces, if they want effective action to be taken. As Hillman and Whalley say:

> Regrettably, people are killed and injured on the roads in a fairly random geographical pattern so that the impact is diffused. Moreover, the very fact that accidents occur so frequently seems to dull instinctive responses of sympathy, and demands for ameliorisation of the situation then becomes more apathetic. Additionally, the media often see their function more to capture the public imagination than to inform it. As a consequence front page headlines and photographs are used to dramatise the horrific loss of life in an air or train crash (both of which occur extremely infrequently but with relatively large numbers of people involved), but only a few column inches are devoted to each year's toll of death of the roads. The statistics are then presented with a degree of cold bloodedness more appropriate to statistics on annual rainfall.[15]

Only political action will bring home to local and national authorities, what these statistics mean.

6.4 Physical Access to Public Transport

There are two principle reasons for difficulty of access to public transport. The first is that it is simply no longer there to be used – competition from the private car and constantly rising costs having made the old rural transport networks no longer viable. The second is that, where buses and trains are still running in adequate numbers, poor design and unhelpful drivers and conductors can make them uncomfortable, dangerous or impossible to use by those who have a temporary or permanent disability (including mothers with young children and people with luggage). The disappearing stage bus and local train is a problem in its own right and there is no space in this short chapter to discuss it. It must suffice to say that UK experience indicates that given sufficient ingenuity, community good feeling and determination, it is possible to devise new forms of local public transport in rural areas which go some way towards meeting the gap.

This section is concerned with what various countries are trying to do to make their surviving public transport systems more accessible to the 9 per cent or so of the average population which is not so disabled as to require door-to-door transport but does have at least some physical difficulty in using buses and trains. More than one third of the population over 65 is in this situation.[16] Only in the United States has it been formally resolved, by the Urban Mass Transportation Act of 1970, that the elderly and handicapped should be given the same rights as others in using mass transit facilities and that all new facilities should be designed in such a way that they are accessible to these groups. This policy has been applied to Rapid Transit systems as well as to buses so that, for example, the Bay Area Transport (BART) in San Francisco was made accessible to people with all types of disability at a cost of $10 million, after a major legal battle.

In most westernised countries, however, the approach has been to make such systems accessible to the moderately disabled, without attempting to provide for the wheelchair bound. For example, London Transport commissioned a firm of architects to study ways in which the Underground system could be made easier for people whose mobility was impaired but who could negotiate escalators. Their suggestions included: the introduction of recessed 'pause' places in long tunnels where people can stop and rest without holding up the rush hour tides of commuters; clearer warnings of change of level and direction; improved lighting to give better definition to steps and treads; use of pictograms to give travelling information; use of colour contrast to help those with poor sight; improved design of handrails; more seats on the platforms; and the introduction of tickets whose return part can be identified by touch as well as by sight. The authors also advocated more rigorous application of the UK Chronically Sick and Disabled Persons

Act 1970 to the design of approach stairs, ramps, lavatories, shops and other parts of station concourses, which are not the responsibility of the Transport Authority.[17] Unfortunately there are no visible fruits of these proposals on the London Transport system at the time of writing.

The problems of adapting buses for easier use by disabled people are very complex. Here there are two types of barrier. One is the hazard resulting from actually using any bus system: for example, getting to the stop; waiting for the vehicle, and perhaps having to stand for some time in bad weather conditions if the service is not reliable; keeping balance in a moving vehicle; finding money while an impatient queue waits; getting through automatic doors; and not being able to see well enough to know what bus is coming or when the destination is getting near. Other hazards arise more directly from the design of buses themselves. Even for those who are not severely disabled, the height of the step, the positioning of bells and handrails, the type and positioning of seating, changes in floor level and a number of other factors can make buses difficult or frightening to use. Efforts to improve matters therefore have to focus both on design, and on attitudes of the staff and travelling public, reliability of service and the provision of sheltered waiting facilities with seats. Improving design by itself will be of only limited assistance.

The United States has now made it mandatory for all new buses which have been bought with the aid of federal money to have a maximum floor height of 22 inches, with an ability to 'kneel' to 18 inches, and to be equipped with a ramp or hoist for boarding by the wheelchair-bound. This policy has aroused much controversy. The improvement in accessibility can mean deterioration in other aspects of the service, arising from increased capital cost, slower operation, reduced proven reliability and high operating costs. Indeed, there is some evidence that elderly consumers in the United States are more anxious to obtain the provision of a basic service network in rural and suburban areas than to obtain redesigned vehicles, and there is a degree of dispute between the elderly and physically handicapped younger people in this connection.[18]

No other country has gone 'all out' on accessibility in the way the United States has done, but in the United Kingdom, a Government circular, issued in 1973, encouraged concern for such matters as step height, positioning of handrails and bellpushes, fare collection systems, seating, and storage space for wheelchairs and this was followed up by a study of the problems by British Leyland on behalf of the Transport and Road Research Laboratory. This study found that probably about four million people in the country (of which two million are over 65) are too disabled to negotiate a step height of seventeen inches (the legal limit) and about half a million could not manage the most modern designs with step heights of ten and a half inches. Proper positioning of handrails was found to be one very important factor in determining whether people could or could not get up the step (87 per cent of British Leyland's sample of elderly and handicapped citizens could manage a seven inch step using handrails, but only 47 per cent without them). British Leyland's researches have resulted in the production of a new double-decker, the B15, which has a step height of twelve inches, a level floor, higher ceilings, improved stability and carefully positioned handrails. They claim that it is accessible to about 2½ million people in the UK who cannot use conventional buses. It is also very expensive – about £5,000 more than standard designs – and so it seems unlikely that most authorities will be able to introduce it for many years.[19]

Access to long-distance trains and air services is yet another problem. Here France appears to have led the way. Article 52 of 'A Law of Orientation of Handicapped Persons' (1975) gave the Government power to regulate vehicle construction standards and modes of access. This was followed in 1977 by the institution of a Liaison Committee for the Transport of Handicapped Persons, with responsibility for developing co-ordination between the interested parties and creating a logical overall concept. The Committee is now planning a feasible programme for modifying scheduled public passenger transport. However, the French railways (SNCF) are ahead of the statutory requirements and have already made a survey of access facilities at their stations and introduced a programme for raising platforms. Other action taken by SNCF includes: reserved parking for those conveying handicapped passengers; wheelchair availability at stations; and mobile steps which can be set up at carriage doors. Since 1976 an experimental pre-booked service has been set up on three routes, providing especially adapted seating and personal help at both ends of the journey on one train a day. This arrangement is said to be responsive to three basic principles: complete service, non-segregated service and service at a limited cost to the general public. Use has not been extensive, but the results have shown where further progress can be made. In particular, a new form of ticket collection, which does away with access barriers, will make access to platforms easier and some of the staff released by this system will be used to man a reception service 'to orient, inform, aid and assist all travellers who are in difficulty, and especially the handicapped'.[20]

In the United Kingdom, British Rail offer special facilities for wheelchair-bound people on inter-city trains, including the loan of especially narrow wheel chairs to enable the traveller to get down the aisles of trains and the ommission of tables in the end bays of coaches so that the traveller can transfer from a narrow wheel chair to a seat and have some freedom of movement when seated. New first-class coaches are being designed so that one seat can be temporarily removed to accommodate a wheel chair and special toilet facilities will be progressively provided 'where it is practicable and reasonable to do so'. In association with RADAR, the Royal Association for Disability and Rehabilitation, British Rail have also produced a guide which gives details of parking, access, ramps, refreshment facilities and toilet facilities, as well as the telephone numbers of 420 stations so that travellers can contact the stations and ask for information and assistance.

All these efforts to help very severely disabled people are to be welcomed, but the fact remains that in many countries the railways system remains difficult for more moderately disabled people to use because of stairs, escalators, poorly provided and sited travel information, and poor waiting facilities. Perhaps the biggest bugbear of all, however, is difficulty with handling luggage. In the United Kingdom, at least, porters are almost non-existent and luggage trolleys only made available at major stations which are all on one level (of which there are not very many). Personal luggage trolleys sometimes offer an answer but these add to the difficulty of negotiating steps and escalators where luggage has to be carried. Until some answer can be found to this problem long journeys by rail (and also on many occasions by air) remain exceedingly difficult for anyone but the young, strong and unencumbered.

6.5 Financial Access to Public Transport

In a period when the cost of running a public transport system is soaring, the payment of a full economic fare is becoming prohibitively expensive for those living on pensions or fixed incomes. Yet, if these people cannot afford to travel, there is a decline in the numbers of passengers carried and this pushes up the cost per passenger mile still further and so creates a vicious circle of rising costs and falling ridership.

There are two (not mutually exclusive) solutions to this predicament. The first is to subsidise the public transport services so that they are able to keep fares down and still maintain an adequate transport network; the second is to offer concessionary fares to specific groups of the population, for travel at off-peak periods when available capacity is not fully used. In the United States these two approaches are directly linked, since conventional transport operators who accept government subsidies are required to implement a regular half-fare policy for off-peak travel by elderly and handicapped people. Virtually all commercial transit companies in the United States servicing cities of 50,000 or more (some 200 in number) are in receipt of such 'Section Five' funds and so offer these fare reductions. Attempts are now being made to gauge the ridership impact of this policy.[21]

In England and Wales the situation is far more complex because in rural areas the provision of concessionary fares is usually in the hands of the lowest tier of government – the District Council – while responsibility for subsidising the public bus companies and maintaining a basic public transport network lies with the county councils. Many districts operate schemes which offer only a few pounds worth of travel tokens a year to elderly people, sometimes with some kind of means test or other restriction on eligibility – and in mid-1978 nearly 50 non-metropolitan districts in England and Wales (covering some 800,000 people over retirement age) offered no concessions at all. In some rural counties, however, a county-wide scheme has been developed, and in the great conurbations the metropolitan county authorities, which run their own bus services, offer concessions which provide all pensioners with free or very extensively reduced fares for off-peak travel.[22] The inherent unfairness and inefficiency of these disparities has been generally recognised, and shortly before it went out of office in 1979, the Labour Government announced its intention of introducing a national scheme which would offer a nation-wide, off-peak, half fare pass to people of pensionable age, on payment of a prescribed charge, while at the same time allowing local authorities to make more generous provision where local circumstances demanded a relaxation of the off-peak rule, or where more generous pass schemes were already in operation.

The government fell before this scheme could be discussed with the local authorities, transport operators and potential beneficiaries, but it is at least encouraging that the discussion paper which was issued publicly recognised that close links exist between providing concessionary travel, operating transport subsidies and maintaining a basic public transport network. It also recognised that while the bus companies should be reimbursed for the fare revenue lost from people who would have travelled even if they did not enjoy a concession, this should be balanced against trips generated by the concession. This challenges the traditional UK method of costing concessions as if all the passengers carried would have travelled in any case.

It is clear from British studies that where a free bus pass or other generous concessionary scheme is provided, and an adequate transport network exists, elderly people do make enthusiastic use of it. For example, on Tyneside a change in the concession from half fare to a zero fare and a change in availability to include Saturdays up to 10 p.m. meant that each concessionary pass holder made a third more bus journeys. In London, a change to a fare of 2p or 3p and then to a zero fare resulted in existing concessionary fare travellers making 30 per cent more bus journeys. In the West Midlands, concession holders said that they would not have made about 30 of their trips if the concession (zero fare at certain times) was not available.[22]

Undoubtedly the cost of transport does act as a severe deterrent to non-essential travelling by elderly people and thereby considerably restricts the quality of their lives. For this reason alone, much greater attention should be given to lowering the financial barriers to travel on public transport. But this is not the only, or indeed the most important, aspect of the matter. As the National Corporation for the Care of Old People said in its response to a Government Discussion Document entitled *A Happier Old Age*:

> public interest in concessionary fares too often contains a patronising element. Concessions are not a 'charitable handout'. They have an important role in that generous bus pass schemes generate passenger journeys at little extra cost to the operator, so that when the local authority pays the bus company concerned on the basis of the full fare for an estimated number of journeys made, the result is a hidden subsidy to the bus operator. It follows that concessions and subsidies should be considered together and that both should be related to the debate about economic pricing of transport, the minimum acceptable level of rural transport provision, and the case for a general provision of off-peak return fare concessions. Travel concessions for the elderly cannot and should not be considered in a vacuum.[23]

The relevance of that comment is not confined to the United Kingdom. There is certainly a case for increasing the basic level of pensions so that elderly people can afford to buy the travel which they need, but it is not only the elderly who are severely disadvantaged by exorbitant travel costs. Unemployed or low-paid rural workers and their families, and members of large or single-parent families, also have serious difficulties with fares. If the countryside is to be kept alive and these people are to be enabled to obtain the goods and services which they require, the provision of adequate public transport at reasonable cost will have to be considered as a basic national essential, on a par with clean water, an efficient sewage system and nation-wide electric power. The fuel crisis is now ramming this point home.

Use of Taxis by the Elderly

It is becoming evident that commercial taxis are an important transport resource for the elderly people who are not fit enough to use public transport or who have no public transport available to them. A study by the Institute of Public Administration found that in many American communities (particularly those under 100,000 in population) taxis were the only form of public transport, but that even where a bus service did exist, taxis might be preferred, in spite of the cost, because of the door-to-door flexible service which they offered.[24] However, in some parts of the USA it is legal for drivers to charge passengers separate fares so several strangers can be carried on one trip from different starting points and to different destinations. In the UK where this is not allowed, taxis are still seen by elderly people as an expensive luxury, only to be used as a last resort. The Guildford study found that two thirds of the respondents never used taxis and another quarter used them less than once a month. Only 4 per cent used them once a week or more often and this use was clearly related to a higher income.[25]

A number of schemes have now been devised which offer taxi transport at a reduced rate to the disabled, or to elderly people who are without public transport. In the United States, the Urban Mass Transportation Administration (UMTA) has sponsored three interesting experimental projects which provide elderly and handicapped people with a subsidised service. These experiments are proving very successful: they benefit the taxi drivers, who have proved willing to cooperate; they require no capital expenditure; and they are less costly than alternative demand-responsive systems. Also they can cater for limited and scattered demand, and they only cost the use which is actually made of them.[26] A similar but more ambitious scheme is working successfully in Stockholm where 72,400 disabled people of whom 80 per cent are pensioners (26 per cent of the pensioner population) are entitled to 72 single journeys per year for leisure purposes and any necessary number of journeys for work, school or medical treatment. The cost to the passenger is three crowns per journey (approximately £0.33) for any distance up to 30 kilometres taken within the county. This service is very extensively used. During 1977, 4.3m trips were made, representing about 40 per cent of total taxi production and over 5.5m were expected by 1980. Leisure trips averaged 42 a year. The service also runs 135 special buses for transport to school, etc. Its total cost in 1977 was about £20.2m of which 5 per cent was covered by fares.[27]

Clearly, such a service is of great value, but its usefulness may be limited by faults in taxi design which make entering and leaving the vehicle difficult for arthritic or otherwise disabled people. Perhaps the worst offender in this respect is the traditional London taxi which is extremely difficult to enter for wheel-chair bound people, or those who have difficulty with steps, or are dependent on a walking frame. Other designs are by no means faultless however. A Swedish study of five vehicles in most common use as taxis (Ford, Mercedes, Opel, Saab and Volvo) found that all of them had some design details which made it difficult for disabled people to use them – for example, three had unsatisfactory threshold height and/or width; two had an inadequate angle of door opening; and every model was lacking in at least two respects out of twelve characteristics being tested. The researchers concluded that the cars tested could be improved immediately by one or more of the following measures:

(1) Providing a firm cushion on the front passenger seat covered with a material that does not offer great friction while turning and sliding.
(2) Modification of the slope of the seat.
(3) Moving the seat as far back as possible with extended runners.
(4) Improvement of the profile of the threshold by making it flat at the inside edge and covering it with suitable material.
(5) Increasing the door-opening angle to 80-90°.
(6) Providing suitable handles on the dashboard, inside the doors and on the window pillars.
(7) Removing protruding glove compartments on the insides of the doors.[28]

Surely these relatively simple measures could be made a condition for the licensing of taxis, and their importance for the private car could be brought more strongly to the notice of manufacturers?

The steep rise in fuel costs and general inflation will inevitably make taxis an increasingly expensive resource, but they are still often cheaper in the provision of one-off, door-to-door transport than any alternative, except volunteers using their own cars. Those who are concerned to provide such services need to look carefully at how taxis can be most efficiently used. In the UK we also need to consider whether it would be desirable to change the law in order to allow taxis to pick up passengers along their route and operate on regular routes.

6.7 Special Transport Schemes

The mushroom growth of lunch clubs, day centres and other specialised facilities for people who are elderly, disabled, or otherwise disadvantaged has entailed the proliferation of specialised transport services intended to meet particular needs. The haphazard development of these services has resulted in a great deal of waste in terms of duplicated effort, under-used vehicles, inadequate vehicle maintenance and poor service provision. In the US Department of Health, Education and Welfare alone, for example, there are 65 Federal programmes which allocate funds for client transport as well as numerous other Federal, State, local and private programmes which also spend money on transport for specialised client groups. Operational policies such as client eligibility, service type and quality, geographical restrictions, etc. vary according each individual agencies' statutory and administrative requirements and the result, as Sahaj has pointed out, is 'duplicative expenditures and services among programmes, service gaps, overlaps and fragmentation, failure to serve broader transit-dependent populations, and failure to take advantage of the benefits of existing Federal and State transportation resources'.[29]

In the United Kingdom specialised transport is paid for from charitable funds, fare collection and local government support, not from central government resources, but as in the United States such provision is often complex and wasteful. A recent study in Birmingham identified no less than 187 voluntary bodies which arranged transport services for clients. Between them they owned 106 passenger vehicles and employed 1,008 volunteer car drivers. Twenty-one of the organisations surveyed were exclusively concerned with the elderly but pensioners also benefited from 27 bodies such as churches and community centres which provided 'non-specific' services.[30]

Serious attempts are now being made to enable and encourage agencies to organise their transport provision more efficiently. In the UK, for example, experiments are testing the effect of providing paid co-ordinators to recruit and deploy volunteer drivers on behalf of all the social services and voluntary bodies in a particular area and also to encourage the sharing of minibuses.[31] In the USA, agencies are being encouraged to co-ordinate and/or consolidate their funding and equipment among themselves. This can be done by incremental steps, starting with joint purchase of fuel and supplies, and moving on to joint information and referral, centralised vehicle maintenance, centralised dispatching and, most difficult of all, the actual pooling of vehicles under one consolidated operation. An alternative approach is to employ a commercial transit operator to run a specialised service on behalf of all the agencies involved. This has been tried out in Portland, Oregon, where the public transit authority operates fifteen lift-equipped buses supplemented by taxis and a private wheel-chair service on behalf of the relevant agencies.[32]

Another form of specialised transport is the provision of some kind of demand-responsive minibus service which can collect and deliver disabled passengers at their own request. The problem with such services is that they require the user to have easy access to a telephone (still not common for most elderly people in the UK) and cannot give the personal support at both ends of the journey which really frail or disabled people require. In the United States, extensive and sophisticated experiments are being made in this field, for example by the Central New York Regional Transport Authority.[33] Six other demand-responsive systems in the United States and Canada are said to 'represent the most innovative and promising approaches yet tried out for the transportation of the transport-handicapped' and are being subjected to systematic monitoring.[34] In Australia also, 14 Regional Councils for Social Development are trying to provide special services of this kind for the 'transport disadvantaged',[35] and an ambitious scheme is run in West Berlin where thirty adapted minibuses provide door-to-door on-demand transport for about 11,000 people who are too disabled to use public transport. The project, which is known as 'Telebus', is being treated as a research exercise and should provide a great deal of information about specialist vehicle design and transportation need.[36]

Much as one welcomes this evidence of growing awareness of the necessity for demand-responsive and specialised transport services for those who need them, it is regrettable that provision is so piecemeal and haphazard, depending on local initiative and goodwill and often arbitrary in its criteria for eligibility and suitable use. We need an overriding *political* decision such as that taken in Stockholm County, to provide door-to-door services for all who cannot use public transport and this decision needs to be followed through with thorough local assessment of the best means by which such a decision can be put into practice. At present these services are still too often considered as a bonus, a charitable donation to the disabled, and not as the provision of a reasonable level of mobility as a matter of social justice.

6.8 Conclusion

This brief review has tried to sketch the severity and complexity of the mobility difficulties which are faced by a large proportion of elderly people and to indicate some of the ways in which the problems can be tackled. But it must be remembered that no action of this kind can be taken in a social vacuum. Attitudes to transport and mobility reflect our concept of 'the good life', our concept of community and our social and ecological priorities. For example, how much should we be prepared to spend on maintaining a public transport network which is not financially viable? At what point should speed of traffic flow take precedence over pedestrian comfort and safety? Is a high level of personal mobility a luxury which we cannot afford in a world of fuel shortage and economic recession? Should we put less emphasis on getting people to centralised services and more effort into bringing essential facilities back to the local community? Should we worry less about providing transport for the disabled and more about providing the research and treatment needed to prevent rheumatism and arthritis and strokes from crippling such a high proportion of our elderly population?

Some of these questions affect not only the mobility of the elderly but all our lives on this planet, and the evidence indicates that it is high time we began to face them rather than continue to yield passively to the commercial and industrial pressures which force an ever-greater measure of centralisation and mechanisation upon us.

But although we need to think in global terms about planning for the world of the twenty-first century, we must at the same time keep our concern about how Mr Brown and Mrs Jones can get to the shops and the post office, the doctor, the church and the pub; how their friends can come to see them and they can visit their friends; how they can be enabled to cross the road without fear; or wait for a bus with a reasonable expectation that it will arrive punctually and carry them at a price which they can afford to pay. Effective action depends on keeping this dual perspective of the needs of the individual and the wider implications of social policy. It depends also on finding the political will to translate words into deeds. Only if we can find such a political will is there a chance that the nations of the industrialised world will make a serious effort to pursue transport policies which are genuinely directed towards the common good.

Notes

1. A.J. Norman, *Transport and the Elderly* (National Corporation for the Care of Old People, London, 1977) p. 9.
2. N. Ashford and W. Bell (eds.) *Mobility for the Elderly and Handicapped* (Loughborough University of Technology, 1978) hereafter referred to as *Conference Report*.
3. UK Department of Transport, *National Travel Survey 1975/6* (unpublished) STA Division, Department of Transport, 2 Marsham Street, London SW1P 3EB.
4. M. Wachs, 'Lifestyles and Changing Transportation Needs of the Elderly in Los Angeles', *Conference Report*, pp. 130-40.
5. J.M. Hopkin, P. Robson and S. Town, *The Mobility of Old People: A Study in Guildford* (Transport and Road Research Laboratory, Crowthorne, Berkshire, 1978), TRRL Laboratory Report No. 850, pp. 7-8.
6. P. Robson, *Profiles of the Elderly – their Mobility and Use of Transport* (Age Concern, London, 1978), Vol. 4, No. 6, pp. 23-24.
7. Ibid., pp. 17-18.
8. J. Barker and M. Bury, 'Mobility and the Elderly: a Community Challenge', in V. Carver and P. Liddiard (eds.) *An Ageing Population* (Hodder & Stoughton, in association with the Open University Press, Sevenoaks, Kent, 1978), p. 190.
9. D. White, 'How to Build a World that's Fit to Walk in', *New Society* 19 July, 1979, p. 124.
10. Ibid., p. 125.
11. S. Dahlstedt, 'Walking Speeds and Walking Habits of Elderly People', *Conference Report*, pp. 243-9.
12. N.G. Skelton, 'An Investigation into the Travel of Elderly People in Urban Areas' (unpublished PhD thesis, University of Newcastle upon Tyne, 1979).
13. P. Robson, *Profiles of the Elderly*, p. 7.
14. Ageing International, Vol. 6, No. 2, 1979, quoting R. Wittenbuerg, *Accidents and Security Problems in Traffic* (*Unfall-und Sicherheitsforschung Strassenverkehr: Strassenverkehers-beteiligung älterer Menschen*) (University of Bielefeld, Federal Republic of Germany, 1977).
15. M. Hillman and A. Whalley, *Walking is Transport* (Policy Studies Institute, 1979), Vol. 14, No. 583, p. 17.
16. See the *Conference Report* for national estimates of the percentage of the disabled in the community – in particular, J.R. Revis, 'Transportation Problems of the Elderly and Handicapped – an Overview of United States Experience', pp. 11-13 (USA). See also J.M. Hopkin, P. Robson and S.W. Town, 'Transport and the Elderly: Requirements, Problems and Possible Solutions', pp. 98-9 (UK); S. Simonsen, 'Special Transport Service and Modification of Conventional Public

Transport Services', pp. 215-16 (Norway); F. Blennemann and E. Pajonk, 'Additional Costs in Designing Public Transport Systems', p. 62 (West Germany).

17. J.H. Penton, 'The Use of the Underground System by People of Impaired Mobility', *Conference Report*, p. 73.

18. J. Fisher, 'The Texas Experience', *Conference Report*, pp. 192-3.

19. B.M. Brooks *et al.*, *An Investivation of Factors Affecting the Use of Buses by both Elderly and Ambulant Disabled Persons* (British Leyland, Truck and Bus Division, Leyland, UK, 1974). For a preliminary account of research relating to passenger problems on moving buses, see also B.M. Brooks *et al.*, 'Passenger Problems on Moving Buses', *Conference Report*, pp. 91-4.

20. J. Artaud-Macari, 'French Policy in Relation to the Transport of Persons with Reduced Mobility', *Conference Report*, pp. 20-6.

21. Editorial Summary, *Conference Report*, p. 153.

22. P. Robson, *Profiles of the Elderly*, p. 12.

23. *Annual Report 1977-8* (National Corporation for the Care of Old People, London, 1979), pp. 31-2.

24. J. Revis, *Conference Report*, p. 14.

25. J.M. Hopkin *et al.*, *The Mobility of Old People: A Study in Guildford*, p. 10.

26. L. Sahaj, 'Recent USA Experience with Transportation Service Innovations for Elderly and Handicapped Persons: User-side Subsidies, Accessible Transit and Co-ordinated Services', *Conference Report*, pp. 185-7.

27. I. Berg, 'Public Transport for the Handicapped in Stockholm', *Conference Report*, pp. 299-303.

28. S.O. Brattgard, 'Swedish Experience in Modifying Vehicles and Infrastructure', *Conference Report*, pp. 51-3.

29. L. Sahaj, *Conference Report*, p. 189.

30. J.M. Bailey, *Voluntary and Social Services Transport in Birmingham, Redditch and Bromsgrove* (Transport and Road Research Laboratory, Crowthorne, Berkshire, 1979), TRRL Supplementary Report 467, p. 4 and Table 1.

31. *Annual Report 1978-9* (National Corporation for the Case of Old People, London, 1980), p. 11.

32. L. Sahaj, *Conference Report*, pp. 189-90.

33. J.W. Przepiora and T.O. Wallin, 'Transport for Elderly and Handicapped Persons', *Conference Report*, pp. 227-37.

34. D. Texeira, 'State of the Art Demand Responsive Systems for the Transportation Handicapped', *Conference Report*, pp. 304-12.

35. K. O'Flaherty, 'Using Community Resources to Develop Mobility for the Disadvantaged', *Conference Report*, pp. 114-20.

36. V. Sparmann and E. Pajonk, *The 'Telebus' in Berlin (West) an International Comparison with Other Transportation Services for the Handicapped*. Part 1, SNV Studiengesellschaft Nahverkehr MBH, Zweigniederlassung Berlin, Joachimstaler Str. 17, 1000 Berlin 15.

7 CARING AND DEPENDENCY

Olive Stevenson

The purpose of this chapter is to explore some of the implications of dependency for those who need a greater degree of care in the last phase of their lives than heretofore, and for those who provide such care. But, first, let us clear away any possible misunderstanding about the use of the word 'care' and the associated term 'dependency'. Donne's perfect expression of human interdependence 'no man is an island, entire of itself' has been trivialised by over-use.[1] It remains a clear, beautiful metaphor to express the fact that human life is meaningless without opportunities to care and to be cared for, to have others depend on us and to be dependent upon others.

Before considering the problems which arise in these relationships, it is important to acknowledge that there is no value judgement inherent in the words 'independent' and 'dependent'. They are morally neutral. It is the context and manner in which independence and dependence are displayed which cause us to define behaviour as appropriate or inappropriate, or as normal or abnormal, and to consider the ways it affects other people, for good or for ill. No one challenges the need of the newborn infant for a high degree of dependence upon its parents in every aspect of life; a parent who openly fears or resents it is perceived to be abnormal (although it has to be said that such emotions may play a greater part in early relationships than is usually acknowledged). Nor, indeed, is the greater physical dependency of the aged unacknowledged.

> When thou wast young, thou girdest thyself and walkest whither thou wouldest; but when thou shalt be old, thou shalt stretch forth thy hand and another shall gird thee, and carry thee whither thou wouldest not.[2]

Thus, this discussion is founded upon the assumption that our physical, social and emotional well-being rests upon mutual interdependence and that the balance between dependence and independence will change during the span of our lives, in varying degree and in different aspects of living. For example, the emotional dependence of teenagers in love may be of an intensity unrivalled in the rest of life.

It may reflect, in part, the trauma of necessary separation from the family of origin to achieve a separate identity. Thus the very striving for 'togetherness' may reflect an inability to achieve that separation from the family by oneself.

When, therefore, we turn to consider old people we are not addressing new issues or new problems. We are seeking to relate what we know to a particular phase of life. It is important to reiterate that this chapter focuses upon that phase of life when an increased degree of physical dependency is inevitable. (How far this brings with it increased social and emotional dependency is variable but some such associated increase is likely). It is obvious that the extent of such dependency and the span of time involved vary greatly between individuals but it may be argued that physical dependency is only exceptionally found in those between retirement and (say) 75 years. There is no point in setting an arbitrary age, however, since most of the matters under discussion apply to any adult whose physical disability or frailty brings increased dependence on others, whether he be a man of 30 with multiple sclerosis or (more commonly) a stroke victim of 60.

Such persons, sad as their predicament may be, are, however, exceptional. In caring, or being cared for, physically, similar emotions will be aroused as in the case of the frail elderly. But, perhaps by the very fact of their occupying, unequivocally, 'a sick role', more attention has been given to the feelings of all concerned than to those of the frail elderly, and those who care for them. For example, these issues are sensitively explored by Miller and Gwynne in a study of the disabled living in a home run by the Cheshire Foundation.[3] We are only beginning to examine feelings and attitudes about dependency about and amongst a group distinctive in the combination of the following characteristics, first, their age; secondly, their numbers; thirdly, their diversity of economic, social and familial circumstances.

Whilst the multiple sclerosis or stroke victim is defined as 'morbid' – in the clinical, medical sense of the term – we are constantly being told that old age is not an illness. Such a social stance is in some ways helpful. It discourages old people from sinking readily into a sick role and encourages social expectations of normality. However, it may be confusing, especially in relation to the topic under discussion. On the one hand, if such pleading leads to a lack of interest in the health problems common in old age and to an acceptance of their inevitability, that is undesirable. On the other hand, since it is true that a degree of frailty is an inevitable concomitant of very old age, even if not to be regarded as 'sickness' in the clinical sense, this does not mean that the implications for care are very different from those which apply to the sick or disabled, conventionally defined. So the reassurance that 'old age is not an illness' is ambiguous, if not ambivalent.

A further aspect of dependency in old age concerns its onset. Sometimes this will be sudden as in younger people, for example, following an accident. But it is just as likely that it will be gradual. For those in direct contact with such old people, there are sensitive and complex problems concerning the appropriate response to the gradual increase in dependency. We shall return to this later.

The second peculiarity of dependency in old age is the sheer size of the problem. Of course, to the individuals concerned, each situation is unique and it should be thus. But every developed country is struggling with a community problem of the sheer numbers of very old people in proportion to the younger generation. There is thus a total 'community' burden of dependency which affects us all. For example, people put limits upon the numbers of involvements with older relatives they feel they can manage. Bluntly, if they are caring for mother, can they manage auntie or a second cousin as well? (And it is not unlikely that the last will have no surviving children.) Neighbours may, similarly, limit their commitments, knowing how hard it is to ration the time and emotion offered to particular old people, once the involvement is established.

It is suggested, therefore, that numbers *per se* complicate social attitudes to dependency on two levels; first, the purely practical – there are limits to the time available to support the aged and dependent. Secondly, it is not, I believe, fanciful to suggest that the aggregate of need raises anxieties and fantasies in the potential carers – that they could be overwhelmed, even devoured, by these needs.

The third distinctive element in consideration of our topic relates to the diversity of economic and social familial circumstances amongst very old people. This could be the subject of a chapter in itself. It is referred to here in relation to dependency to emphasise that its psychological aspects, to be discussed later, do not operate in a vacuum and that many aspects of the environment interact with the individual case, for better or for worse.

The extent of poverty amongst old people within the United Kingdom is well documented. The most recent study of Poverty in the United Kingdom by Townsend finds that 44 per cent of men aged 65 and over and women aged 60 and over (approximately 3.7 million) were in or on the margins of poverty, according to the State's definition.[4] Furthermore, the elderly poor comprised 36 per cent of the poor. There is every indication, given present government policies, that the old will become relatively poorer. There are innumerable ways in which physical dependency is increased by poverty. To take but a few examples; convenient transport cannot be readily hired to go shopping; food cannot be bought and stored in large enough quantities; housing and furniture may make free movement more difficult; chronic shortages of essential paramedical services, such as chiropody, affect mostly those who cannot pay; and so on. Nor are we solely concerned about the poverty of those who are 'old and alone'. We have yet to see, for example, the extent of the cost to the old of increased unemployment. When the middle-aged breadwinner becomes unemployed, will there still be money for regular visits?

Social and familial circumstances, again, affect dependency in many ways, some of which are too familiar to rehearse here. Suffice it to say, the latest study by Abrams of 844 respondents aged 75 or over in three areas of England should give pause for thought to those who suggest that the mobilisation of better family support systems can be readily accomplished.

> Less than 70% had any living siblings and many saw these brothers and sisters rarely.
> Two thirds of the women were either widowed, divorced or separated; and another 18% had never married.
> Over one third had either never had children or else had outlived them. Among those living alone as many as 45% were childless . . .
> Less than 60% . . . had grandchildren; but almost half these grandparents had either not seen any of their grandchildren during the four weeks before the interview or had seen them only once . . .
> Less than 30% . . . had had a visit from any family member during the weekend before the interview.[5]

Such findings have major implications for the dependency of the old on people who are *not* relatives, whether they be neighbours, friends, volunteers or paid workers. They also raise fundamental questions, the answers to which are uncertain and will in any case differ from one person to another, as to whether dependence on voluntary help has more or less stigma for the old than dependence on 'professionals', who are known to be paid for the work they do.

In short, specific community patterns, geographical and sociological, must be studied in relation to the needs of very old people who live in a given locality. Only in this way can an attempt be made to maximise independence, and yet to meet the inevitable dependency needs of this group. Plans for service provision, whilst individually tailored, need to be linked in to an appraisal of a locality's strengths and weaknesses for these purposes. The structure of women's employment, the extent of family dislocation, 'the shape' of public transport – all these and many more elements enter into such an analysis.

All this being acknowledged, however, it remains a central assumption of this chapter that psychological factors are of profound significance in attitudes to dependency, in those who care and in those who are cared for. There would seem to be two main sources: first, there is the balance, whether satisfying or unsatisfying, between dependence and independence in relationships in earlier years, especially in childhood. Secondly, in adult life, aspects of daily living which have assumed particular significance to the individual, affect adjustment to later dependence. Psychologists and psychoanalysts have paid much attention to the processes of bonding, upon the impact of loss and related areas in early childhood and the subsequent effects upon adult behaviour.[6]

Whilst there is much that is contentious, quite a solid body of empirical evidence is now available which stresses the importance of these early processes in parent-child relationships and the emotional dangers of premature 'breakage' of these bonds. Very little research is available to link these early experiences with reactions in old age, although there is evidence that depression in women may be significantly associated with loss of a mother in childhood.[7] One can easily be trapped between, on the one hand, a determinist view which overemphasises these connections, and, on the other, the impertinence of denying to an old person the unique significance of earlier experiences which are part and parcel of a human being, whether he be five, 50 or 100 years old.

It is commonly suggested that old people hark back to childhood and that their memories and interests are often more keenly focused upon that phase of life than those of their maturity. Above all, memories of parents surface with remarkable clarity. What we do not know – and it would take a long longitudinal study! – is the extent to which satisfying and unsatisfying experiences of dependency in childhood affect attitudes towards it in old age. Nor do we know how far the 'corrective' experiences in adult life – for example, of a happy marriage – soften the impact of earlier suffering in these last years.

Thus, despite much evidence about child development, its connections with behaviour in old age are not clearly understood. When, for example, a degree of physical dependency becomes inevitable, we do not know the extent to which earlier experiences of 'being handled' affect the reactions of the old person. My hypothesis is that there would be a strong association and that some of the seemingly irrational fears and anxieties of those who are demented may be related to childhood fantasies or real experiences. It is reasonable to suppose that some of the patterns of defence of earlier years will persist. Thus, if a defence against childhood deprivation has been a life long determination to deny dependence, major difficulties may be experienced in adjustment when it is enforced by physical frailty. Yet, if, as seems sometimes to be the case, certain defences of adult years are weakened in old age and earlier anxieties and fears rise to the surface, then childhood deprivation may reassert itself quite explicitly. One way in which dependence manifests itself and which is often experienced as threatening and intrusive by younger people is, indeed, focused on separation. 'When will I see you again?'

To suggest that there may be a link between the past and the present is not to suggest that such separation anxiety has not also within it the reality of present emotional loneliness and the fear of being left alone without physical resources to cope. Nor is it to suggest that great anxiety in this area necessarily implies externally demonstrable experiences of parental deprivation (although it would be extremely interesting to examine this further). Rather, it is to emphasise that, in my view, greater physical vulnerability must reawaken some of the fears which are inherent in childhood – when the bough breaks, the baby will fall.

Another kind of behaviour which gives 'the carers' cause for concern and irritation may be what is described as excessive dependence. How often one hears (or says) 'she could perfectly well have done it for herself!' There are many questions surrounding that perfectly understandable reaction. One is – 'could she really?' That is to say, has the assessment of the old person's condition fully taken into account the difficulties with which she is labouring? These may be physiological or, often missed, psychiatric, in the area of depression and anxiety, for example. It is also possible that, at an unconscious level, the person concerned is determined to get her psychological money's worth to make up for what has been missed earlier. One of the difficulties in this is to disentangle the feelings of the carer from those of the old person. The carer may experience the demands as excessive because of her own problems or those of the working environment, or because she is in truth picking up a *very* demanding message from the person concerned. This interactional component will be considered later. It is impossible, for the carer to sort her feelings out without help. There is room for much more experiment in such supportive counselling or consultation.

Thus, in the absence of evidence to the contrary, it would seem important for the 'carers' to listen to the stories of earlier experiences and consider what their implications are for the present processes of care. In this way, listening to reminiscences becomes purposeful or 'functional' as Cormican puts it.[8] In this context, however, the function may be more to guide the carers in their task than to effect change in the attitudes of old people.

A second aspect of dependency, which relates to adult achievement, is easier to delineate. A proper sense of self-esteem is reinforced by the achievements of adult life. It must follow that if the growth of dependence on others is related to an area of living in which the individual took a particular pride, and which had been a source of ego strength, the reactions or adjustments are likely to be painful. This poses a major problem for those who provide care. If it is possible to preserve a degree of autonomy in some area of life which was especially meaningful to the elderly person, this may usually take up more time than doing things 'for people' or require some special provision to be made to permit the activity to continue. There are particular difficulties in responding to those unique needs (and gifts) in group living, which may, of course, thus compound the processes of depersonalisation which have been observed in institutional life.

In addition to those achievements which are specific to individuals, there are those which, although commonplace, nonetheless play a crucial part in the maintenance of self-esteem and thus a proper sense of independence. One has only to reflect upon the significance a young child attaches to acquiring the skills of dressing, eating and toileting himself to see the threat posed to the individual's sense of autonomy when she can no longer perform some or all of these functions without aid. How to offer that aid without undermining the dignity of the individual is one of the central challenges to sensitive care and especially difficult in group provision.

Intellectual interests and educational achievement also affect the impact of physical dependence. There can be little doubt that both offer opportunities for the assertion of independence, whatever level of physical dependence is enforced upon the individual. This assertion goes to the roots of being; it offers the possibility of freedom when the body is confined. Those whose satisfactions have been in this area of life have, therefore, an advantage over those who have depended on physical mobility. The importance of this in promoting intellectual interests in the newly retired is self-evident. There is evidence of much untapped potential, as the British Open University experiment has shown.

Thus far, the discussion has centred upon aspects of dependency in old people. It has been suggested that greater understanding of the variations between individuals in the extent of dependency, of the reasons why it may be welcomed or rejected and of the areas of life in which its impact is greatest is important and that these are in part related to past experiences.

However, as was suggested earlier, dependence implies interaction. It is a dynamic situation in which the feelings of the parties involved constantly affect each other. It is therefore unhelpful to lay all the stress on the needs, feelings and attitudes of the old people when 'the carers' – whoever they may be – have their own attitudes towards dependence and independence, derived in turn from earlier experiences, and, of course, particular reactions to the old people for whom they care. Although the intensity of the feelings experienced by relatives in the caring role is crucially important, one should not underestimate the strength of similar feelings which may well up in anyone whose caring role brings them in intimate contact with those whose level of dependency is high. This is especially significant when it involves the performance of basic bodily tasks, which have associations both with infancy and with sexuality. Menzies' work on the nursing profession and its defences against anxiety is equally appropriate to the care staff of old peoples homes.[9] Theories of transference and counter-transference have a bearing on this. Yet even if one does not subscribe to that theoretical framework, it seems virtually certain that earlier experiences with real parents, whether in a dependent role or, later, being depended upon, will have a bearing on the way the supposedly 'unrelated' carer looks after the dependent old person. This has vital implications for the selection and training of care staff in homes for the elderly.

However, many people are caring for those who brought them up, and were influential in their childhood, or with whom they lived for many years. The emotional luggage is carried round in these relationships. Some of the feelings involved are conscious and explicit; others may be unconscious or, at least, firmly stowed away. If those whose task is to support the carers do not take account of these feelings and, on occasion, seek to help the carers acknowledge and discuss them, well intentioned efforts to provide practical support may founder. We have yet to discover in which cases the breakdown of the caring networks could have been averted by a greater input of domiciliary support and in which relief of emotional strain, mostly engendered by guilt and anger, was the key factor. This is a matter which empirical research could examine. It would be simplistic to suggest that the greatest difficulties amongst the related carers were experienced by those who had been ill-treated as children, although research into the non-accidental injury of children suggests an area for investigation here.[10] But one would certainly want to examine the patterns of dependence and the effects this had upon their children who care for them. The key areas in childhood – feeding and toiletry – once again assume major significance in the last years of life and it is around these experiences that feelings about dependency, on both sides, are keenest.

The problems of caring for very dependent old people cannot be completely explained – least of all explained away – by considerations of the earlier experiences of the parties involved. It is argued, however, that such factors should be taken into account in the provision of service. To take two examples: suggesting possible explanations for behaviour may help puzzled 'carers' to understand better the interactions which may take place; and this may serve to protect old people from the employment of those whose drive to care, ostensibly benign, is in fact malign and derived from a desire to get their own back for past ill treatment and rejection of their own dependency needs. In any case, whilst such extreme pathology may be rare, the potentiality for the hostile exercise of power over dependent people exists in many (perhaps in all?) of us. Whatever its origins, it must be noted, controlled and, at times, rooted out.

There is one matter – that of 'risk-taking' – which is closely associated with dependency and which is, of late, receiving more attention.[11] It is an issue of importance and complexity for old people and those who work with them.

Let it first be said that a good deal of the anxiety generated about risks could be alleviated if we could provide an environment less hazardous, both inside and outside the home. There are many small, and some large, steps which could be taken to contribute to greater safety. Despite the huge cost to the United Kingdom National Health Service of accidents to old people, very little has been done by successive governments. This suggests a lack of imagination, 'lateral thinking' and coordinated action which is necessary to take into account the effects of some general changes upon the older generation.

A small example concerns the shift to 'one man' buses. Some old people stopped going on buses when the automatic doors without a conductor were introduced. There were, of course, important financial reasons for so doing. What seems regrettable is that so little was done to help old people with their fears about the transition and to make some special provision for them. (Old people are major consumers of public transport.) Similarly, it would not be difficult at a local level to institute a service to old people to check for 'hazards at home'; frayed carpets, faulty switches, and so on. In fact, this might be an area of voluntary activity in which contact between helper and helped was easier because it was practically focused.[12]

However, even if we were much more foresightful, the fact remains that risk-taking would still be a social and psychological problem of magnitude. For children, we have a tested set of developmental norms which can be used to construct guidance and educational programmes for parents. They have clear implications as to what can and cannot be expected of children at certain ages and hence for reasonable risk-taking. In any case, whether through processes of socialisation or some more basic learned behaviour, parents seem to have a pretty shrewd idea about the boundaries they need to put round their children to protect them from physical hazard. It is interesting to note where they are less successful: first, in areas where social change has created more hazards rather quickly – for example, in accidents caused through misuse of drugs or other chemicals; secondly, in the protection of adolescents at the point where physical maturity is not paralleled by social and psychological maturity and where clashes of value, as in sexual conduct, are involved.

The relevance of these observations to our care of the very old is threefold. First, we have not got a comparable set of developmental norms for ageing. How can we hope to have one since the processes of ageing are much more diverse and less precisely timed than those of childhood? There is no substitute for the assessment of each individual and this may involve the interaction of bodily functions with mental state, the latter referring not only to mental impairment but to the kind of anxiety which precipitates accidents.

Secondly, old people are having to adjust rapidly to technological innovation which brings into their daily lives gadgets, many of which make life easier but some more dangerous. (Some also indirectly increase the dependence of the old on the young.)

Thirdly, just as parents are posed with a moral dilemma over their adolescents and risk-taking, so those who care for old people are similarly challenged. It is, of course, the other side of the coin. Instead of 'Is she ready to *assume* full adult responsibilities for some of her decisions?', it is 'Is she needing to *renounce* full adult responsibility for some of her decisions?' The word *needing* raises the question – whose need is involved?

If what has been argued earlier is accepted, then it follows that the carer's anxiety about risk will be influenced by a variety of personal factors, partly but not wholly determined by her feelings about the individual concerned. It has often been suggested that some over-protectiveness is a manifestation of repressed hostility and certainly it can feel like that to the recipient! Equally (and probably related) it can be experienced as a wish to control rather than to protect, even to infantilise. Yet again, the levels of anxiety in those who care are variable and it would not be right to attribute this solely to suppressed or repressed hostility.

All these emotions interact with those of the old person, producing very different reactions from clashes to collusions. Behind them lie other social pressures, powerful and at times none too subtle. We have not worked out a social code to support those who care in their attempts to balance dependence and independence in relation to risk. The example of fire precautions is topical. Carried out to the letter, as presented by law, they can result in buildings so constructed by heavy fire doors that old people's mobility is severely curtailed. (There are also some faintly ludicrous stories of old men repeatedly setting off the smoke alarm in their sitting room by puffing their pipes.) Less serious, but of considerable psychological importance, one knows of some homes which allow residents to make their own tea and others who do not 'because of the risk'.

These examples are concerned with old people in residential care which highlights a familiar problem – that, in assuming responsibility, either directly through statutory provision or, indirectly, through the voluntary sector, for the physical care of the vulnerable, society is more sensitive and more vulnerable to criticism. There are oddities in this. Perhaps because of the intractable difficulties in providing individualised, dignified care in large groups, 'scandals' periodically erupt. There is an explosion of concern. It dies down but change for the better is not always apparent, perhaps because we do not know how.[13] Yet it is broadly true to say that where any form of institutional care is provided, there is a greater degree of formal control and concern about risk. Thus, when I worked in child welfare in a seaside county, fostered children were allowed to swim without an adult present but not their peers down the road in a children's home. Such an example represents a different sense of accountability rather than any difference in the children's needs.

However, old people in residential care in the United Kingdom are, on the whole, more frail and more vulnerable than their counterparts who stay at home. Thus, it is to be expected that greater attention will be paid to the reduction of physical risk. The problem which falls to those who staff the establishments is how to balance this against a different kind of risk – that of creating an environment in which dependency is maximised and anxiety reinforced (if not created) which reduces the quality of life of the residents. The practical and administrative elements in this are complex but they can only begin to be worked out if the basic premiss is accepted – *that a degree of physical risk is inherent in maintaining some degree of personal autonomy*. That premise also has to be accepted by those to whom the staff in charge are accountable, because their support will be crucial in devising and maintaining the equilibrium between risk and protection.

Very few old people in the United Kingdom live in special homes, however, or even in sheltered accommodation. Most will be by themselves, with elderly spouses or with relatives. Again, societal vacillation is apparent. There are strong pressures against interference 'with private lives'. Legislative powers which permit an old person to be removed from home for self-neglect are very sparingly used. Yet there are intermittent public outcries when elderly people are found dead and alone, and strong neighbourhood criticism if a relative is thought to be allowing her mentally impaired relative to wander. So far, we have not heard many allegations of abuse by relatives but my prediction is that this will increase over the next decade, paralleling the increase in public awareness of child abuse in the 1970s.[14] It can only be a matter of time before questions of the type 'did she fall or was she pushed' so common in child abuse, will be asked more frequently by professionals and neighbours.

That those who care for the very old in their own homes or nearby will be sensitive to public attitudes, there can be no doubt. As with residential care staff, there is a need for the question of taking risks to be discussed openly and responsibly. The media has an important role in this.

This chapter assumes that the dynamics of interaction, whether familial or quasi familial, are truly generic; specifically, that professionals, in particular doctors and social workers, can use the same frames of reference for the understanding of behaviour of the old and those who care for them as they would any other human interaction. There are, of course, special problems of which senile dementia and the strain it imposes upon the carer is probably the most striking example. But such a generic focus helps to counter-balance a tendency observable in the United Kingdom to talk and write about the delivery of practical services to the elderly and those who care for them without regard to their emotional needs. I am reminded of a similar tendency in the late 1960s and 1970s, in which, in the flood of proper indignation about the extent of poverty in supposedly developed countries, it seemed to be implied that the poor had no need of any help except the relief of their poverty. If one suggested that man did not live by bread alone it was taken as meaning one was not concerned to provide bread.

As has already been stressed and as other chapters in this book illustrate, we face massive economic and social problems in the western world simply to provide for old people a standard of living and of comfort which compares relatively well with their younger contemporaries. Nothing in this chapter should overshadow that central challenge. It nonetheless seems important to stress the common humanity of old people, through the identification of emotional problems which exist for them and those who care for them. Apart from its moral justification, it also affords a rationale for the involvement of those in the helping professions who see themselves as working at the interface of environmental, emotional and social problems.

In the United Kingdom, current research has produced somewhat depressing evidence that so-called generic social workers rarely engage in work with the families and relatives of the elderly or with the elderly themselves in the way they do with families and children.[15] It is also well-known that geriatrics has not been a popular or prestigious specialism amongst doctors. The deeper reasons for this, embedded in social attitudes, cannot be explored here. But one way to break into a vicious circle is to stimulate enthusiasm so that work with the very old is seen to be professionally demanding and stimulating; linkages with theories of human development and socialisation afford a genuine intellectual challenge seen clearly in relation to dependence.[16]

By chance, I have recently seen two examples, one of groupwork and one of brief focused psychotherapy with the very old. In the first, a small-scale but exciting example has been provided by the work of a social worker, recently retired from a senior management position, whose field experience had only been in child welfare. She set up groups for old people in an acute hospital ward, whose anxieties naturally focused a good deal upon dependency – would they be able to cope when they got home? The group by its nature was not constant in membership; over 100 took part in some 20 meetings, most were in their late 70s, and disabled in some way. The sessions demonstrated the potentiality for purposeful, dynamic discussion which was a far cry from the 'oppressive dejection' noted at an early visit to the ward. The most frequent comment made by members after the groups was the equivalent of 'I have used my brain today'.[17] This is a form of independence, perhaps more precious than any other.

The second concerned an old man who was showing symptoms of extreme regressive dependence – refusing to get up, incontinence, etc; the therapist (again formerly a social worker in child welfare) focused upon unresolved tensions surrounding the death of his wife and relationships with his son, and, by the end of a relatively brief period, the man improved to the point of keeping out-patient appointments without undue difficulty.

Such examples challenge us to think again about the exchanges which are possible and desirable between the old and their helpers. Whether the professional's role is to work directly with old people or to support those who do so, the need is to tease out the different elements in dependency. A degree of physical dependency in very old people is inevitable. The questions to be addressed concern the match or mismatch between physical and emotional dependency, the areas in which it is most resented or welcomed. The objective is not to assert independence as preferable to dependence – a common assumption. It is to work out a balance which is right for each individual and to do as little as possible through our social institutions to undermine aspects of independence which are valued by the old person concerned.[18]

Notes

1. J. Donne, *Devotions*.
2. St John, 21, 18 (note that one may be carried where one does not want to go).
3. E.J. Miller and C.V. Gwynne, *A Life Apart* (Tavistock Publications, London, 1972).
4. P. Townsend, *Poverty in the United Kingdom* (Pelican, Harmondsworth, 1979) p. 819.
5. M. Abrams, *Beyond Three Score and Ten* (a second report) (Age Concern, 1980).
6. J. Bowlby exemplifies this work, see for example, *Attachment and Loss*, Vols. 1, 2 and 3 (The Hogarth Press, London, 1969, 1973 and 1980).
7. J. Bowlby, Childhood Mourning and Psychiatric Illness', in *The Predicament of the Family* LOMAS (ed.), (The Hogarth Press, London, 1967).
8. E.J. Cormican, 'Task Centred Model for Work with the Aged', *Social Casework*, October, 1977, pp. 490-4.
9. I.E.P. Menzies, 'A Case Study in the Function of Social Systems as a

Defence Against Anxiety', *Journal of Human Relations*, Vol. 13, 1960.

10. B.F. Steele and C.B. Pollock, 'A Psychiatric Study of Parents Who Abuse Infants and Small Children' in C.H. Kempe and R.E. Helfer (eds.), *The Battered Child* (University of Chicago Press, 1968).

11. See, for example, C. Rowlings, *Social Work with Elderly People* (Allen and Unwin, London in Press).

12. In 1977, approximately 3 million people over 65 died from accidents in the home, against approximately 307,000 children under 5. Falls and fires accounted for the majority of the deaths in the elderly, Social Trends, CSO, 1980.

13. See for example, (a) *Report of the Committee of Inquiry into allegations of ill treatment of patients . . . at Ely Hospital, Cardiff*, HMSO, 1969; (b) *Report of Committee of Inquiry into Normsnfield Hospital*, HMSO, 1978. These reports, separated by 9 years, revealed disturbing similarities in the problems of hospital care for the mentally handicapped.

14. Between 1974-80 there have been in the UK, a substantial number of enquiries into the circumstances surrounding the deaths of children at the hands of their parents: the first of these which aroused extensive public concern and interest was: *Report of the Committee of Inquiry into the Care and Supervision provided in relation to Maria Colwell*, HMSO, 1974.

15. See, for example, *Social Service Teams: the Practitioner's View*, HMSO, 1979.

16. See, for example, I. Roscow, *Socialisation to old Age* (University of California Press, 1977). This well exemplifies a generic sociological approach, in which a systematic attempt is made to link general concepts to ageing.

17. J. Cooper, *Social Group Work with Elderly Patients*, Monograph, Beth Johnson Foundation, England, in Press.

18. The author is indebted to Cherry Rowlings, who has shared her ideas and thinking on these matters and whose contribution to this chapter will be apparent in: Rowlings, C. *Social Work with Elderly People*, Allen and Unwin (in Press).

8 AGEING AND THE DOCTOR

Bernard Isaacs

'I don't envy you your job, doctor, it must be so depressing working with old people.'

'It's no use going to my doctor. All he ever says is – what else can you expect at your age? You're lucky to be still alive.'

'I hear you are going into geriatrics. You must be crazy. You are committing professional suicide.'

'Geriatrics – I just *hate* that word.'

These remarks recently addressed to me or made in my hearing illustrate the public's sympathetic incomprehension of how the medical needs of the aged are to be met. There are many to instruct us about the dignity, the individuality, the uniqueness, the human worth of old people; but when a soiled bottom has to be wiped, or the cause of a soiled bottom determined, the task is happily left to others.

The quest for better care for old people is in essence a quest for a better old people's doctor; one who can provide philosophy at one end of the patient and absorbency at the other.

In the United Kingdom this question has been approached by the formation of a cadre of specialist geriatricians. Other countries are debating this policy, and look to the British experience for guidance. The British are not quite certain that they are correct. Geriatric medicine has more than 300 consultant geriatricians, one for every 20,000 population aged 65 and over. That is an impressive number, but it is not enough; and recruitment is difficult. The psychiatric care of the elderly is in a muddle in much of the country, despite the emergence of a small but splendid group of specialists. The debate continues as to whether geriatrics should be strengthened, integrated or abandoned. Academic development proceeds. One-third of our medical schools have professorial departments of geriatric medicine, further new chairs are planned, and instruction in geriatric medicine is provided to undergraduates in practically every medical school.

I believe that recruitment to geriatric medicine will never be easy, because this speciality is concerned with the period of life most remote from the experience of the young graduate. Negative attitudes to the speciality are reinforced when the student and the young doctor see the poor facilities and low status accorded to geriatric medicine. These are to some extent dispelled by exposure to the enthusiasm, humaneness and excellence of many specialist geriatric services. Recruitment may be less than satisfactory, but students at least see beyond the poor resources to the excellent philosophy of care; and would not do so if specialisation is abandoned.

This theory is often challenged by those who ask what is special about the medicine of Old Age which, after all, is now of necessity practised by virtually all physicians. My belief is that the care of old people is best entrusted to doctors who have made a special study of this subtle and demanding branch of their profession; and who derive from its practice interest, enthusiasm and commitment, to the unique opportunities which it provides for personal, professional and scientific fulfilment.

8.1 Medicine in Old Age

The aged are survivors: their maladies disable but do not kill. Disease hounds them from all sides, but despite structural imperfections, impoverished nutrition, defective immunity and bombardment with multiple drugs, lethal illness is held at bay, and we witness the 'survival of the unfittest'.

This melancholy stereotype is not true of all old people; but it need only be the fate of 10 per cent – as indeed it is – for an enormous demand to be unleashed for medical and social services.

The multiple diseases of very late life converge into four major disabilities, which are called the 'giants of geriatrics'. These are:

(1) immobility;
(2) instability;
(3) incontinence;
(4) intellectual impairment.

These four giants have four common properties:

(1) they have multiple causes;
(2) they destroy independence;
(3) there is no simple treatment;
(4) they need human helpers.

The 'giants' are not exclusive to old people, nor are they the only illnesses of old people. Other conditions which are extremely common in old age include disturbances of vision and hearing, diseases of the heart and kidneys, feet troubles, cancer and the toxic effects of drugs. These, however, are found and dealt with at all ages. The giants are distinctive, and my case for specialisation hangs on the quest for better care of those who fall victim to them. I believe that many doctors have in the past been emotionally blocked when confronted with the giants of geriatrics. These are too widely assumed to be the inevitable and untreatable consequences of old age. They too often evoke a cry for removal and storage, rather than for investigation and treatment. A reason for this may be sought in an analysis of the medical encounter.

8.2 The Medical Encounter

The encounter between doctor and patient contains two elements which will be called 'transaction' and 'reaction'.

Transaction. A 'transaction' is the performance of a technical act unhampered by emotional penetration. Most of adult medicine, surgery and obstetrics is conducted through 'transactions', to the satisfaction of both parties. The doctor exercises his skills in diagnosis and treatment, while the patient perceives competence and derives benefit. The doctor preserves his detachment and the patient preserves his privacy. The human bond of concern and trust is present between doctor and patient, and is reinforced by the efficiency of the transaction; but each remains firmly within his own skin.

Reaction. In a 'reaction' a bond of mutual recognition occurs between the two parties, so that for an instant each knows what it is like to be in the position of the other. Such moments are rare in the course of medical practice, but their occurrence enriches medical life. They occur during work with children, with women in labour, with alcoholics and cancer victims and in much of psychiatry. The doctor need not have experienced the patient's plight in order to gain understanding, but he must be able to encompass it within his imagination. Most doctors base their professional satisfaction on a series of successful transactions. Some avoid 'reactions' of the type described; others seek them out and find them a rewarding aspect of their practice.

The Elderly. Those who contemplate the elderly from a position of limited knowledge find them unlikely to offer the professional satisfactions of successful 'transactions' and even less of 'reaction'. Even communicating effectively with them seems a daunting prospect. Their poorly verbalised complaints and the limitless signs of past disease seem to offer little scope for therapeutic intervention. The idea that their world can be encompassed, their outlook understood, their vision seen through their eyes, must seem bizarre. This may be why some doctors seek alternative and less satisfactory approaches to elderly patients. Three such mechanisms are frequently observed.

Fractionation. The doctor who finds it difficult to form a relationship with a whole elderly patient may successfully do so with a part. He becomes attached to the patient's heart or lung or kidney, investigates and treats it, and makes a very good job of it. It may then be sent home with its owner attached, and with the transaction completed to the satisfaction of the doctor.

Abrogation. A less satisfactory process is to blame the patient for the impotent situation in which the doctor finds himself, thus justifying abrogation of medical responsibility. Letters of referral to departments of geriatric medicine frequently illustrate this attitude. Patients are described as having been fully investigated and nothing has been found, so could they please be accepted by the geriatric unit for permanent care. Doctors claim that they have done all they can for the patients, who are advised to console themselves with the fact that they have attained a great age and should not expect health. Some are given the wise advice that they should 'live with' their disability. (The alternative is not spelt out.) Statements of this nature imply abrogation of further medical responsibility.

Defamation. Regrettably the process does not end there and intemperate and defamatory language is sometimes used. Patients are described as 'blocking beds'. Wards are 'cluttered' with elderly patients; and I have even heard holders of medical degrees describe their fellow human beings as 'old crumble'. Defamatory language is accompanied by the symbols of medical exasperation: the cot sides, the barrier chair, the catheter bag and the massive usage of sedatives. These to me do not represent the needs of the patients, but rather the frustrations of the doctors who have been unable to perform the effective transactions with their patients on which their professional satisfactions are based.

8.2.1 What does Specialisation Offer?

Can the specialists do better than this? One of the specialist's skills is in securing an effective transaction with the patient. Conventional methods of history-taking and physical examination require modification. For example, elderly patients are sometimes described by inexperienced doctors as 'poor historians'. Now, a historian is one who records history – in this case, the doctor, not the patient. Historians carefully sift evidence. An elderly patient's capacity to provide his doctor with a 'good' history may be impeded by the very length of years over which health has been failing; by deafness which prevents him hearing the question; by aphasia which prevents him expressing the answer; by incomprehension of a questioner's language or idiom or words; by inability to recall answers, or reluctance to admit of inability; by the use of confabulatory responses designed to protect him against the suspicion of intellectual failure; by delusions which obscure his view of reality; by failure to recall a question or part of it; by unwillingness or refusal to impart the information; by apprehension, fear or suspicion of the motives or manners of the questioner; or by inexperience of the verbalisation of unfamiliar bodily sensations.

The compilation of a 'good' history from ostensibly poor material necessitates the ability to recognise these obstacles. It needs confidence in working with old people, knowledge of their words, their ways and their world; and this can be learned only by long apprenticeship at the bedside. The geriatric specialist learns also how to use the information from relatives, neighbours and others which is part fact and part interpretation. He learns the difference between gaining this insight in the hospital corridor and in the patient's home. Indeed only in the patient's home does the story come to life; and the geriatrician's day is programmed to allow him the opportunity of seeing patients in their own homes.

Physical Examination. The conventional physical examination is conducted with the patient prostrate in bed. This is convenient for the examination of chest and abdomen, but prevents adequate examination of mobility and stability. Observation of the ability to perform the functional activities of daily living is absent from the conventional physical examination. If the facts are not recorded by the doctor, they may not form part of his mental map of the patient's world and of his estimate of the patient's needs. Yet the clue to the patient's illness may be in some disturbance of speech and language, abnormality of gait pattern, error in dressing or defect in spatial orientation which is not picked up in the conventional medical examination.

Investigation. Doctors who work with old people sometimes face the charge of 'over-investigation'; but they are trained to seek additional information only when this will influence their management of the patient. Sometimes the charge of 'under-investigation' may justifiably be levelled at non-specialists who fail to appreciate that the temporary discomfort and trivial cost of a special test may well be justified if it can improve the quality of life of one who may still have two or three years to live.

Social Assessment. In conventional medical work, the social assessment is a transaction designed to facilitate the discharge of the patient. To the specialist, however, the social assessment is part of the education of the doctor. Through it he comes to learn of the stresses within the ageing family. The specialist's concern is not solely with whether the relatives will or will not accept responsibility for the continuing care of the patient. His object is a study of the 'residual family', faced with the last stresses of a long life together. The doctor has a unique opportunity of observing a new facet of human behaviour. He may see the utmost devotion or the most abysmal selfishness; the working out of guilt feelings; the eruption of old hostilities; the clinging to lost love; a degree of devotion and a depth of human understanding beyond his former compass. There is unending fascination in observing the mechanisms of family cohesion and dehiscence; in gaining an enriched understanding of the greatness of our patients; and in achieving knowledge of what we do when we send them to their homes.

Rehabilitation. Treatment of the elderly patient requires the collaborative working of doctor, nurse, physiotherapist, occupational therapist, speech therapist and social worker. Conventionally, each looks after his bit of the patient and expects the others to do likewise. Not so in the geriatric unit where each specialist must be prepared to modify his view of the patient in the light of the perceptions of another team member; otherwise a team does not exist. The necessary humility is not easily acquired.

8.3 The Case for Specialisation

The content and the method of geriatric medicine make its proper practice very different from that of general medicine. Reluctance to accord to geriatric medicine the status of speciality rests on reluctance to hand over a large number of patients and corresponding resources to a group of people with no visible tools. The tools of the geriatrician, though less tangible than the fibreoptic scope or the cardiac catheter, are no less penetrating. They are the insights into the world of old age.

8.3.1 Obstacles to Specialisation

The major obstacle to the further development of geriatric medicine is recruitment. Only a tiny proportion of recent graduates rate geriatric medicine as their career choice. This is not in itself surprising, since at that early stage of their career most young doctors seek general medical experience; and an interest in the elderly may not develop until a later stage. Any upsurge of interest in the elderly is likely to be discouraged by contemplation of the poor facilities an enormous work loads in geriatric departments; by the exclusion of many geriatric departments from general hospitals; by the relatively poor material rewards of the speciality; and, not least, by the derision and incredulity of well-meaning friends.

The argument that recruitment to geriatric medicine is poor has led to the suggestion that specialist physicians in geriatric medicine should be replaced by consultant physicians with an interest in geriatric medicine. Much the same happened in the public transport system, where the natives drive taxis and the immigrants drive buses; but no-one has suggested the abolition of full-time bus-drivers and their replacement by taxi-drivers with an interest in driving buses. There are some successful examples of posts of physicians 'with an interest' in geriatric medicine; but in general I have difficulty in seeing how people who do not wish to be full-time geriatricians will wish to become part-time geriatricians; nor do I see how a geriatric service which is having difficulty in meeting its commitments with full-time doctors will manage better with part-time ones. This compromise is an expression of no confidence in the hard road that has already been tramped by pioneer geriatricians. It denies the advances made by those wholly committed to the speciality. It also fails to acknowledge that difficulty in recruitment, which is by no means unique to geriatric medicine, is as much due to failure to provide the resources which the speciality requires as it is to any inherent repulsiveness in the practice of the clinical art of medicine in old age.

8.4 Geriatrics as 'Managing'

The preoccupation of the geriatrician is in the management of resources. The needs of the elderly are unlimited: the resources of Health and Social Services are severely limited. The optimum use of limited resources is a skill in itself, which necessitates that the individual case should always be considered against a clear picture of the total. It is very easy for the inexperienced or ineffectual geriatrician to accept all requests for admission and transfer of patients in chronological order and to admit them when a bed becomes available. This soon leads to the accumulation of a waiting list. When pressed for speedier removal of a patient to hospital, the geriatrician replies that the case is on the waiting list and will be admitted as soon as possible. He appears to have taken some action, but in effect nothing has happened. A second doctor may decide to avoid accumulating a waiting list by refusing to see cases unless a bed is available. A third may prefer to ensure that beds are available by pursuing a relentless policy of early discharge. A fourth doctor may see his responsibility as being solely to the patients under his care, proving indifferent to all pressures.

All these systems of management can be criticised. The fully trained specialist geriatrician sees himself as one among many who provide care for the elderly in a community. His particular set of resources must be used in collaboration with those provided by general practitioners, general hospital physicians, psychiatrists and social service departments. He must keep the balance right, ensuring that patients whose needs can be met only by the use of his facilities are given early and appropriate access to them; while those who could more appropriately be dealt with by another part of the system are encouraged to go thither. He acquaints himself with the resources and restraints of the other parts of the system, helping when help is needed. A public relations and educational role is part of his position, as is the responsibility to acquaint himself with the health needs of the community which he serves. He must have a coherent philosophy behind his decisions, and must be prepared to explain them to his patients and their relatives, to the general practitioners with whom he works, to the members of his team, and to his medical, surgical, psychiatric and social service colleagues. He must also be prepared to fight for his care-group in the political quarters where decisions are made regarding the allocation of resources to his speciality. His fighting must be not merely pugnacious, but informed; he must know the facts of the case and speak of them. Of all the roles of the geriatrician, this is the most daunting and forbidding. The sight of a geriatrician at a committee, his back to the wall, with few voices to support him, is a sad one. He is fighting not for his own empire, but for a little place in the sun for a neglected group of patients.

These managerial skills do not come easily to one trained in clinical medicine, but they are a formidable educational experience. After running a department of geriatric medicine, it would, I sometimes think, be child's play to run a multi-million pound business or a government department.

8.5 Geriatrics as 'Man Ageing'

The other great fascination of this specialty is that it affords a unique opportunity for studying a new biological phenomena, Man Ageing, unknown before at any time in human history. This is the survival of the unfittest; the novel and awesome spectacle of vast numbers of people surviving beyond the capacity for independent existence. The medical and social intricacies of this situation represent a potential field of enquiry as broad and as unexplored as Antarctica. Fascinating medical questions jostle one another, awaiting codification and answer. Why do women live longer than men? Why is brain failure compatible with long existence? What sustains balance and what impairs it? Why do some people survive into the tenth decade without deterioration? How is the bladder controlled? What are the stresses of community living? Opportunities for observation of new and hitherto undescribed clinical phenomena abound. Rich harvests await the patient investigator. The comparatively low level of study of these questions in the past has been due to the immense routine commitments of geriatricians and the failure of non-geriatricians with research resources to perceive these problems. It is greatly to the credit of geriatricians that they have sustained research interests for many years and have advanced knowledge very considerably. But this is as yet only a beginning; a very much greater investment is necessary in the study of ageing man, if the enormous problems are to be reduced.

8.6 Structure of Geriatric Services

8.6.1 A 'Standard' Service

The standard British geriatric unit serves a population of approximately 250,000 people in a health district. This population includes about

30,000 people aged 65 and over, of whom 10,000 are aged 75 and over, 2,500 of these being aged 85 and over. The department is headed by 2 consultant physicians in geriatric medicine, supported by a handful of junior doctors.

In a fortunate unit there are 300 beds, of which 50-100 are in a general hospital, with ready access to all emergency, diagnostic and specialist services. The remainder may be in one or more less central units – often a converted fever hospital, a tuberculosis sanatorium, or former chronic sick infirmary or a Poor Law institution. The buildings may be modern, modernised or ancient, well or poorly adapted to their function. The location may be central, peripheral or isolated.

The department will also have one or more day hospitals, providing some 60 places, usually located adjacent to the in-patient unit and sometimes on an isolated site. Each consultant generally has one or more out-patient clinics a week.

In addition to the geographical separation, there is often functional division into admission, rehabilitation and long-stay wards. Beds in the district general hospital are preferentially used for emergency, short-term cases; those in remote hospitals tend to be reserved for longer-term cases. There is a fair amount of patient flow within the department, mostly in the direction of admission to rehabilitation to long-stay.

8.6.2 Admissions

Admissions to departments of geriatric medicine come from three sources:

(1) Direct admissions of medical and medical/social emergencies on the day of occurrence either by direct telephone referral from the general practitioner or by unheralded arrival at the hospital casualty department.

(2) Planned admission of patients referred by the general practitioner from their own homes, whose needs have been assessed at an out-patient clinic, a hospital or usually on a domiciliary visit by the consultant geriatrician, either alone or occasionally in the company of the general practitioner or a social worker.

(3) Transfer of patients from medical, surgical, orthopaedic or other hospital wards for further care. This may be for specialist rehabilitation, e.g. patients' with stroke, fractured femur, or amputation; for general, short or medium-term rehabilitation; or for continuing care.

8.6.3 Activities

Most geriatric units describe themselves as undertaking active investigation and rehabilitation, using the services of an integrated, multidisciplinary team, and with the object of early, planned discharge and continuing community supervision. The degree to which this is practised depends on such factors as the selection of patients, the availability of staff and the philosophy of care. The 'standard' unit is able to muster sufficient dedicated staff in the disciplines of medicine, nursing, physiotherapy, occupational therapy, speech therapy, and social work to create an effective team in at least part of the service. This necessitates concentration of effort on the recently-admitted. The level of activity falls off sharply after a stay of two to three months, and the implicit identification of the patient as being 'long-stay'. There is then relegation to an alternative facility which is less well staffed to carry out rehabilitation.

The 'standard' unit invests much effort in the preparation for discharge home of those patients capable of being maintained outside the hospital. This involves repeated assessment by members of the multidisciplinary team, of the patient's competence in activities of daily living; and in the capability of the family and the environment to sustain them. Hospital assessment and training are supplemented by assessment visits paid to the patient's home in the company of the patient and his carer; and by such additional devices as the trial weekend. The final decision to discharge is made in consultation with the community nurse and the general practitioner, and in accordance with the expressed wish of patient and relatives. Special attention is devoted to two common situations: the stubborn insistence of a disabled patient of her competence to manage at home; and the apparently unreasonable resistance of relatives to the discharge home of a patient judged to be competent to manage. These situations call for delicacy, skill and judgement in their handling; and the team is accustomed to sensitive negotiation.

After discharge follow-up care is provided by the patient's attendance at the day hospital and out-patient clinic; and by visists to the home by liaison nurses attached to the geriatric department.

8.7 Variants

There are many variants on this organisational pattern.

8.7.1 The Age-related Department

Several departments of geriatric medicine in the United Kingdom define their purpose as providing comprehensive medical care for all patients over an arbitrary age. Usually this is 75, but in some units it is 65 or even 60. The argument of such units is that the blurred division between 'geriatrics' and 'general medicine' perpetuates the view that geriatrics is inferior medicine practised on inferior patients by inferior doctors in inferior buildings. A geriatric unit located beside a general medical unit will receive, they believe, only what is rejected by the medical unit. By taking all patients over the arbitrary age, whatever that might be, they ensure for themselves a fair spread of the work load. They claim the additional advantage that nobody is left in any doubt about what is or is not a suitable patient for admission to the geriatric unit.

In practice, of course, there has to be some flexibility. A patient over the age of 75 who is of special interest to or who already 'belongs' to a general physician may still be accepted in his wards; and a patient whose needs can best be met by the geriatric department, even though he is under the arbitrary admission age, must still be accepted. The operation of this system requires that a high proportion of the beds of the geriatric department should be in general hospitals. Where this is provided, the system works well, but it uses a lot of resources.

8.7.2 The Integrated Department

There are a few units in the United Kingdom in which the geriatrician is a member of a team of physicians who admit all patients of all ages to a common pool of beds. The geriatrician demonstrates his competence as a general physician by dealing, on his day on duty, with emergency medicine in all age groups; just as his general colleagues, on their duty days, deal with the medical-social emergencies of late old age. After emergency care has been provided in the common area, patients are transferred to specialist areas for continuing care. The geriatrician receives other admissions from conventional sources. This system is possible only when resource provision is adequately balanced.

8.7.3 Other Variants

In between these extremes are many variants. A snapshot view of the working of a department can be gleaned from the figure of the number of patients treated to completion per bed per year. This ranges from 2-10, with an average for the country of between 3 and 4. This indicates that most units are unable to practise very 'high turnover' geriatrics, for the excellent reason that they are doing the job of a geriatric service, which involves the rough with the smooth, not excluding patients who require the services of the unit. Very low turnovers are associated with a very low proportion of emergency admissions; while very high turnovers necessitate a policy of early discharge.

8.8 Boundaries

Departments of geriatric medicine are thought of as having boundaries with general medicine, psychiatry and residential care; and definitions of their respective roles have been composed. The concept of boundaries is damaging and erroneous. Where they are boundaries there are boundary disputes. The good name of geriatric medicine is jeopardised by squalid arguments whether some poor soul is a 'medical', 'geriatric', 'psychiatric', or 'social' problem, when manifestly she is all four; or more correctly she presents problems for all four services. There are no real boundaries, merely overlapping areas of expertise; and the problem is often solved and always soluble by courteous consultation. Guidelines and definitions should be used to aid planners in determining a desirable level of resource provision, rather than to direct individual patients towards (or more often away from) individual resources.

The definitions delineate responsibilities of the four services respectively, for the acutely ill, the physically disabled, the mentally disabled and the socially deprived. Unfortunately these define entrance but not exit criteria. In order to enter a medical ward, the old person has to demonstrate that she is acutely ill; but once her acute illness has been relieved she no longer satisfies the entrance criteria. In order to enter a residential home the old person has to be capable of limited self-care; and if she becomes no longer capable she fails to satisfy the criteria. The staff must then either negotiate the patient's ejection, or accept her inappropriate retention. A similar process occurs in geriatric and psychiatric units if, after appropriate admission, the balance between physical and mental ill-health alters. Since removal of the patient from part of the system which she has entered is often inadmissible or unavailable, all four services perceive a proportion of their resources as being 'blocked' or inappropriately used. These patients may become disadvantaged, unless the inevitability of the situation is accepted and due provision is made for it.

8.8.1 Alternatives

The alternative to the provision of separately defined services is to group all ill and disabled old people in an undifferentiated resource with no corporate purpose other than custody and no corporate skill other than care. Experience has shown that this deprives the system of the will to investigate, the skill to rehabilitate and the thrill to discharge home those brought under its charge. A differentiated system, especially one which can be made to work in a collaborative manner, is surely to be preferred.

8.9 The Geriatrician

The British-style geriatrician is presented as one who has acquired the transactional skills and the emotional insights to understand the needs of ill, old people and to meet them humanely and effectively. He is also seen as one who is capable of working collaboratively within a team, to promote rehabilitation and restoration to normal living. He is a resolute and informed manager of complex resources; and he has a curiosity about the nature of the problems with which he grapples daily.

8.10 The Specialist as Educator

Specialist geriatricians will never be responsible for the total care of all ill old people. Primary care, emergency treatment, surgical and psychiatric care will always be in other hands. The practice of non-specialists largely reflects the training which they received as undergraduates many years previously. Few who hold senior positions today have received undergraduate education in geriatric medicine. The local community geriatrician must be an educator in modern and better ways of thinking about and caring for old people. This role is very well performed in local communities by local geriatricians. Academic departments can make a contribution; but essentially it is within the local medical community, in the day-to-day contact between geriatrician, general practitioner and others, that the educational process grows.

8.11 Alternatives to the Geriatrician

The abandonment of geriatric medicine as we know it in the United

Kingdom would not, I believe, be in the interests of old people. Custodial systems were tried and failed, when needs and opportunities were less than they are today. At a time when the Royal Commission on the National Health Service is considering the partial abandonment of geriatric medicine, visitors from all over the world are flocking to our shores to see our system in the hope that they can adapt it to their needs. Geriatric medicine in the United Kingdom depends on a strong bond of trust between specialists in hospitals and primary care doctors at home, providing a continuing responsibility for elderly people from the first signs of dependency to their death, months or years later. I believe that we have found a good system which stimulates and challenges the doctor and goes a long way to meeting the needs of the community. I hope that this system will be strengthened and not abandoned.

9 THE SOCIAL WORKER AND THE PROBLEMS OF AGEING

Cherry Rowlings

This chapter explores some aspects of social work with elderly people. Olive Stevenson, in her chapter, has already described the concepts and the experiences with which much of social work with old people is concerned. The management of dependency is a *leit motif* of social work with this group of clients, involving the social worker in managing his/her own feelings as well as those of the dependent person and of the person(s) providing direct care, and this is reflected in the content of this chapter.

Not all old people, or their families, will require or wish for help from a social worker or from any outside agency. Others may require advice, for example on financial benefits; they may welcome the use of certain facilities, such as clubs; or may need more protected living conditions, such as are provided by a complex of bungalows or flats which have a warden on the premises. Many old people will require help with some aspect of daily living – shopping, cooking, bathing or walking. But such need or wish for what might be termed social *services* is not *prima facie* evidence of a need for social *work* and it would be inappropriate and professional arrogance to make such advice, facilities and resources available only through social workers.

Some elderly people, however, face complex or severe problems of an inter- or intra-personal nature; for example those who are 'desolated' by their loneliness and isolation;[1] those who have been unable to adjust to multiple and accumulated loss; those who are depressed; those whose degree of mental and/or physical frailty poses problems for themselves and for their carers. Social work can make a major contribution towards the well-being of people in such circumstances.

In making this statement, I do not wish to imply that social workers hold a monopoly of skills to help elderly people with psychosocial problems, nor that such problems are the province only of professionals. (The word 'professional' is used throughout not in its more technical, sociological sense, but as a synonym for occupational groups which may include some who may be considered to be 'more professionalised' and some 'less professionalised'.) Occupational therapists, for example, bring a particular expertise to the management of dependency and the assessment of risk; home helps often provide not just the important support services of shopping, cleaning, collecting pensions and so on, but also a warm and consistent relationship which is vital to the emotional well-being of their clients. Elsewhere in this book, there is an account of the role that may be played by volunteer counsellors – including those who themselves are old – and later in this chapter, there will be an account of a project where statutory and voluntary help are sharing the care of some very frail elderly people in the community.

Nor, by focusing on the role of social workers which, in this context means staff who have received the Certificate of Qualification in Social Work (CQSW), do I deny or undervalue the contribution of unqualified and ancillary staff in social services departments, who at present undertake the major part of work with elderly clients. There are of course exceptions to be found, notably in the hospital setting, but in general, qualified social workers are involved mostly and at times solely with the care of children, whilst the caseloads of unqualified or ancillary staff are composed largely and sometimes exclusively of elderly clients.[2, 3] The level of intuitive understanding and skill and the experience of many of these staff is undoubted, but to acknowledge this does not answer the issue raised by this method of deployment. For example, it is highly questionable that untrained staff and those in (officially) ancillary posts should carry the level of responsibility that many currently do – supporting families where the care of an elderly relative has caused a good deal of emotional and physical strain or working with lone elderly people in the community who are suffering from senile dementia.

Secondly, it is difficult, if not impossible to uphold the present system of work allocation which depends so heavily upon client group (children, mentally ill, the elderly, and so on) rather than the task to be performed. Thus the task of reception into care, for example, or supervision of a client 'at risk' is likely to be undertaken by a qualified worker if the client is aged eight years but by an assistant if the client is aged 80 years. The priorities for attention by a qualified social worker have been succinctly summarised as 'first child care, second mental health and third the elderly'[4] – a hierarchy which stems not just from the primacy accorded to work with children but also from a reluctance amongst many social workers to face the problems that may accompany ageing and a pessimism about the potential for change or amelioration.[5, 6] One of the most significant tasks facing social work is to find the means of moving away from this emphasis on client groups as the indicator of need and to develop systems of work allocation which pay greater attention to the nature of the task(s) to be undertaken and the level and type of training, experience, knowledge and skill which are therefore appropriate. Social work teachers, social work practitioners and senior staff within social services departments all share a responsibility here.

It is probably true that social work in the UK nowadays enjoys little sympathy from the general public. Publicity following child abuse tragedies has focused attention on the short-comings of practice; the social work strike in the winter of 1978/9 affected by no means all parts of the country but national media coverage tended to emphasise the 'who needs social workers? We didn't notice they weren't there' reaction. (One study of the effects of the strike suggested that those who *did* miss social workers were the most vulnerable members of society – children in care, families close to breakdown, very frail elderly people – few of whom wish or are able to advertise why they need social work help.)[7] There has in the past been no shortage of criticism of social work and consideration of the social work task with old people raises again questions and issues which previously were discussed largely in relation to other client groups. Two examples illustrate this: first, the value of social work when people are socially and economically deprived and secondly, the place of welfare rights within social work.

There are critics of social work who argue that it does no more than tinker at the edges of problems which require action on a wider scale aimed at changing fundamental injustices and inequalities in our society. However, to deny that people who are socially, educationally and economically disadvantaged may also have personal problems which cannot be solved by the provision of better housing or higher incomes is an attitude as narrow as that which focuses on the personal problems to the exclusion of the others. This is highly relevant to social work with old people, especially those who are very old, whose income and standard of housing compare so badly with that of the rest of the population.[8, 9]

The constraints that relative deprivation of this kind places upon people (irrespective of their state of health and mobility) cannot be stressed too heavily but this should not obscure the fact that some of the difficulties experienced by elderly people cannot be solved or ameliorated solely by much needed changes in social policy. Social workers have an obligation not to conceal the extent of poverty associated with old age and to ensure that their clients have received the full range of services and benefits to which they have an entitlement, but some of the problems that may arise following bereavement, loss of function or stressful family relationships require attention to individual worlds and group processes rather than to wider structures in society.

A related and long-standing criticism of social work as a profession is that it is insufficiently involved and inadequately skilled in the field of welfare rights and the allocation of resources.[10, 11] Shanas and Sussman[12] develop this in relation specifically to elderly clients when they argue that social work with elderly people should concentrate on the formation of links between old people, their families and the many voluntary and statutory agencies which dispense discretionary and non-discretionary services to old people. Social workers are of course already extensively engaged in rationing resources – be these located in their own departments or in other agencies or voluntary societies to which the worker may or may not refer a client. Shanas and Sussman point out the complexity of organisations concerned with the needs of old people, the variety of services available and the intricacies of different referral procedures. This leads them to stress the importance of developing expertise in what might be termed 'brokerage skills'. However, whether that expertise is, or should be, a *social work* expertise is unclear. Liaison, referral and advocacy are skilled tasks, but it may be that a thorough knowledge of welfare rights legislation and a familiarity with resources in the statutory and voluntary sectors form a specialism in their own right, distinct from social work, although it may be located within social services departments.

Clarification of the social work role with elderly people cannot, therefore, be separated out clearly from the debates and discussions about the development of social work as a helping profession. In some respects, however, consideration of fundamental issues can be illustrated with a particular sharpness by reference to work with elderly clients. The extent to which social workers should be concerned with seeking out need (however defined) as opposed merely to responding to demand is a case in point, given that elderly people are often not vociferous on their own behalf. I shall develop this in relation to just one dimension of possible need or disease, namely the identification of emotional and psychological problems.

As a client group, elderly people have certain features which distinguish them from other client groups referred to social services. First, elderly people, and especially those aged over 75, are major consumers of social services (though not, as was mentioned earlier, of social work time). In 1977/8, residential care for old people absorbed one fifth of the total net expenditure of social services departments; to this must be added the cost of other services – domiciliary care such as the services of a home help (homemaker/home aide) or the delivery of meals; day care such as is provided at day centres and clubs; aids for walking, bathing and other aspects of daily living and adaptations (ramps, widening of doors to enable wheelchair access, rails on stairs, perhaps even building a downstairs bathroom) which may be provided. When the cost of residential care is added to these other services, the total of services and resources for elderly people comprises over one third of total net expenditure – that is expenditure after any contributions made by the clients have been taken into account.[13]

Secondly, the findings of a study of a year's work in an office of a social services department where the population was close to the national average in age distribution, economic and social status, housing, etc. showed that referrals concerned with disability and frailty in old age amounted to nearly 30 per cent of the referrals to that area office in one year – and this did not include requests for domiciliary services only.[14] Thirdly, relatively few of the referrals were self-referrals – a finding which is not surprising, given the extent of unarticulated need that has been found amongst the elderly population in relation to their health care,[15] and to their eligibility for additional financial benefit from the state social security system.[16] Health care personnel were the most frequent referral agents, and many referrals concerned very old people, often reflecting the strain experienced by relatives caring for those who were mentally or physically very frail – a situation likely to become more severe during these years of rapid growth in the very old section of the elderly population at a time when the cuts in local government spending have affected, and continue to affect, both the quantity and the variety of services available.

Fourthly, a comparison of referrals concerning old people with those on other clients shows that, of all client groups, the elderly are most likely to have their needs presented in the form of a request for a specific service or resource. Referrals were rarely for help with emotional problems for which some form of counselling/casework help could be seen as appropriate. This indicates the extent to which the needs of elderly people and also of their carers are often seen *solely* in practical or resource terms, to the exclusion of any emotional and psychological needs which may be present alongside the practical.

Information from a variety of sources indicates that emphasis on the practical is a misrepresentation of the full extent of need in the elderly population. For example, Goldberg *et al.*[17] found that in their sample of elderly people referred for practical services, one third needed precisely that but the remaining two thirds had problems, of varying degrees of severity, which the researchers considered to need some form of social work (i.e. of a counselling/casework nature) in *addition* to the services requested.

More recently, a social worker on a project which provided intensive domiciliary care estimated that as many as 72 per cent of the referrals that had come for these intensive services also required additional help with unresolved grief and adjustment to bereavement.[18] A study which examined the work of young Task Force volunteers with elderly people estimated that nearly one third of their sample, most of whom were aged 80 and over, were 'dominated' by a sense of loneliness. The researchers described how the replies of these people 'frequently suggested confusion and fear of the future, and sometimes seemed to indicate a diminution of their sense of identity . . . [They said] 'Sometimes I can't sort of face myself. I can't see how it will all end up.'[19] This combination of bewilderment and purposelessness has been identified as a possible consequence of profound loss.[20] It represents a serious threat to mental health and indeed to the preservation of life itself, perhaps offering an important explanation why an estimated 30 per cent of all successful suicides occur in the elderly population.[21]

At present in most, if not all, social services departments, referrals for a specific service are likely to be passed direct to the worker responsible for organising this work. Thus, a request for a home help will go to the home help organiser; referrals for meals to be delivered will go to the meals-on-wheels organiser (or to the home help organiser if her job includes the delivery of mobile meals). These staff rarely have a social work training but they are engaged in a number of assessment interviews either of clients previously unknown or of clients who are in receipt only of domiciliary services. The expectation in most departments is that they will 'refer back' if a need for social work help is discovered. I do not know of any systematic study of the way in which home help organisers fulfil this part of their job, but the small number of interviews that I undertook with home help organisers and occupational therapists in one authority indicated that there was considerable variation between individuals as to how they interpreted both the needs of their elderly clients and the role of the social worker.[22]

In an attempt to identify those clients (or potential clients) for whom practical help alone is not sufficient, it is possible to adopt at least two strategies. One is to single out those referrals for services which seem most likely also to present other needs. For example, advanced age is significantly associated with the presence of need, which is likely to be multiple, complex, perhaps well camouflaged and probably also involving medical as well as social factors.[23] It could be argued that in view of what is known about the social and psychological circumstances of people aged over 80, *all* referrals of people in this age group should be routinely assessed by a social worker, in addition to that undertaken by a home help organiser or an OT. A recommendation of the working party of the British Association of Social Workers on the social work task was that complexity of task(s) to be undertaken should be one criterion on which work is allocated to a social worker.[24]

Alternatively, it would be possible to decide that certain events which precipitated the referral might indicate the need for a social *work* assessment – bereavement or sudden handicap for example. These are established events which old people themselves often regard as marking the beginning of a new and unhappy phase of their life.[25, 26] They are events which considerably increase vulnerability to mental and physical ill-health – which are a crisis in the literal sense of the word, meaning a decisive moment in one's life. It is at such times that people may be most open to being helped, before they have developed possibly inappropriate or unhealthy coping mechanisms.[27]

It is, however, possible and maybe more practicable, to concentrate on maximising the assessment role of the non-social work staff whose services have been requested. The development of more systematic and rigorous interviewing, designed not just to assess the need for the required service but also to investigate the presence of social, emotional and psychological problems would involve non-social work staff in a 'screening' role more positive than the one in which they are at present widely deployed. It would also be a form of out-reach which had the potential to identify problems before it is 'too late', thereby offering the opportunity for preventive work to take place. But it would mean that greater attention would be required to the actual content of the interview – the topics covered, the way questions were phrased, the explanations given to the client as to why the scope of the interview was more wide ranging than might be reasonably expected given the nature of the referral, and so on.

The records of such interviews might then be routinely seen by a senior social worker or team leader who would decide, on the basis of the information, whether a social work assessment was also advisable. Separating out the information gathering from the decision-making about the likely need for social work, would seem to be an important element in this process to ensure that elderly people have *access* to social work which takes into account the many obstacles that at present result in the under-reporting of their social and psychological needs.

Bearing in mind the number of referrals on non-elderly clients which concern advice on welfare rights, financial problems, housing, etc. which currently form a considerable (and widely disliked) part of the work of social workers on duty, it may be that there is scope to develop the role of staff trained in interviewing but not necessarily in social work. (It is the responsibility of social workers 'on duty' to deal with any enquiries/referrals made by telephone or by personal callers. This task is usually undertaken on a rota system, with one or perhaps two workers being on duty for a day or half-day at a time.) They could be involved in the initial interviews with a wide range of clients, obtaining information which would indicate whether welfare rights advice was all that was required or whether it seemed to be the 'presenting problem' behind which there were family, marital or personal difficulties for which social work help should be offered. Social work staff, thereby freed from some of the time-consuming tasks of duty, could devote more of their attention to clients and problems which seemed to require their particular training. (It is worth noting that staff given in-service training in basic interviewing have been used, with apparent success, to screen all incoming patients on a geriatric unit.)[28]

The second part of this chapter focuses on three aspects of work with old people where social work might be seen to have a particular contribution to make: the management of care systems in the community; life in residential establishments; and caring for the carers.

The Management of Dependency in the Community

Olive Stevenson's chapter refers to the findings of the study by Abrams,[29] which graphically demonstrate the number of elderly people who have no close family – over 30 per cent had no living sibling; over two thirds of the women were without a spouse; over one third had no children, and so on. Those who are very old are also most likely to live alone and those who live alone are the most disadvantaged in terms of social contacts, income and housing.[30] It is, of course, the number and proportion of the very old which are increasing at the fastest rate. Even before the current economic restraints began to take effect, the resource implications of these increases were enormous and unlikely to be fulfilled. In 1978, one director of social services spelt out what the population increase meant in terms of his own authority's provision:

> Assuming the present balance of care to be broadly correct, demographic information suggests that one new 36-bedded old people's home will need to be built every eight months in order to maintain existing levels of provision; to improve the level of service significantly it would be necessary to hold every other service to its present level and invest all available finances in old people's homes.[31]

The Kent Community Care Project is one example of how an authority has sought to develop resources from within the community.[32] The aim of the project is to provide care of frail elderly people within their own homes (or at the very least make it possible for them to remain at home if they so wish – a choice which many dependent elderly people on their own no longer possess). Volunteers, paid a nominal sum, undertake to perform certain specified and agreed tasks for an old person – for example, providing a meal, shopping, providing companionship, so many times a week. The project offers a useful example of how voluntary help can be introduced and, equally importantly, sustained. A project worker, who is a social worker, establishes with the volunteer and the elderly person the task(s) to be carried out; and through joint discussions, the role and expectations of all parties concerned (including the project) are clarified and made explicit. The purpose is thereby to establish a basic level of involvement, but from this there is the opportunity for 'extras' to develop with a degree of spontaneity as client and volunteer get to know each other, and if they wish this to happen. The relationship between them can be shaped according to the inclinations and capacities of each, in a manner similar to the normal process of developing an acquaintanceship or friendship.

A significant element here is that 'packages of care' can be put together taking account of the needs of individual clients and the availability of volunteers; there is the potential for a flexibility of care which it is almost impossible for a statutory agency to provide from its own workforce. The social worker is seen as having a vital role in assessing need and then in assembling the appropriate 'package'. Secondly, care systems such as these are likely to flounder if no support is offered. A responsibility of the social worker is to keep in close contact with the volunteers and to find out how their clients experience the help being offered. It is perhaps appropriate here to quote Challis and Davies on the role of the social worker in the project:[33]

> Firstly, a close assessment of client need; secondly, choosing amongst alternative ways of providing care; thirdly, providing the necessary degree of psychological understanding that should suffuse such a care system.[33]

They further conclude that it is appropriate for a social worker to manage such care systems because 'the responsibility demanded by this kind of activity cannot be relegated to the level of routine procedures'. Certainly, social work involvement in this kind of activity is supported by those like Morris who advocate that 'the core of social work development' lies in the assumption of greater responsibility for the provision of care for those in the population who depend on others for their survival.[34] Caring *for* people rather than caring *about* them is work for which the ethics and knowledge base of social work may be seen to be particularly appropriate.

Life in Residential Establishments

Residential social work in the UK has for a long time been something of a 'poor relation', with conditions of employment, opportunities for training and availability of consultation/supervision generally more limited than those enjoyed by field social workers. There are signs now that this is changing and the development of the Certificate of Social Service (CSS), as an alternative training for social service staff for whom a CQSW is not appropriate, is already making its presence felt in the residential sector. This is not without potential complications, since CSS training is expanding despite the lack of clarity about the CQSW role in residential work, but it is nevertheless meeting a need amongst staff who, for whatever reason, could not avail themselves of CQSW training and whose job seemed to require a differently structured training.

Social workers have not on the whole been much involved in the residential care of old people – at least not after a client has been admitted and adjudged to have 'settled down'. Usually this has meant that six weeks or two months after the admission, the admitting social worker withdrew, unless 'problems' had arisen. Such practice is, of course, quite different from that thought necessary with children in residential care, for whom regular visiting is at least an aim even if not always achieved. The distressing consequences of insufficient attention to social care are visible only too clearly in the lounges of many old people's homes. However, there are signs of change: some authorities are transferring to old people's homes the practice of regular reviews, which include a social worker, such as are undertaken in children's homes.

The potential social work role in old people's homes has been convincingly expounded by Brody, many of whose ideas and practices transfer without too much difficulty to the British scene.[35] Some are quite simple: for example, relatives may be helped to manage the artificiality that is often part of visiting people in institutions by bringing the family photograph album to look at, cards or dominoes to play, a magazine which has pictures or articles of mutual interest. These can become important aids to communication and may well enable old people to engage in conversation.

Brody's underlying philosophy, however, is that social workers have a vital *promotional* role in the provision of care. This changes their job from that of a 'trouble shooter' called in when things have gone wrong, to one which involves them in the development of a care régime which individualises the residents and is attentive to the social and emotional aspects of caring and being cared for. As with many aspects of work with people who are very dependent, it is important to find ways of minimising the 'learned helplessness' that often results from residential care and maximising the choices that are still available to them. (It is unfortunate that admission to an institution often deprives residents of one of the basic choices in life – that of what food to eat. Yet this may be one of the few areas of some discretion left to individuals who are dependent on others to meet most of their daily living needs.) Mercer and Kane also draw attention to the creative role which social workers might adopt:

> Social workers can help develop programs and policies within homes that will increase the degree of control, choice and predictability available to residents. In addition, it seems important that such programs are contingent on an individualized assessment of the residents of the home to insure that the control and choice being offered correspond to what the residents themselves value . . . With their professional penchant for individualization, social workers would do well to expend their energy in determining what is important to each individual rather than focusing exclusively on the residents' problems.[36]

That such work may take the form of apparently minor innovations is illustrated by Mercer and Kane's study which demonstrated that positive results could come simply from involving residents in the selection and care of indoor plants. Of crucial importance, however, was the fact that the residents were not simply given a plant but were encouraged to take the opportunity of selecting a plant and were later involved in taking cuttings, repotting, and so on. In this way the plant became a focus for conversations and shared activities both between residents and between staff and residents. The residents in the home came from a rural area and most of them had been directly involved with horticulture and agriculture throughout their lives; hence the deliberate choice by Mercer and Kane of an activity which would evoke memories of past experiences. For residents in an urban community or for those who are members of particular ethnic or religious groups, there are likely to be other activities which may form the focus of work.

Caring for the Carers

In her chapter, Olive Stevenson described the complexity and the strength of feelings which are inherent in the relationship between those who provide care and those who are cared for. Social workers, together with doctors, have been described as 'hit and run' professionals: they assess or diagnose, administer some form of treatment and then depart, leaving others to provide the day-to-day care.[37] To borrow Parker's terminology, social workers may indeed 'care' but they do not 'tend'; 'tending' is the work of nurses, of care attendants in residential homes or, above all, of relatives who are looking after a frail or disabled member of their family.[38]

It is often said that families no longer care, or do not care enough about their elderly relatives. The increase in state welfare provision, it is said, has encouraged or enabled families to opt out of their responsibilities. It is interesting that this notion of the uncaring family persists despite the strength of evidence to the contrary. In Britain, successive studies have demonstrated both the extent of dependency amongst elderly people in the community and the extent of family and neighbourhood support that is provided; to take but one example, Isaacs and Neville found in their study of old people in two areas in Scotland:

> For every immobile old person in the sample who was in hospital there were two at home; for every two incontinent persons in hospital there were three at home; and for every three with severe mental

> abnormality there were four at home . . . These figures suggest that the greater part of the care of dependent old people in the survey fell upon their relatives, including spouses, others of the same generation and children; and that hospital beds were used preferentially for those who lived alone and who had no close relatives.[39]

The concentration of scarce services and resources upon old people who live alone or with an elderly spouse has important implications for families who are tending an elderly relative or relatives – especially since the main burden may fall upon one person.[40] What is his or her equivalent of the nurse's time off? What sources of emotional and physical support are available? Looking after someone on a full-time or near full-time basis can be a very isolated and lonely task, for all that it provides opportunities to demonstrate love and care.

Attempts by the health and social services to share the burden of care and to enable families to continue caring without their being brought to the point of breakdown are only just beginning to develop. Periods of short-term care are offered in some hospitals and some residential homes; day centres (usually run by the social services department) and day hospitals may offer relief from care for a day or more per week. However, both the level and the type of provision vary from one part of the country to another. In areas where provision is grossly inadequate the social worker has an important role to play in identifying the extent of need and the potential for a more flexible use of resources. This may, for example, take the form of encouraging one home to accept a few frail old people for what is termed 'intermittent' or 'rotating' care; where an elderly person spends, say, three weeks in care and six weeks out. Given this time span, one bed can offer some relief to three families or carers. This system is a good example of how a partnership between welfare services and the carer can be put into practice; the partnership can of course be equally effective between a hospital and the carer, with a number of beds on the geriatric unit being reserved for rotating care.

Without in any way underplaying the physical strain of tending, perhaps accompanied by the misery of constantly interrupted sleep, and the restrictions placed on normal social activities because of the need to be 'there' all the time, it is important, as Olive Stevenson pointed out, to take account of the emotional strain of being intimately involved in the gradual physical and possibly also mental decline of someone whom you love. Social workers have hitherto been little involved in helping the carers or, to put it more accurately, social workers tend to be called in when caring systems have broken down, when families or the carer have been defeated and when attitudes and behaviour have become entrenched. The challenge is to find a 'way in' before this happens, when an appropriate amount of support stands a better chance of preventing or at least delaying the need for urgent or emergency action.

It may be that through closer links with doctors and other professionals in primary health care, social workers may be alerted to the presence of those who tend before it is 'too late'. There does, however, seem to be a clear indication that, since families and carers do not usually refer themselves until they have reached a certain stage of desperation, a policy of out-reach may need to be adopted more often than is usual in the UK.[41] This raises serious questions about intrusion into people's lives before they have requested involvement and it would alter the traditionally reactive practice within social services, which broadly speaking respond to demand rather than seeking out unarticulated need. Yet, as is evident elsewhere in this chapter, in many aspects of the care of old people, a reliance on a reactive response has severe limitations and the failure (even before present economic stringency) to be explicit about provision has in effect limited the access of many old people and their carers to social work and social service.

It is not unusual in the psychiatric setting for social workers to work with the parents or the spouse of the patient, focusing on their needs, on the way their behaviour and attitudes may help or hinder the patient and on the nature and purpose of the doctor's treatment of the patient. Such work may take the form of groups (such as for parents of schizophrenic people) or of sessions with individuals. There is scope for work of this kind to be undertaken with those who tend very dependent elderly people. Support groups for the carers of people with dementia can offer the opportunity for advice on management, the sharing of the hurt, the anger and the bewilderment plus the welcome contact with others who know something of the meaning of caring in such stressful circumstances.[42] Some carers may value help on an individual basis, with the opportunity to express their feelings and, moreover, to be helped to understand that the ambivalence is *normal* and not a sign of being uncaring. Others may need help to acknowledge that they can no longer provide the level of care they would like to; facing the limits of one's capacity to meet the needs of a loved one is not easy.

The focus has thus far been on helping families and individuals to continue providing the type of care that otherwise would require the admission of the old person to hospital or residential care. Tending is however frequently the work of the least experienced or the least trained members of nursing and social services staff (indeed, the care attendants in residential homes in the UK are categorised as manual workers, which reflects the status according such work). They may, therefore, need help in understanding their feelings about tending and in examining the way in which they respond, consciously and unconsciously, to the helplessness of many of their patients or residents. The social worker may well be the professional whose training and value system is the most appropriate for exploring and explaining concepts such as loss, ambivalence and the dynamics of the caring relationship.

There may, however, be specific occasions when it is especially important for a social worker to be seen to be part of the caring team or system. For example, the effect of several patients or residents dying over a very short period of time (perhaps the consequence of a flu virus) can be extremely demoralising for staff and *they* may need to be shown that someone cares about *them*. It may be appropriate in such circumstances for the social worker to 'be around' more than is usual; his or her presence may be as important, if not more so, than any action he might take, since being there is an acknowledgement of the sadness and the weariness.

It is also possible to see a role for social work support to staff in residential homes (most of whom are not trained in social work although they may have a nursing qualification). Recently, the author was engaged in training sessions for officers in charge of old people's homes. It emerged during the sessions on dependency, loss and grief that some of these officers had reached their senior position at a time when their own parents were becoming more frail and needing care not dissimilar to that required by residents. This had raised some acutely uncomfortable feelings. One officer was distressed that she found herself unable to do for her mother those intimate care tasks which she could do without difficulty for residents. Another, whose parent had died about a year previously, found that each death in the home reawakened her grief at his own loss. A third felt torn between the needs of her residents and the needs of her mother; whenever she tended the one, she was conscious of the needs of the other. The kind of support available to residential staff in the UK seems to be directed more towards such issues as budgeting, diets and replacement of furniture than towards the emotional demands of their work; it would seem imperative for this to change, especially given the high level of dependency to be found in many establishments providing long-term care.

In conclusion, two points need to be made. First, it must be acknowledged that much of this chapter concerns how social work *could* contribute to the well-being of elderly people who are under stress. It is a sad reflection on the social work profession that the problems of people who are old in general occupy low status; the fact that similar attitudes can be found within medicine and nursing does not excuse social work in its failure to bring to the problems of old age the understanding and commitment accorded to the problems of the young. Some social workers are welcome exceptions to this gloomy picture and it is to be hoped that their enthusiasm and their skills will encourage others to become thus involved.

Secondly, a more equitable distribution of social work time amongst *all* clients who seem to need such help will not be quickly achieved. It requires a considerable change in social work education and practice and in the operational priorities of employing agencies. Ways must be found of helping social work students to apply their knowledge and skills across client groups and problems, so that they do not come away thinking that social work is 'not about' old people. Within social services departments, closer attention must be paid to the appropriate deployment of staff with different levels and types of training. Social work time is a finite resource and in some parts of the country, where the level of qualified staff may be as low as 20 per cent, it is very scarce. All the more reason, therefore, that it is rationed on a more sophisticated basis than is at present the case in most authorities. For social workers this might mean moving away from the one worker-one case model of practice to one of case-sharing, where certain prescribed tasks are undertaken by staff who do not have a CQSW training; this would allow social workers more time to focus on those aspects for which their qualification seemed particularly appropriate.

Social workers have yet to develop their potential for helping elderly people, their families and carers. Until this has happened to a far greater extent, it is difficult to see how the recommended 'team work' or 'multidisciplinary' approach to the care of old people can become a reality. It is a matter of some urgency that social workers become more directly concerned with the well-being of elderly people.

Notes

1. P. Townsend, 'Isolation, Desolation and Loneliness', in E. Shanas, P. Townsend, D. Wedderburn, H. Friis, P. Milhoj and J. Stenhouwer (eds.), *Old People in Three Industrial Societies* (Routledge and Kegan Paul, London, 1968) pp. 258-87.

2. A. Holme and J. Maizels, *Social Workers and Volunteers* (George Allen and Unwin, London, 1978).

3. DHSS, *Social Service Teams: The Practitioner's View* (HMSO, London, 1978).

4. C. Rowlings 'The Allocation of Work' in DHSS 1978, pp. 57-76.

5. C. Hallett, 'Ancillaries' in DHSS, 1978, pp. 137-68.

6. C. Rowlings, *Social Work with Elderly People* (George Allen and Unwin, London) in Press.

7. DHSS, *An Investigation into the Effects on Clients of Industrial Action by Social Workers in the London Borough of Tower Hamlets* (HMSO, London, 1980).

8. A. Hunt, *The Elderly at Home: a Study of Peopled Aged Sixty Five and over Living in the Community in England in 1976*, Office of Population Censuses and Surveys (HMSO, London, 1978).

9. R. Layard, D. Piachaud and M. Steward, *The Causes of Poverty* Background Paper No. 5, Royal Commission on the Distribution on Income and Wealth (HMSO, London, 1978).

10. B. Wootton, *Social Science and Social Pathology* (George Allen and Unwin, London, 1959).

11. A. Sinfield, *Which Way for Social Work?* (Fabian Tract 393, 1969).

12. E. Shanas and B. Sussman (eds.), *Family, Bureaucracy and the Elderly* (Duke University Press, Durham, N. Carolina, 1977).

13. CIPFA, *Personal Social Services Statistics: 1977-78 Actuals* (Chartered Institute of Public Finances and Accountancy, London, 1979).

14. E.M. Goldberg and R.W. Warburton, *Ends and Means in Social Work* (George Allen and Unwin, London, 1979).

15. J. Williamson, I.H. Stokoe, S. Gray, M. Fisher, A. Smith, A. McGhee and E. Stephenson, 'Old People at Home: Their Unreported Needs', *Lancet* Vol. 23, May 1964, pp. 1117-20.

16. Supplementary Benefits Commission, *Annual Report for Year ended 1978* (HMSO, London, 1979).

17. E.M. Goldberg, A. Mortimer and B.T. Williams, *Helping the Aged: a Field Experiment in Social Work* (George Allen and Unwin, London, 1970).

18. N. Dunnachie, 'Intensive Domiciliary Care of the Elderly in Hove', *Social Work Services* No. 21, November 1979, pp. 1-3.

19. R. Hadley, A. Webb and C. Farrell, *Across the Generations* (George Allen and Unwin, London, 1975).

20. P. Marris, *Loss and Change* (Routledge and Kegan Paul, London, 1974).

21. K. Shulman, 'Suicide and Parasuicide in Old Age: a Review', *Age and Ageing*, Vol. 7, 1978, pp. 201-9.

22. C. Rowlings, 'Social Work with the Elderly: Some Problems and Possibilities' (University of Keele, Keele, Staffs. 1978).

23. B. Isaacs and Y. Neville, *The Measurement of Need in Old People*, Scottish Health Service Studies No. 34 (Scottish Home and Health Department, Edinburgh, 1976).

24. BASW, *The Social Work Task*, BASW Working Party Report (BASW, Birmingham, 1977).

25. J. Tunstall, *Old and Alone* (Routledge and Kegan Paul, London, 1966).

26. Hadley *et al.*, 1975, p. 40.

27. L. Rapoport, 'Crisis Intervention as a Mode of Brief Treatment', in R.W. Roberts and R.H. Nee (eds.), *Theories of Social Casework* (University of Chicago Press, London, 1970).

28. R. Ricketts, 'Screening the Old', *Community Care* No. 231, 20 September, 1978, p. 23.

29. M. Abrams, *Beyond Three Score and Ten: A Second Report on a Survey of the Elderly* (Age Concern, Mitcham, Surrey, 1980).

30. Hunt, 1978.

31. W. Harbert, 'Wanted – a Policy for the Elderly', *Social Work Service* No. 16, July, 1978, pp. 26-8.

32. D. Challis, and B. Davies, 'A New Approach to Community Care for the Elderly', *British Journal of Social Work*, Vol. 10, No. 1, Spring 1980, pp. 1-18.

33. Ibid. p. 10.

34. R. Morris, 'Caring for *vs* Caring about People', *Social Work*, Vol. 22, September 1977, pp. 353-9.

35. E.M. Brody, *Long Term Care of Older People* (Human Sciences Press, New York, 1977).

36. S. Mercer and R.A. Kane, 'Helplessness and Hopelessness amongst Institutionalised Aged: an Experiment', *Health and Social Work*, Vol. 4, No. 1, February, 1979, pp. 91-116.

37. A. Kushlick, 'Some Ways of Setting, Monitoring and Attaining Objectives for Disabled People', Health Care Evaluation Research Team, Research Report No. 116, 1975.

38. R. Parker, 'The Future of the Personal Social Services', Unpublished paper delivered at a Seminar at the University of Bath to mark the anniversary of the Seebohm Report, September 1978.

39. Isaacs and Neville, 1976, p. 64.

40. B. Isaacs, 'Geriatric Patients: do Their Families Care?', *British Medical Journal*, Vol. 4, 1971, pp. 282-6.

41. Ibid.

42. J. Fuller, E. Ward, A. Evans, K. Massam and A. Gardner, 'Dementia: Supportive Groups for Relatives', *British Medical Journal*, Vol. 1, 23rd June, 1979, pp. 1684-5.

10 AGEING AND THE COMMUNITY COUNSELLOR

Sally Greengross

For at least one hundred years, writers studying society and the social order have tried to pinpoint the essential features which make a community. What emerges is some consensus on the importance in a traditional community of personal relationships, based on something deeper than encounters arising merely through the work situation. People in such communities know one another as whole, many faceted personalities, not simply by their occupation.

A contemporary student of communities and neighbourhoods, Philip Abrams, has pointed to the circumstances favouring the emergence of traditional community life.[1] Kinship ties are usually of overriding importance, the population tends to be fairly homogeneous in terms of employment and informal caring networks are strong. The existence of adverse living conditions, with extreme hardship and sickness usually not far away makes a community of interest in survival paramount. While other writers have looked back in romantic vein to pre-industrial static social networks in which people knew the traditional leaders and experts to whom they could turn for help in adversity, Abrams sees the decline in such community care as an inevitable trend in modern industrial society, together with higher living standards and increased mobility and choice for the majority. Such opportunities affect many aspects of life including a widening pool of acquaintances from whom friends are drawn. To go back to the traditional community and with it the good neighbourliness it offered, would mean going back to totally unacceptable living conditions.

Even if a return to the past is both undesirable and unlikely, certain groups in society have probably lost more than others through the destruction and decline of traditional community life, especially in urban areas. Those who have most to lose and the strongest ties in an area are often the elderly population. As the rate of social change itself increases and young people tend to move away, those who survive in ever greater numbers into very old age are increasingly going to experience isolation and acute loneliness.

In inner city areas the total population has been steadily declining for a number of years. This in turn results in a contraction of the rate base which finances many public services such as transport. Yet the number of elderly people is rising in absolute terms at a time when the services on which they are most dependent are beginning to disappear. The problem is made more acute by the fact that concentrations of elderly people are often to be found in 'twilight zones' which are particularly deprived environmentally.

The trend towards large-scale and cheaper supermarket shopping in decentralised precincts, the decline of corner shops, the Sub-post Office, the local chemist and many local churches also affect the elderly adversely. In most areas the virtual extinction of delivery services means that the postman and the milkman play an increasingly important social role as the 'eyes' of the neighbourhood. They know better than most about any changes in a particular person's daily routine and are often the first to give the alert when help is needed, but they cannot be expected to provide more than fleeting, though essential, social contact.

Mark Abrams' research for Age Concern has demonstrated that, among those over 75, 35 per cent have no living children and almost half live totally alone.[2] Of those living alone about a third expressed feelings of extreme loneliness. The Office of Health Economics published statistics which indicate that more than 80 per cent of people over 80 are single, widowed or divorced, and in this country people who are 75 years and over are going to increase by half-a-million in the next twenty years.[3] Elderly people particularly suffer from the break-up of closeknit neighbourhoods because those within them have historical, not merely geographical, ties. They share, as individuals and as members of a group, experiences and a culture. Mere proximity is not usually enough in itself to create deep and lasting personal bonds.

Schutz in his essay 'The Stranger' described the difficulty experienced by anyone who comes to settle in a well-established community and wishes to become part of it.[4] He can never assimilate totally because he has not grown up in the same culture and learned its subtleties and nuances at the same pace and in the natural way that a child, and later a young adult member of the group, does over many years. For those people who have spent a lifetime in one particular environment, affecting it by their presence and drawing from it support and a framework for living, it is difficult to communicate with other younger people its total significance and character. When we speak, therefore, of informal networks of care and support in the community, we are describing relationships which exist over time as well as space, with many interlocking bonds of kinship and reciprocal ties which often cross generational boundaries. Help given to someone today might relate to help received at some former time in a person's life or indeed to other members of a family. These are, nevertheless, reciprocal relationships and need to be recognised as such.

In a recent discussion document on collaboration in community care, attention is drawn to the fact that the term 'community care' usually means care outside an institution, but in the 1960s and 1970s the term developed to incorporate an element of public participation in the caring task, or care by the community rather than merely in it.[5] Within the concept of neighbourhood care, Abrams has pointed to the same ambiguity of meaning, the term applying to organised service delivery or to informal care based on genuine feelings of concern or affection for others. People do not need to know one another for effective 'service delivery' to take place and geographical neighbourliness will not in itself ensure that informal mutual systems are set up.

Proximity is an enabling factor and can reduce costs, but no more than that. It is obviously an advantage if people derive mutual benefit from community relationships and often the valuable contribution that old people themselves could make is virtually untapped. Time to spare, compassion, a sympathetic ear and understanding are important factors in caring for any age group, and while elderly people do a lot for others in this respect, they could be much more involved, given adequate opportunity and encouragement.

There are many examples of the solidarity of a group of people against adverse external conditions. Many newly arrived immigrant groups appear to care more for their dependent elderly relatives in the face of a strange and difficult environment. Age Concern is currently conducting research into the needs of older members of ethnic minority groups whose families are no longer immigrants but British-born citizens; this is designed to help us discover, among other things, whether this network of informal care given by close relatives and friends is indeed greater, whether it will decline, and whether different needs will emerge as the situation of the total group becomes more stable.[6]

It is not a new phenomenon in this country for the elderly to be left on their own. Britain has been an almost continuous net exporter of population since the Industrial Revolution and harsh necessity has forced many young people away from home to other parts of the United Kingdom in the search for work, a factor which is still very important in today's areas of declining industrial activity, but the present population of elderly people is much larger and much older than ever before. With increased age people are more vulnerable to the debilitating disorders which can accompany old age. They are more likely, therefore, to be left without the company of close relatives, particularly of their own age group, and to be more frail and far less mobile than younger people living nearby. Self-imposed solitude which many people enjoy and choose is very different from the despair of loneliness and the feeling that one is useless and unwanted by society in general and one's family and friends in particular.

Even where a well-established 'natural' neighbourhood exists and where informal care systems flourish, there are likely to be lonely, friendless old people who slip through the caring network and are excluded from the mainstream of social life. They may themselves resist overtures by neighbours, who in turn find it hard to appreciate the contribution which a difficult, unfriendly or perhaps confused person can make in a relationship which is usually carefully geared to be of mutual benefit. In urban areas, particularly where people have little time to spare, neighbourly relationships are constrained within certain boundaries and the encroachment of privacy is avoided whereever possible. In these situations some less 'natural' caring system has to be developed if such people are to be protected from risk, both physical and emotional.

Inevitably therefore longevity and a greater ease of mobility, together with smaller families, must increase the likelihood of loneliness in the elderly, although research on the subject, even among the highly mobile population of the USA, shows a high degree of 'intimacy at a distance' and that most of the care of frail elderly people is still carried out by the family and is often at enormous personal cost to those involved. This cost of caring is borne directly in most cases by women. However, the emotional strain of what can be twenty or more years of caring for a dependent and increasingly frail relative, often at a time when adolescent children also demand and need attention from their parents, or when the adults themselves are facing their own retirement and ageing, is immeasurable.

As more women demand full equality of opportunity, the willingness of the multi-generational family to continue to be the greatest caring agency in society well may decline further, contrary to much current thinking on this matter. In fact, most elderly people cope until their death, living independently in the community with little or no outside help. As a result of this, degrees of greater ageing can almost be equated with degrees of greater isolation, as more contemporaries who share a similar past die and with them their part in the shared culture. This culture has bequeathed to those left behind many attitudes (both positive and negative), fears and beliefs based on real life experiences which are meaningless to the young unless they are capable of real empathy and understanding and have the ability to listen in the fullest sense. This seemingly rare quality is latent in many people and can be encouraged and developed with adequate preparation through training. Failing this, sadly, the ability to listen to people and to talk with them about the problems they face after a bereavement or similar painful and acute loss is often totally missing. Death in today's society is hidden from sight and the loss suffered by those left behind is contained and repressed, together with any outward display of emotion and other trappings of mourning which used to serve as clues to suitable and appropriate behaviour by others.

One elderly woman expressed her feelings about this recently to the writer Jeremy Seabrook:

> Death has been removed from sight, hasn't it; made shameful; a bit disreputable. An unfortunate accident that only happens to those who are careless. Of course the whole tenor of life has changed, and in a way that makes life more enjoyable; but whereas my parents used to dwell on the more sombre things, we seem quite unable to face them today . . . I can think of death quite coolly, but you can't help being infected by the changed attitudes towards it. That's why I sometimes feel afraid in a way that I used not to. It isn't that I am afraid of going to everlasting torment, it isn't even the fear of the unknown. But I have to pull myself together and remind myself that with birth, it is the most universal experience. A world which thinks that death is shameful has lost touch with its own reality. It isn't I who am wrong, it is those who insist on the illusion that pain doesn't exist and loss can be ignored. I think perhaps the tragedy is that I feel I have to wrestle with my feelings in isolation. Although we and only we can experience our own death, in another way, it is the least individual problem there is.[7]

Alison Norman, in a recent publication, demonstrates vividly how decisions to move people into residential care are sometimes made because relatives or other carers cannot manage any more, rather than because the old person's condition makes such a move inevitable.[8] She argues that it is much easier to lose one's home and with it one's independence by going into residential care or to live with relatives than ever it is to regain this independence at a later stage. She also points out, as have Murray Parkes and others, that the loss of one's home and personal possessions may produce a pattern of grieving similar to that which follows the death of a loved one.[9]

Those who come through the experience the least harmed and manage to adapt well to a new way of life in a residential setting tend to be those who are strongest; they may not have needed to go into residential care in the first place, if a viable community alternative support system had been available. The weak and the most frail who suffer the most through the change of life-style often never fully recover, sometimes dying in the process. The very condition of others would make some form of residential care desirable and necessary if adequate foresight was used in planning the move, retaining friends and giving advice and counselling in preparation for this major change in life.

While Simone de Beauvoir's own fear and distaste of the ageing process are apparent in much of her writing on old age, her description of the shattering effect of bereavement or similar loss on the body and not merely on the personality, is revealing:

> It is not the organs that abruptly lose their powers in the case of illness, stress, bereavement or serious misfortune; it is the build-up which hid their deficiencies that falls to pieces. The individual's body had in fact undergone the decay, the involution of age, but he had successfully dealt with the situation by conscious or unconscious compensatory reactions; all at once he can no longer make use of these forms of defence and his latent old age becomes apparent. The spiritual or psychological collapse has physical repercussions, and it may even lead to death.[10]

We are made aware in examples such as these of the need to help people work through the grieving process and to give them more of the support which they need at this vital stage in which so much change and adaptation to a new life situation has to take place.

We should perhaps consider, in trying better to understand the ageing process, the different sort of problems which people face and whether those that emanate from external situations can be solved, or at any rate mitigated, through conscious effort.

Many problems which old people face need practical solutions. They seek basic but specialised information, often on housing matters or welfare rights, or on the availability of practical aids and domiciliary services.[11] Some problems are exacerbated through restricted mobility due to the ageing process and can result from new initiatives in the neighbourhood, such as medical centres which are situated far away, from the closure of a bus route or difficulties in finding a chiropodist. Such problems are among those to which skilled and highly trained staff sometimes apply themselves, although in many areas they are dealt with entirely by voluntary agencies or ancillary workers.

Elderly people have a right to help from skilled social workers and other professionals, if they desire it, in proportion at least to their numbers but more properly according to their need. This need is far from met, partly due to overall shortages of staff (a situation which is rapidly deteriorating as the population of the very elderly increases), partly due to insufficient financial resources, and partly due to a well-known reluctance on the part of social workers and other skilled personnel to work with the elderly.[12] Social services have few statutory obligations to meet with regard to adults, but many towards children, so the trend is reinforced in recruitment and training to specialised fields in the social work career structure.

In the area of emotional problems, some are best met by professional workers whose skills, resulting from appropriate training and experience, enable them to form judgements, assess situations demanding radical action and take full responsibility for any such action that follows. There are other types of emotional problems, however, which can be met not simply as effectively, but more so, by people who are themselves members of the community. Their knowledge of local resources and 'natural helpers' or informal carers is invaluable and derived from an intimate and often long standing experience of local life. In some ways the strength of the Home Help Service, though part of the statutory provision of the local authority, is due as much to its reliance on people who share similar backgrounds and experiences with their clients, as the fact that it provides practical help with problems that elderly people themselves recognise.

There are many among the elderly who are fiercely independent and who will resist seeking help from 'the Welfare' even at high personal cost to themselves; they may do so to avoid the stigma of accepting what they consider to be charity. Some thoughtless intervention by social services can indeed reduce individual autonomy and lead to dependency in a previously self-sufficient and vital person, whose personal problems at one point seemed insuperable but need not have been so had suitable counselling been available.[13, 14]

With elderly people a multidisciplinary and 'global' approach to care, involving professionals, family and the elderly clients themselves, is widely acknowledged to be desirable but rarely takes place outside the hospital setting. In the community this task is often allotted to unqualified members of the team.

Elderly people are particularly likely, therefore, to be deprived of the sort of help which social workers could provide if they had the time, training and the inclination. Given the available resources, however, they could not in any circumstances meet the growing need of this client group but, as Holme and Maizels have demonstrated, volunteers are not usually given the responsibility of working closely in depth with clients, and social workers are reluctant to pass on skills to willing volunteers, who can offer that most scarce of commodities, time, but who themselves need support and backing from qualified professional staff.[15]

Jonathan Barker has argued that, unless the professional or 'outsider' sees his role as supporting the efforts of the indigenous (or accepted) informal network – or in its absence, as trying to promote it – he will end up trying to substitute for it. Barker believes that such professional substitutes cannot enable the client to retain certain key means of satisfactory survival. These include dignity, self-esteem and active membership of the community

Like Abrams, Barker believes that paternalism or the takeover of responsibility from a client/patient is disabling and confirms the recipient of help in what is, in effect, a deviant status.[16]

The elderly are more likely to accept help from others if they feel that in some way they can reciprocate. This in itself maintains for them the status of 'contributor' to society, a status which the working population has and needs to maintain in the struggle most people face to earn enough to meet their expected standards of living.

The professional, to achieve a balance, must act as an enabler, rather as a community worker who supports and encourages local people to use their own skills, and to give invaluable spare time to the betterment of life for others and, through others, to enrich their own lives.

A community-centred approach to intervention would, argues Hadley, maximise the capacity of the community to provide care and encourage local people to accept greater responsibility for those at risk.[17] The central role of the informal or voluntary sector, with the state providing the necessary support and backup, is one way of trying to cope with the increasing need of the frail elderly over the next twenty years, and the system of breaking down social service areas into small local patches, where 'key workers' mobilise all the domiciliary services and helping agencies, together with local caring individuals, may be one way, now in the experimental stage in a few places, of using our very limited resources of skilled and qualified staff more rationally and effectively. The use of local people in the front line, constantly backed up by professionals, could lead to a greater integration of informal care and bring in many more active elderly people as carers for their own and younger age groups. Families, the community and the state will need to work together far more effectively if the challenge posed by the ageing population over the next twenty years is to be met.[18]

There are preliminary indications that this approach helps to provide genuine encouragement to family, community and neighbourhood care, and that there is more opportunity for preventive work and, therefore, less concentration on crisis intervention in most areas where it is being tried out. Preventive and supportive work with families is often as important as direct work with elderly people themselves. Bergmann found, in a study of severely impaired day-patients using psychogeriatric services that the crucial factor differentiating those who remained viable in the community and those who did not was not the condition of the patient so much as the level of support given to caring relatives.[19]

A combination of circumstances, therefore, demonstrates a need for community-based help for those suffering from loneliness, grief or despair either directly or as a result of being involved in caring for elderly people, or with problems of relationships between old people themselves or across the generations.

Counselling itself has been defined in many ways, from the need for information and advice on specific matters like housing or income maintenance to the need for help with one's deepest feelings, when the facts under discussion are not as relevant as the way they are interpreted and their meaning to the person concerned. Problems for which counselling techniques are appropriate with older people often result from retirement itself which can have profoundly disorientating and even tragic effects on individuals and their families. In-depth counselling is usually defined as being derived from the theories of Carl Rogers, in which people are not told what to do but helped to make informed decisions themselves, having come to a true understanding of what their problem is and what their future situation will be. Such counselling involves a relationship which develops and can change over time, in which the client's right of self-determination is respected and during which process, if direct advice is given over practical matters to reduce anxiety, it is not itself part of the counselling process.

Voluntary organisations have played a major role in the United Kingdom in pioneering counselling services, and the work of the Samaritans and Marriage Guidance are well known examples. Cruse

Self-help Groups draw directly from the community, and widows and widowers use their own understanding and experience to help others who are bereaved. It goes without saying, however, that many professionals may use counselling skills as part of their every-day work and this applies particularly to the clergy, the medical profession and to social workers.

If community counselling schemes are to be set up, professionals must be willing to share some of their skills and pass them on to volunteers. Initiatives taken by Age Concern in training volunteer counsellors are designed to provide a service for elderly people whose emotional problems are very often at present totally neglected, while at the same time, benefiting from the expertise of newly retired professionals to co-ordinate the schemes and drawing on the resources of active older people living locally as potential counsellors. The schemes are operating with the full support of social services area teams and the co-operation of local education authorities in providing training facilities.[20]

Research has demonstrated that lay counsellors can be as effective as professionals provided they are trained. Carkhuff and Truax found that approximately a hundred hours of training was appropriate; but in many cases committed people, with adequate time to give their clients to express hidden and repressed feelings and an ability to retain some measure of detachment, can achieve excellent results with far less training and preparation, if the latter are carefully planned, sensitively carried out, and prepare people to work in specific problem areas, rather than in general counselling situations.[21]

Counselling often has to be limited to specific and realistic goals and, as Brearley has argued in discussing social work for the elderly, towards the acceptance of a changed situation and the ability to cope with it.[22]

While the help can at times be limited to befriending people, as is the case in many self-help schemes, there is also a great need among older people for counselling in the fullest sense, for which adequate preparation by professionals is required. Both the clients and the befrienders need access to such counsellors for problems which arise and which need to be worked through at a deeper and more profound level. Even though in theory the method of counselling can be taught, the personality of the counsellor has been found to be of fundamental importance. Empathy, warmth and non-possessiveness are among the essential qualities, as is an optimistic attitude and the belief that the work is worth attempting because one is able to help achieve beneficial results.[23]

Counsellors need some preparation in order, among other things, to examine their own motives and to ensure that they are not working out their own problems through others. They must be certain that their own values do not prevent them from accepting the other person totally and any subject, however extraordinary or even repugnant to themselves, as suitable for discussion. Counsellors have to learn the limits of self-disclosure, how to be open and friendly without burdening the clients with their own anxieties. The absence of professional status and the equality of lay people should be used to the benefit of their clients who may feel reluctant to approach professionals, who can be far younger than themselves and attached to what appears to be a remote and rather bureaucratic authority. While many people have within them the skills necessary to become effective counsellors, training can help them recognise the meaning of non-verbal communication and to use it skillfully themselves to increase empathy and understanding. They will not always be aware of the need for repetitive unburdening of guilt and for the possible transference of guilt and hatred onto themselves.

Specialist training can help volunteers to understand the feelings of others, including the stages most people experience following bereavement or other loss. They can learn to recognise symptoms of abnormal grieving or extreme depression for which psychiatric help is needed, and they can be partially compensated for years of experience if taught how to predict the outcome of certain types of situation with which they may be faced and to aim for realistic goals.

Some of the stark facts of widowhood need to be examined during the training process; how elderly women whose whole life was devoted to marriage and motherhood are particularly ill-equipped to cope with a total loss of role and are generally reduced to a level of poverty compared to their married life, which makes visits to relatives infrequent or even impossible. This can also create barriers to involvement in new activities, even if they have the will to explore such possibilities. Butler has described desperate and pathetic efforts by older women to remain young when shocked through bereavement into facing their own mortality and the imminence of death.[24]

Some understanding is needed of the extent of paranoid behaviour, so that expert help can be sought when necessary, and also the frequency with which physical illness can follow bereavement.

The degree and duration of numbness, apathy and the wish to die, which so many bereaved people feel need to be understood as well as the extent to which older people experience total hopelessness when grieving the loss of a loved one.

Whitehead has drawn attention to the danger of old people suffering from clinical depression being wrongly diagnosed as senile because so many of their presenting symptoms are identical, and counsellors need to understand the difficulty of getting through to 'shocked' people who are unable to ask directly for help.[25] Elderly people may express grief less overtly than the young, and some people can appear to deny it altogether. This denial, especially when prolonged through the use of drugs, is especially dangerous, argues Murray-Parkes whereas early concern and understanding by a counsellor can enable the bereaved person to get in touch with denied feelings and begin the long process of healing.[26] Pincus has described the life cycle as a 'continual flux of gains and losses' which can only have meaning if seen in perspective.[27]

I have not intended to suggest in this chapter that professional social work can be dispensed with or reduced as community counselling schemes increase. The professionals will always be needed because they should have the skills to cope with a whole variety of situations, are able to identify underlying needs, instigate appropriate courses of action and to act as a major resource in the community.

Ian Galloway, in discussing the need for a professional amateur, emphasises that counselling must always form a major part of the social worker's task.[28] After the professional has made his assessment, the volunteer comes in, working to clearly defined and set limits. The social worker should be involved in the selection and supervision of the volunteers and in supporting them with regular case reviews. Counsellors need regular support, even counselling themselves, if they are to cope with demanding and at times very difficult work, and Galloway's model is of a social worker whose primary case load consists of volunteers, each working with two or more clients. A partnership between the professional and the volunteer would thus provide, in his view, an infrastructure of care. There are, however, many complex situations in which a vulnerable person's right to skilled help should not be overlooked and the professional may need to work directly with the client.

Not all community counselling is developed on a one-to-one basis. Much valuable help is provided through groups of people coming together, sharing experiences and giving each other mutual support.

Relatives of stroke patients, severely handicapped or mentally frail elderly people can often themselves be elderly and, even if this is not the case, their problems and the stress they suffer are largely due to their involvement and often unselfish devotion to an old person. Some group support schemes for the elderly mentally infirm have brought relief and help to many caring relatives and therefore performed a most effective preventive role in keeping such frail people far longer in their own homes.

Married couples with problems which are intensified after retirement may also benefit greatly from group counselling. Understanding the similar plight of others and realising one is not unique or inadequate can do a lot to ease the situation and enable people to discover for themselves new negotiated relationships, better suited to their changed circumstances. Groups can help people to explore their feelings about retirement, about the future when the death of one partner must inevitably occur and when the other will face living alone. They can be of enormous help to people working through the emotional trauma following strokes, physical handicap or serious illness and involve a wider network of people than might otherwise be known to those involved.

People facing a new life-style resulting from what they see as a stigmatising 'illness', resulting in the loss of an organ or a limb, can often experience a sense of normality when together with a group of similarly afflicted people. The restricted world of the group can be a source of great comfort to such people.[29]

Peer-group counselling can, in such situations, be less resented and more approachable to many people. Members of the peer group can be very helpful in clarifying problems and in enabling people to gain a better understanding of possible future strategies for living and for planning their lives. Whether on a one-to-one basis or through a group, the overall aim of this type of counselling is to lessen dependency in the long run and to increase self-determination, personal responsibility and self-acceptance.

Counsellors working with old people have to overcome problems within themselves. They have to come to terms with their own feelings about ageing, physical and mental decay and death. They have to cope with rejection and apparent failure and they have to judge when to end the counselling relationship with a client. This can be very difficult with frail old people, especially if independence has been difficult to re-establish; but it is essential, and a well-established network of caring organisations locally can ease the transition.

The evaluation of counselling schemes can be lengthy and difficult. Success cannot be measured realistically for at least a year and probably needs longer. The best assessment might come from the clients' own views about the help they have received, and another indicator would be how long counsellors stay with the schemes and whether they are joined by previous clients who wish to help others by training to become counsellors themselves.

C.G. Jung wrote:

> The sole purpose of human existence is to kindle a light in the darkness of mere being.[30]

Jung's philosophy of life, reflected in his work, contained the belief that a truly enriched and fulfilled life can be experienced fully only by those fortunate enough to live to an advanced age. It is not until the personality reaches maturity that it can draw together the many threads of external life experiences, the web of personal relationships, the totality of living and the joy and sorrow it brings, and use them to achieve the next stage, that of the true integration of the personality.

While some people can accept that this continuing growth takes place in the individual, many more adopt, albeit unconsciously, the powerful competing theories of personality development, which concentrate only on the early years of life and believe them to be the foundation upon which all future behaviour depends and by which it is determined. Such theories inevitably lead to the conclusion that old age is at best static, more likely a period of decline.

The counselling process has been likened to other learning experiences, incorporating self-discovery and change and so it can only succeed if the counsellor believes that age does not form a barrier to such learning and to opportunities for personal growth and development.

Gail Sheehy writes:

> As age increases there is a decreasing tendency to compare oneself with others. People become more preoccupied with the inner life, benefiting them with two of the most salient characteristics of the mature years; insightfulness and philosophical concern.

She ends:

> The courage to take new steps allows us to let go of each stage with its satisfactions and to find the fresh responses that will release the richness of the next. The power to animate all of life's seasons is a power within us.[31]

Just before his death, Ernest Becker said:

> Joy and hope and trust are things one achieves after one has been through forlornness.[32]

Those best qualified to help others come through a period of grief or emotional stress must very often be people whose age, life history and experience give them an insight into the situation of afflicted people in their own community, which outsiders could never acquire. Their power to identify closely with those they help makes their help more acceptable to many elderly people, even if at the time it cannot be reciprocated. If they are well prepared for the difficult situations they will undoubtedly encounter and are supported by skilled professionals when the need arises, they can offer a realistic appraisal of what life in the future has to offer those they are prepared to counsel. In this way, in the future, they can help people come to terms with such a situation they now face and in so doing find meaning and purpose in their own lives as valued older members of their own community.

Notes

1. P. Abrams, 'Social Change, Social Networks and Neighbourhood Care' paper given at DHSS Social Work Service Conference, 1979.
2. M. Abrams, *Beyond Three Score Years and Ten*, First Report (Age Concern, England, 1978).
3. G. Thomas, speaking at the Age Concern England Conference 'Ageing in the Eighties', 1980.
4. A. Schutz, *The Stranger*, collected papers (Martinus Nijhoff, The Hague, 1967).
5. 'Collaboration in Community Care', discussion document, Personal Social Services Council (PSSC), Health Service Advisory Council (HSAC), 1980.
6. *The Needs of Ageing and Elderly People from Ethnic Minority Groups*, Age Concern England Research Unit, 1980.
7. J. Seabrook, *The Way They Are* (Age Concern, England, 1980).
8. A.J. Norman, *Rights and Risks*, National Corporation for the Care of Old People (NCCOP), 1980.
9. C. Murray-Parkes, *Bereavement: Studies of Grief in Adult Life* (Tavistock Publications, London, 1972).
10. S. De Beauvoir, *Old Age* (Weidenfeld and Nicholson, London, 1972).
11. J. Barker and M. Bury, 'Mobility and the Elderly: A Community Challenge', in V. Carver and P. Liddiard, *An Ageing Population*, Open University (Hodder and Stoughton, Sevenoaks, 1978).
12. E.M. Goldberg and R.W. Warburton, *Ends and Means in Social Work* (Allen and Unwin, London, 1979).
13. P. Parsloe and O. Stevenson *et al.*, *Social Services Teams: The Practitioners' View* (HMSO, 1978).
14. A. Webber and B. Gearing, *Crisis. Unit 8. An Ageing Population*, Open University (Hodder and Stoughton, Sevenoaks, 1979).
15. A. Holme and J. Maizels, *Social Workers and Volunteers* (BASW and Allen and Unwin, London, 1978).
16. J. Barker, 'The Relationship of "Informal Care" to "Formal" Social Services', in *Teamwork in Personal Social Services and Health Care*, S. Lonsdale, T. Briggs, A. Webb (eds.) (Croom Helm, London, 1979).
17. R. Hadley 'Social Services Departments and the Community', paper presented at Policy Studies Institute, May, 1980.
18. R.M. Moroney, *The Family and the State* (Longman, Harlow, 1976).

19. K. Bergmann, 'How to Keep the Family Supportive', *Geriatric Medicine*, August, 1979.

20. *Volunteer Counselling Schemes*, Age Concern Scotland, Age Concern England preliminary report.

21. H.R. Carkhuff and C.B. Truax, 'Lay Mental Health Counselling: The Effects of Lay Group Counselling, *Journal of Consulting Psychology*, Vol. 29, 1965.

22. C.P. Brearly, *Social Work, Ageing and Society* (Routledge and Kegan Paul, London, 1975).

23. C. Sutton, *Psychology for Social Workers and Counsellors* (Routledge and Kegan Paul, London, 1979).

24. R.N. Butler, 'Towards a Psychiatry of the Life Cycle. Aging and Modern Society', American Psychiatric Association, 1968. In *Readings in Aging and Death*, Zarit (ed.) (Harper and Row, London, 1977-8).

25. T. Whitehead, 'Dementia or Depression: Do we Always Spot the Difference?' *Modern Geriatrics*, January, 1978, pp. 21-5.

26. C. Murray-Parkes, 'Facing the Reality', *Age Concern Today*, No. 23, Autumn, 1977.

27. L. Pincus, *Death and the Family*. Quoted in *Age Concern Today*, No. 23, Autumn, 1977.

28. I. Galloway, 'Volunteers – the need for a Professional Amateur', *Social Work Service*, Vol. 20, June, 1979.

29. E. Goffman, *Stigma* (Prentice Hall, Hemel Hempstead, 1963).

30. C.G. Jung, *Memories, Dreams, Reflections* (New York Vintage Books, 1961).

31. G. Sheehy, *Passages* (E.P. Dutton, New York, 1976).

32. S. Keen, 'A Conversation with Ernest Becker', *Psychology Today*, April, 1974; *Readings in Aging and Death*, Zarit (ed.), Harper and Row, London, 1977-8.

References

Batten, T.R. *The Non-directive Approach in Group and Community Work* (OUP, Oxford, 1976)

Vaughan, T.D. (ed.), *Concepts of Counselling*, SCAC (Bedford Square Press, London, 1975)

Watts, A.G. (ed.), *Counselling at Work*, SCAC (Beford Square Press, London, 1977)

11 PROGRAMMES AND SERVICES FOR THE ELDERLY IN INDUSTRIALISED COUNTRIES

Charlotte Nusberg

It has been observed that the two most important factors influencing welfare expenditures of different countries are their economic well-being and the proportion of the population that is old.[1] These two factors so far have coincided with advanced industrialisation. It is not too difficult to see how industrialisation increases a country's wealth and why the greater a country's wealth, the more it has available to spend for welfare purposes *if* it so chooses. However, the reasons why the number and proportion of the old tend to correlate positively with industrialisation and welfare expenditures may not be as apparent.

Industrialisation and welfare expenditures have in all cases been accompanied by improvements in health and sanitation; these have both contributed immeasurably to decreased infant mortality and morbidity in later life. Life expectancy in the industrialised countries of the world is the highest it has ever reached in the history of the world. In fact, the large majority of the population of developed countries can expect to reach old age. At the same time, modernisation has been accompanied by sharp reductions in fertility, so that the increased numbers of the aged account for ever larger proportions of the population.

While this successful ageing of the population should be primarily viewed as a major benefit of industrialisation, it is not an unmixed blessing; both the normal and pathological processes of ageing require an extensive social support system unique to this age group. In large part, this is a function of yet another consequence of industrialisation – the breakdown of extended family patterns which traditionally provided most of the support to the relatively few persons who did survive into old age. It should be noted that the continuation of extended family patterns, which is, for example, still largely the case in Japan today, does not preclude the need for ever increasing public interventions to improve the support system for the elderly. Many of the problems that can accompany ageing are simply too great to remain the sole responsibility of families; this is recognised by policy-makers in all the developed countries.

11.1 What are Some of the Problems?

The most basic is that of providing *income security* in old age. This, of course, becomes necessary with the almost universal acceptance of retirement as a legitimate goal for all. While the normal retirement age may vary from as low as 55 to as high as 67 in different countries, increased life expectancy has resulted in the need for huge income transfers from the working population to the retired. Although some developed countries provide only means-tested retirement benefits, most provide practically universal systems of publicly supported retirement benefits. So far, there has been little opposition to the large assumption of public responsibility for income provision for the elderly, although there are indications this attitude may be changing.

A second basic need is for *health care* in all its aspects – preventive, curative, rehabilitative and chronic care. The elderly suffer in disproportionate numbers from poor health and account for a very large part of most developed countries' health care expenditures. At any point in time, they may occupy as much as 35 per cent (in the US) to 50 per cent (in Sweden) of a nation's acute care hospital beds and the overwhelming majority of long-term care beds.[2] Health care for the elderly has also become recognised in most developed countries as a public responsibility which is usually exercised through the provision of either a national health service or third-party reimbursement for medical costs.

The *housing* needs of the elderly are increasingly being accepted as a major public responsibility, because of the importance of adequate shelter to the total well-being of the lives of older persons, and the inadequacy of provision for many of them at the present time. The assumption of public responsibility still varies greatly from country to country, but most have adopted measures to increase the number of housing options available to their older populations.

The elderly also differ from other age groups in that many more require one or more *personal social services*, such as home help assistance, home nursing, chore services, etc. on a permanent, on-going basis. This is a function of their greater vulnerability to chronic health problems, as well as particular social factors, and the policy goal of assisting the elderly to remain in their own homes and out of residential institutions – both in recognition of their personal preferences and the higher public costs that are believed to accompany institutionalisation. Age 75 is considered by many policy-makers as a pivotal age in that the need for both health and social services seems to increase dramatically thereafter.[3] And the over-75s are the fastest-growing age group in many of the developed countries (and in some developing countries too!). Countries will also vary greatly in the extent they have comprehensive and co-ordinated personal social services in place; but again, public responsibility in this area also seems to be in the ascendancy.

Finally, the institution of retirement raises many questions about the use of leisure time, the need to find continued meaning in life, and the means of keeping the elderly integrated into society. The public sector continues to share responsibility with the private sector in addressing these issues.

All of the programmes outlined above form part of a *continuum of care*, each of whose components are necessary to the adequate functioning of the whole. They are not substitutes for each other, although to some extent an increase in provision of one form may decrease the need for another in ways that are not yet thoroughly understood. Inadequacies in any one area, in turn, may place insupportable strains on other components of the continuum. No country claims to have a comprehensive and co-ordinated system of provision for its elderly, although it is clear that some countries come closer than others.

Developed countries are also strongly alike in recognising the need for such a continuum of care irrespective of their economic, political and cultural differences. The needs of the elderly in developed countries are greatly similar; hence, it is hardly surprising that the societal responses are extraordinarily alike. This common response has also been facilitated by the exchange of knowledge among countries through international travel and study. At the same time, practically all countries are worried about the costs of providing an ideal balance of services.

Where countries do differ, as Sheila Kamerman has pointed out, is in the emphasis they may place on particular programmes, the adequacy of coverage, eligibility requirements for entitlement, administrative auspices under which programmes are run, the extent of provision by the public, voluntary and proprietary sectors, and co-ordination in planning and service delivery.[4]

It is unusual to find a programme for the elderly that is unique to one particular country. What is more common is to find that a programme, run as a demonstration project in one country, has been a long-accepted practice or part of a national thrust in another.

In the following sections, we will examine each of the major forms of service provision in greater detail, including some of the major country variations.

11.2 Income Support for the Elderly

11.2.1 Replacement Income

With the universal acceptance of retirement as a legitimate social institution in the developed countries, the first and most basic policy adopted was to provide some income protection in old age. Although some systems originally viewed publicly supported social security as insurance against lost earnings (and some still do, e.g. the US), most countries now view publicly supported pensions as a right to be drawn upon on reaching a certain chronological age, usually after having worked a given number of years. Where pensions are viewed as a right, there is less likelihood that earnings limitations will be imposed – an individual retains the right to draw a full pension while conceivably remaining in the work-force full-time. The more mature the system, the less likely there are to be any earnings limitations.[5]

There seems to be a consensus that retirement income should permit individuals to continue more or less to live in the style to which they have become accustomed. As a result, economists suggest that retirement income be equivalent to anywhere from 65-80 per cent of pre-retirement income.[6] (It is assumed a lesser amount is required because the expenses associated with work are no longer necessary.) Where there is less consensus among countries is the extent to which publicly supported pensions or social security, private pensions and individual savings or assets should be counted on to make this vital proportion. In the US and Canada, for example, public debate continues on the respective roles of social security and private pensions in providing income adequacy in old age. Although at the time social security was adopted in the US, it was meant to be only one source of retirement income for pensioners, today it is the source of 90 per cent or more of the retirement income of some 30 per cent of all people over age 65.[7] Relatively few have adequate private pensions or generous savings.

In countries such as Sweden and France, on the other hand, practically the entire labour force is covered by private pensions, and Switzerland and the Netherlands are, in addition, considering mandating private pension coverage for all workers as a key element in providing income security in old age.[8] Then, of course, there are also countries which rely practically entirely on publicly supported systems, e.g. Italy and the socialist countries of Eastern Europe.

11.2.2 The Structure of Public Pension Programmes

Countries differ in how they have chosen to structure their publicly supported systems. Some, such as Canada and Denmark, provide universal entitlement upon reaching a certain age – participation in the labour-force is not required; these pensions are usually referred to as *demogrants*. Demogrants are usually paid for through general tax revenues. Countries such as the US and the Federal Republic of Germany, on the other hand, provide only earnings-related benefits which are tied to labour force participation and a history of employer/employee contributions. In the US, social security is paid for entirely through such contributions; elsewhere, mönies are also drawn from general revenues. Canada and Sweden have both universal and earnings related systems, plus the expectation that private pensions and individual savings will add yet additional tiers of income protection.

Given the present trend towards increased divorce and the barriers that still exist to work-force participation by older women, many women tend to be better protected under universal or demogrant systems, where they are entitled to an old age pension in their own right without having had to accumulate a work history. Dependants' benefits, through which wives were originally protected in earnings-related systems, can no longer be relied on to the same extent as before in light of changing family relationships. The amount provided under demogrants, however, is usually small.

11.2.3 Income Adequacy

Generally, income adequacy does not depend on the particular structure of a retirement system. Sweden – with both a universal and an earnings-related system – and France, Italy and Germany – with only an earnings-related system – come closest to providing adequate replacement income in retirement. The US and the UK, on the other hand, which also both have earnings-related systems, provide much less protection.

In the USSR, 78 per cent of all pensioners in 1970 obtained less than the average industrial wage through the country's earnings-related pension system.[9] And in Japan, there has been considerable hue and cry about the fact that social security coverage with relatively low benefits does not start before age 60, while mandatory retirement generally takes place at 55.

Many countries have also skewed their social security systems so that low-income groups obtain a higher replacement income in retirement than do higher-income groups. However, given the low income base to begin with, such measures are rarely sufficient to reduce income inequalities in retirement.

Table 11.1: Replacement Rate of Social Security Old-age Pensions for Men with Average Earnings in Manufacturing, Selected Countries[a] (Retirement as of 1 Jan. of year indicated)

Country	Years worked	Pension as percent of earnings in year before retirement											
		Single worker						Aged couple					
		1965	1969	1972	1973	1974	1975	1965	1969	1972	1973	1974	1975
Austria	40	67	65	63	62	61	54	67	65	63	62	61	54
Canada[b]	40	21	22	27	30	31	39	42	39	42	46	48	57
Denmark	40	35	29	30	30	30	29	51	42	44	44	43	43
France	37.5	49	42	44	47	44	46	65	56	60	62	60	65
Federal Republic of Germany	40	48	56	49	49	49	50	48	56	49	49	49	50
Italy	40	60	67	65	67	64	67	60	67	65	67	64	67
Netherlands	50	35	36	35	38	37	38	50	51	50	53	53	54
Norway	40	25	34	37	39	40	41	38	49	51	53	54	55
Sweden	30	31	39	45	45	50	59	44	52	58	57	62	76
Switzerland	Since 1948	28	26	31	39	35	36	45	42	46	58	53	53
United Kingdom[b]	Since 1961	23	21	22	22	22	26	36	33	34	33	33	39
United States	Since 1951	29	29	34	38	36	38	44	44	50	57	54	57

[a] Data are for systems at maturity. For Norway and Sweden, data reflect less-than-mature earnings-related pensions: for Denmark, employment-related pension, which is still not payable in full; and, for Canada, pension that reached maturity in 1975.

[b] Based on April rather than January flat-rate benefits in 1973, 1974, and 1975 for Canada and in 1975 for the United Kingdom.

Source: Leif Haanes-Olsen, 'Earnings-Replacement Rate of Old-age Benefits', 1965-75, Selected Countries, *Social Security Bulletin* (January, 1978).

It is important to point out that even in countries with the most generous retirement benefits, poverty can still be found. Many systems are not yet mature, and it will be a number of years before many persons become entitled to draw the maximum benefits under the system. Another problem is that many individuals have not worked the number of years required to draw full benefits. This problem applies especially to women, whose typical labour-force patterns differ sharply from that of men, with many years taken out for child-rearing. This is aggravated by the fact that when they do work, it is generally in low-paying jobs that usually do not have private pension coverage. The result is that single women are disproportionately represented among older people living in poverty in practically all of the developed countries.

Countries which provide less generous publicly-supported retirement benefits still have relatively large proportions of their elderly populations living in poverty, e.g. 25 per cent at or under the poverty level in the US;[10] the majority of the elderly in Japan.[11] Many countries have had to provide means-tested income supplements to complement their social security systems; the assumption that private pensions and individual savings would play an important role in providing an income foundation for the elderly has not proved true for most persons in most developed countries.

A few countries also provide additional protection for women and others who may not be full-time participants in the labour-force. France and the Federal Republic of Germany allow them to make voluntary contributions to the social security system. Japan has established a second public retirement system supported by voluntary contributions. France, in addition, provides a woman with two years of social security coverage for each child she has raised a certain number of years. Switzerland credits all housewives, divorced women and widows with contributions for years spent at home regardless of whether they have had children or not. And the Federal Republic of Germany, upon a couple's divorce, splits the pension credits earned by both during the marriage between the two spouses. The trend seems to be in the direction of providing women with social security coverage in their own right through a combination of work, voluntary contributions, and credits earned through raising a family.

11.2.4 Inflation

A contributor to poverty in old age is inflation, which erodes both public and private benefits. There are few countries that have escaped the deleterious effects of inflation over the last decade. While almost all public systems provide some adjustment mechanism for inflation, countries differ in how frequently and how automatically such adjustments are made. The elderly probably suffer least from inflation in Sweden where the adjustment mechanism is practically automatic. Each time the price index moves by at least three percentage points, retirement benefits are increased the same amount without prior review. In other countries, there may be a review period of one year, and even then the amount of benefit increase to compensate for inflation is subject to debate.

Private pensions systems, unless they are closely tied to the public systems, as in France and Sweden, provide hardly any protection against inflation, and their benefits have been seriously eroded for many recipients over the last decade. The issue of how to make private pensions inflation-proof remains a lively one in many countries.

11.2.5 Adjustments for Growth in GNP

While most public pension systems adjust benefits at retirement so that people will not be penalised by the fact that wages have increased over their work history as a result of increases in the gross national product, almost no country further adjusts benefits following retirement to reflect similar increases. The result is that, over time, pensioners become poorer relative to the active work-force, even if their benefits continue to be increased for inflationary factors. An exception is the Federal Republic of Germany which has incorporated this dynamic factor into its social security system. However, because of recent economic pressures, it has had to postpone providing some of its scheduled benefit increases.

11.2.6 Incentives and Disincentives to Work

Mention has already been made of earnings limitations placed by some countries on a pensioner's ability to work and draw a pension at the same time. Countries, such as the US and the UK, prohibit a retiree from earning beyond a certain amount in wages before a portion of their public benefits are forfeited. Other countries, such as the Federal Republic of Germany and Sweden, impose no restrictions. The socialist countries of Eastern Europe have removed earnings limitations from occupations where they suffer a labour shortage in order to induce pensioners to continue in work, but have kept them in others. The USSR over the past fifteen years has greatly expanded the number of occupational categories which have no earnings limitations. Earnings limitations in countries where they do exist are often an extremely unpopular issue among pensioners, although it is unclear whether in their absence many more would return to work.

Most countries also provide some financial inducement for persons of retirement age to postpone their retirement. These inducements range from a 3 per cent increase in public pension benefits in countries such as the US to 12.5 per cent in Finland. However, the experience to date has been that such incentives have not been successful in persuading people to postpone their retirement.[12]

11.2.7 Flexible Retirement Opportunities

Most developed countries permit retirement before the normal retirement age with actuarially reduced benefits. Most also allow early retirement at full benefits for certain arduous occupations, such as mining. In the Federal Republic of Germany, people can retire between 63 and 67 with full benefits provided they have worked a requisite number of years. So far, however, only two countries, Norway and Sweden, have structured their systems so that older persons may progressively reduce their work hours at their choosing by combining part-time work with a partial pension.

In Norway, older persons may choose to work ¾, ½ or ¼ time following the normal retirement age of 67 and respectively draw a ¼, ½ or ¾ pension. In Sweden, starting at age 60, individuals who have met certain criteria may work anywhere between 17 and 35 hours a week and draw a partial pension for the wages they are forfeiting. At the same time, they preserve their right to draw a full pension at the normal retirement age of 65 by continuing to pay into the system while employed part-time. The Swedish plan has proved very popular and so far, part-time job opportunities have opened up to accommodate the demand. This, however, has been due in part to adverse economic circumstances; employers have eliminated full-time jobs in favour of part-time jobs as a way to save money. It remains to be seen whether part-time jobs will also be available under improved economic conditions.

There has been an increasing trend in favour of early retirement with actuarially reduced benefits in many of the developed countries. In several countries, such as the US and the Federal Republic of Germany, the majority of new applicants for social security have chosen to retire before the normal retirement age. This trend has been encouraged by increases in social security benefits and confidence in the future purchasing power of pensions. At the time of writing, however, there are already signs, e.g. in the US, that worries about the effects of inflation on retirement income are causing many to postpone their retirement.[13] It remains to be seen whether this countervailing trend will become strong enough to overcome the trend towards earlier and earlier retirement.

11.2.8 Employment of the Elderly

While labour-force participation among the elderly has been steadily declining in most developed countries, income from employment remains important to many of those that do continue to work. In general, the experience of the capitalist countries is that they have not been successful in opening up enough jobs to accommodate all those older persons who want either full-time or part-time work. Older persons tend to be neglected in both publicly-sponsored job training and retraining opportunities, and in counselling and other forms of assistance provided by employment bureaux.

The experience of socialist countries like the USSR is quite different. Because they suffer from labour shortages, pensioners have been actively encouraged to re-enter the labour force. However, it seems that unless serious attempts are made at job redesign or providing flexible work hours, additional pensioners will not be drawn to work by existing financial incentives.[14]

11.3 Health Care

11.3.1 Types and Extent of Coverage

Most countries provide health care for their elderly through the same system which serves all age groups, whether it be a national health service, a national insurance programme, private insurance programmes, voluntary sick funds or a public welfare programme. The US is one of the few exceptions, in that most older persons are provided health care coverage through *Medicare*, a form of national health insurance open only to those 65 and older.

Each form of health care coverage has its particular advantages and disadvantages for both the elderly and other age groups. It seems clear, however, that national health services and national insurance programmes provide more adequate coverage. The US, which still relies primarily on private insurance, was forced to adopt Medicare because of the inability or unwillingness of private insurance companies to provide good coverage for the elderly. And it has been Israel's experience that the elderly were under-represented in the voluntary sick funds – the primary form of health care coverage there – because of a tendency to reject applicants who might place a heavy financial burden on the system.

It should be noted that many countries have a combination of health care financing systems, although one tends to predominate, and that health care – at least under national insurance schemes – is often delivered by a combination of public and private resources. Moreover, the fact that a country has a good national health service or insurance programme does not necessarily guarantee adequacy of services, knowledge by the consumer of benefits available, equitable distribution of services, or comprehensive coverage of health care needs. In fact, several – if not all – of these issues remain unresolved in most of the developed countries.

In countries, such as the US, France and some provinces of Canada, for example, the fact that patients must pay a fee for ambulatory services – even though it may be partially or fully reimbursed later on – probably reduces access to health services for low-income elderly persons. In the UK, the Federal Republic of Germany and Poland, no payment is required by patients at the point of health care delivery, whether it be for ambulatory or hospital services. Most of the industrialised countries also exempt the elderly from further contributions to the health care system after retirement – with a few exceptions – e.g. the US and Israel.

Health care systems also differ in the extent of their coverage of health care needs. Britain's National Heath Service makes available at little or no charge to the elderly prescription drugs, optical and audio equipment, dental care, chiropody, etc. In the US, none of these items are covered under Medicare unless related to a hospital stay.

Long-term care, whether in institutions or the community, is another area where health care systems may diverge. In the US, Medicare covers skilled nursing home care for only several months following a hospital stay, and up to 100 visits per year by a certified home health aide. Individuals who require extensive institutional care must be pauperised before Medicaid, the health insurance for the indigent, will begin to cover long-term stays. At the other extreme are countries like the Netherlands where the Exceptional Medical Expenses Compensation Act covers many forms of institutional care from the day of admission. Patients are asked to contribute part of their pensions towards their care only after the sixth month.

11.3.2 Geriatric Medicine

While typically, the elderly are not differentiated as consumers for health care coverage in most countries, the fact remains that they are disproportionately large consumers of many forms of care. In Sweden, for example, people over 70 require 50 per cent of the hospital care, 25 per cent of all other forms of acute care, 30 per cent psychiatric care and 75 per cent of long-term care in institutions.[15] The preliminary findings of a longitudinal study being conducted in Manitoba, Canada reveal that it is a relatively small percentage of the elderly who consume the majority of health services. It is hoped that further analysis will provide more detailed profiles of those elderly most at risk.

A major consequence of older people's greater need for health services has been the development of geriatric medicine as a specialty in several countries, e.g. the UK, the USSR (Sweden has developed a specialty in long-term care). Geriatricians usually serve as consultants to general practitioners and work in geriatric departments of general hospitals. They provide acute, rehabilitative and some long-term care. The need for a geriatric specialty was seen to arise from the multiple pathologies that older people often experience, making diagnosis an especially important and difficult task, and from the close interrelationship of health and social problems commonly found among the elderly.

Solutions require an interdisciplinary approach, and geriatricians have learned the necessity of co-operating with other health care and social services personnel. Geriatricians, unlike general practitioners in many countries, recognise the importance of visits to the home of patients in order to determine, for example, the extent of the social supports available following hospital discharge. A study recently completed by the National Corporation for the Care of Old People in the UK found that the quality of aftercare for older patients following hospital discharge was much better in hospitals with geriatric departments than in those without any.[16]

It should be noted that, even in countries with a specialty in geriatric medicine, only a minority of the elderly ever pass through a geriatrician's hands. Only 14 per cent of hospital beds in the UK are geriatric beds![17] As a result, a complementary effort has been made in some countries to include training in geriatric medicine as part of the general medical school curriculum. The UK now requires a certain amount of course work in geriatric medicine care of all medical students; and in the US, a number of efforts have been undertaken to encourage medical schools to modify their curriculum in a similar fashion. Interestingly, the US National Institute on Aging has recently come out against establishing geriatrics as a separate specialty; instead, it urges that all primary care physicians and specialists be trained in the biology of human ageing and geriatric medicine.

Table 11.2: Patterns of Provision of Medical Care to the Aged in Various Countries, by Payment at Point of Delivery

	Ambulatory care	Hospital care	Prescription Drugs	Dental Care	Medical Appliances
United Kingdom	No payment	No payment	No payment	Contribution at the rate of 50% of costs, up to a ceiling.	Loaned by voluntary organisations or at a low price. Spectacles without payment, up to a ceiling.
Germany	No payment	No payment for 78 weeks every 3 years for the same disease, in a class C hospital.	No payment	Contribution at the rate of 1/3 of the costs.	Various rates of contribution in different sick funds.
France	Full payment	First month 20%; over 30 days or expensive care — no payment.	Full payment and reimbursement of 70% of the price, or 90% of the price of expensive drugs.	—	—
Poland	No payment	No payment	No payment	No payment	No payment
Yugoslavia	**No payment**	No payment	Contribution at different rates in the various Republics. No payment in Serbia.	Contribution at different rates in the various Republics. No payment in Serbia.	Contribution at different rates in the various Republics.

	Ambulatory care	Hospital care	Prescription Drugs	Dental Care	Medical Appliances
Canada	No payment or or payment with reimbursement of 85-90% at standard rates.	No payment or nominal payment ($1 per day for hospitalisation in British Columbia).	No payment in only two provinces.	No payment in only one province. Full payment in others.	
United States					
a) Medicare	No payment, or reimbursement at standard rates.	Nominal payment for 60 days hospitalisation for any disease, a smaller payment for 30 additional days. Partial coverage of physician's fees.	Full payment	Full payment	Full payment
b) Medicaid	No payment	No payment	No payment	—	—
Israel	**No payment.** Partial payment for house-calls.	No payment	Nominal payment of IL 1 for each drug prescribed.	Full payment	Full payment

Source: Abraham Doron, *Social Services for the Aged in Eight Countries*, Brookdale Institute of Gerontology and Adult Human Development, Jerusalem, Israel, 1979.

The USSR has established a number of geriatric consulting rooms in the larger towns where old people are treated and given instruction on preventive health measures. Retired physicians are widely used on a part-time basis in these out-patient clinics. In addition, the USSR has established specialised dispensaries for the treatment of chronic conditions, such as cardiovascular and gastro-intestinal disease, from which older people suffer in disproportionate numbers. They are encouraged to visit frequently in order to avert deterioration in their condition.

11.3.3 Long-term Health Care

Institutional Care. It would be hard to find an industrialised country that is not expanding its community services in order to avert inappropriate institutionalisation – both in recognition of the desire of older people to remain in their own homes and what is believed to be the lower costs of non-institutional care. Yet at the same time, most countries are finding it necessary to expand the number of long-term care beds because of the growing numbers of the very 'frail' elderly. Generally, about 5 per cent of the elderly population over 65 live in long-term care institutions in both Europe and North America – although the specific figure may vary by a few points in some countries.[18] In the Netherlands, concern over what was considered a high rate of institutionalisation resulted in a central referral system whereby every applicant for institutional care must undergo a diagnostic assessment in order to determine the most appropriate level of care.

Some differences among countries in financing long-term institutional care have already been mentioned. Another important difference is the auspices under which they are managed. Only in the US, Canada and Israel does the private, for-profit sector play an important role in providing long-term care beds. In other countries, nursing homes or skilled nursing facilities are managed predominantly by public or non-profit organisations. One result is that quality of care is generally higher in the public and non-profit homes because the ratio of staff to patients is relatively large, and they are paid at comparable rates to medical personnel in hospitals and other health-related institutions. This results in low personnel turnover and relatively fewer abuses than are reported in for-profit homes. Both Israel and the US have been intent in recent years to improve standards of care in private nursing homes; Israel has introduced a five-star rating system for private homes upon which the level of reimbursement per patient is determined.

Two observers of long-term care in a number of different countries, Robert and Rosalie Kane, also found a greater tradition of service in

European countries where the performance of menial duties did not preclude the development of warm and compassionate relationships with patients. On a more measurable level, the Kanes found that the usual approach to quality care was a structural one, 'One senses an almost tacit assumption that if adequate resources are provided (such as good facilities and staffing patterns), good care will result.'[19]

An issue of concern in most countries is the extent to which long-term care beds should be made available in retirement homes and other sheltered housing facilities as residents become infirm. It is generally recognised that older people do not wish to move far from their familiar environment; yet creating small nursing-home-like units within essentially residential facilities is not always economical. One result has been the expansion in Europe of multi-level care complexes which combine independent living units with sheltered housing and skilled nursing care units to which residents can move as necessary without having to move very far. A disadvantage is that such large complexes need considerable space, which is not often available in the hub of a town where most community facilities and amenities are located. If they must be located outside of town, the possibilities for integrating the elderly into the general community are lessened.

France is encouraging retirement homes to set up medical departments which can provide regular medical supervision and routine care to residents as they become more infirm, in order to avoid the need for transfer to other institutions. Insurance or welfare funds will reimburse the homes 44 FF ($11) a day for each resident cared for by the medical department. However, homes cannot have more than 25 per cent of their beds in the medical department.

While this change in regulations provides homes with greater flexibility, there has been some protest about the inequity involved in the fact that long-term care institutions are reimbursed 83 FF (almost $21) a day for elderly invalids who may be receiving comparable care to that of residents cared for in the medical departments of retirement homes.[20]

Another issue that has not been adequately resolved is the extent to which one mixes the physically frail with individuals suffering from dementia. The common practice has been to separate the two, either within the same institution or in separate institutions. The difficulty of attracting personnel to work solely with demented patients and the desirability of exposing the demented to a more normal environment are producing some rethinking about mixing these two populations together; such rethinking, however, has not yet resulted in widespread applications.

A number of countries are also experimenting with using skilled nursing facilities to deliver services to the elderly in the community. Norway is planning out-patient facilities in its nursing homes. In Denmark a number of nursing homes provide day care for both the physically frail and mentally ill persons still living in the community. Switzerland is contemplating similar measures in order to use existing facilities more efficiently, broaden residents' contacts with the community, and lessen fear among the community-dwelling elderly about one day entering a home. However, it has also been some countries' experience that community-dwelling elderly will avoid services emanating from a nursing home for fear of being identified with residents.

A number of countries are also concerned with inappropriate institutionalisation as a result of the way financial incentives are structured. When funding for different kinds of institutional care emanates from more than one source, incentives may be created to assign individuals to a greater or lesser level of care than required, because it results in less out-of-pocket expense for either the individual or the authority responsible for that individual's well-being. Examples of this have been found in the US, Canada and Norway – to mention only a few; all are concerned about rationalising their systems for long-term care.

A related dilemma is the need to place an individual in a long-term care institution because of the inadequacy of community services. The response in most industrialised countries has been greatly to expand community health services.

Community Health Services. The array of community health services serving the elderly is great; they range from payments to family members who care for an older relative to day hospitals, which provide many of the therapeutic services traditionally provided by acute core hospitals.

Countries such as Sweden, the Federal Republic of Germany, and the UK encourage family care of sick older persons under certain circumstances by providing them with special allowances. In Sweden and the Federal Republic of Germany the allowance is paid to the older person so that he or she can continue to exercise choice over who is to serve as care provider. France only provides an allowance for the care of those who become ill before age 65, although it will be extended if the illness continues beyond that age.

Other services which can be viewed as supporting the family in its care of the elderly include 'night-sitting' to relieve family members of caring responsibilities at night, and short-term admissions to institutional care for respite stays to permit family members to take vacations. Night-sitting is not yet very widespread, but more and more nursing homes and homes for the aged in many countries are providing short-stay beds for respite care.

In addition, the Red Cross in a number of countries is providing short courses to individuals responsible for the care of an invalid in simple home nursing procedures. Courses such as these and other forms of family counselling about caring for an older person are on the increase almost everywhere, and can play a very important role in linking the formal and informal support systems.

Home nursing is one of the oldest of community services and exists in all of the developed countries, although with greatly differing degrees of adequacy and availability. It is one of the health services mandated by law in the UK, along with the services of a general practitioner, health visitor and chiropodist. Home nursing can provide support to both the caring family and to the individual living alone.

Czechoslovakia has recently introduced the profession of 'geriatric nurse,' who works closely with two primary care physicians. She is responsible for home nursing and identifying older people in the community who require assistance – much like the health visitor in Scotland. In this connection, she works closely with the local social worker and visits old people living alone in order to monitor their changing needs. In case of need, the nurse can arrange for domestic help or placement in an institution. She also works closely with the hospital social worker when an elderly patient is discharged. The geriatric nurse works in a catchment area of about 7,000 persons.

While home nursing is a common service, physician diagnosis or treatment of patients at home is much less common. The UK and the USSR are two countries where such home visits are still relatively frequent – at least for older patients. In the UK, an estimated one-third of physicians' consultations with patients 65-74 years old takes place in their homes; this figure rises to two-thirds with patients over 75.[21] In the US, practically no home visits are made anymore, and in Sweden home medical care is considered inadequate.

The most sophisticated form of home health care is probably the *hospital-at-home*, now being experimented with in France, the UK and several other countries. Practically all forms of hospital care, except for surgery, can be made mobile and brought to the patient's home if called for. Hospitals-at-home cost less than full hospitalisation and may often be considered desirable over hospitalisation in certain circumstances – for example, where an older couple has been taking care of each other, and hospitalisation may precipitate a sudden deterioration in the spouse who has been left at home.

The UK pioneered day hospitals in an attempt to separate the custodial from the medical aspects of care; the idea has caught on in many other countries as well. Day hospitals can be free-standing, but are more typically situated in a hospital or nursing home. In Denmark, all newly-built nursing homes must provide 'day nursing homes' for older people in the community, which provide the same care and treatment as is given to residents.

Day hospitals can be used by patients recently released from hospitals or by persons seeking to avert hospitalisation. Transportation to the day hospital is usually provided. Day hospitals also afford opportunities for socialisation, and sometimes the line separating day hospitals from other forms of day care becomes quite thin.

The provision of these and other community services serves as an important back-up to families taking care of older relatives, and is believed to stimulate such care in the knowledge that help is available when needed. For individuals living alone, they permit continued community residence despite deteriorating health.

In some countries, such as the UK, community health services are provided at little or no charge to the older client. Eligibility is usually open to all; where scarce resources limit availability of services, priority is then usually given to low-income individuals. However, means tests are rarely imposed – unlike the US, where means tests are usually the rule. In Sweden, low fees are charged for many community services, but Sweden believes in supplying the retired with enough income so they can purchase needed services. In most countries with advanced welfare systems, health and social services are viewed as a right – lack of funds does not constitute a barrier to service.

11.3.4 Preventive Health

Besides an impressive array of institutional and community services, most countries also have adopted measures which can be considered at least partially – if not completely – preventive health measures. Taking the broadest point of view, social and recreational activities, exercise programmes and transportation availability all serve to keep the elderly active as long as possible, and hopefully ward off premature illness. Sweden very consciously plans to expand such programmes, with a particular emphasis on exercise as an important preventive health measure.

Although not typically considered preventive health measures, outreach and information activities to inform potential users of health and social services about the benefits to which they are entitled are essential. Many older persons suffer needlessly simply because of ignorance about the remedies available. Efforts like that of Sweden, which, in 1968, declared all benefits under the country's social insurance system available to individuals as of right, and ordered local governments to make citizens aware of their entitlements, are particularly dramatic forms of outreach. A less dramatic form of outreach in Sweden, which is being experimented with in other countries, as well, is the use of the postman, especially in rural areas, to check on the well-being of older persons on his route and to dispense information about available services.

In the Federal Republic of Germany, some cities mail out information about services available to the elderly as soon as individuals reach pensionable age.

The UK and especially Scotland, makes good use of health visitors to call upon older persons in the community to both provide general health education and detect early stages of illness. They are knowledgeable about community services and can provide the essential liaison between an older client and the bureaucracy. In parts of Scotland, health visitors regularly visit everyone over 70 years of age. Elsewhere, some localities maintain registries of elderly persons 'at risk', and their conditions are regularly monitored by people such as health visitors.

The USSR places great emphasis on preventive services. Physicians regularly refer patients to 'groups of health' which have been established in major towns. In these groups, older people obtain some education in maintaining health and hygiene, learn first-aid techniques, and are encouraged to exercise. The USSR also sponsors many 'health zones' or spas which are used by older persons and others to help maintain or restore health. Individuals who go to a health zone are prescribed a course of treatment, perhaps including various therapies, medications, exercise or a special diet – all under the supervision of a geriatric physician.

In the US, there are some interesting programmes being conducted by self-help groups with the intent of stabilising or improving health – if not total well-being. One group, for example, helps the elderly accept more health care responsibility for themselves by teaching them when it is appropriate to consult a doctor and to ask the right questions when they do so. Simple home procedures that can be taken during the course of an illness are also taught. In California, the SAGE (Senior Actualization and Growth Exploration) programmes introduces a variety of physical and mental exercises – many of them relaxation exercises – which have been successful in eliminating some of the aches and pains participants have associated with age, and at the same time have assisted in emotional and spiritual growth. Other self-help groups focus on particular health problems, such as stroke, diabetes, cardiovascular diseases, etc. They provide both emotional support and practical advice on coping with illness.

11.4 The Social Care Services

Closely linked to the community health services, in terms of their importance in permitting older people to remain in their own homes despite increasing infirmity, is what Sheilia Kamerman has called the 'practical helping measures', such as home help assistance, chore and escort services, laundry pick-up and delivery, meals-on-wheels or congregate meals, senior centres, telephone reassurance schemes, friendly visiting, transportation, counselling, information and referral, etc.[22] Unlike income and health services, social care services are just beginning to come into their own, as their importance, both as preventive health measures in a broad sense and in maintaining people suffering from chronic conditions in the community, is recognised. Before large numbers of people began surviving into old age, many of these services were only utilised on an *ad hoc* and emergency basis – mainly to support families where the mother, for example, was temporarily incapacitated.

While some countries have experimented with providing additional income in lieu of services on the assumption that the private market would respond to the demand, the experience has not been encouraging – private market forces have not been able to provide services where and when needed. Increasingly, countries like the Federal Republic of Germany have found it necessary to supplement private market forces with publicly-supported programmes. In fact, in Sweden and the UK certain social services, such as home help assistance, are required by law, although each local authority can still determine how and to what extent the services will be provided. (Meals-on-wheels or congregate meals, counselling, and information and advice services are likewise mandated by law in the UK.)

In France, each service area must provide at least three of the following services: pre-retirement training, home help assistance, home nursing, day centres, health education, telephone reassurance, hot meals, referral services and physical exercise.

In the US, States receiving funds under Title 20 of the Social Security Act must provide at least three types of community services to the low-income aged: information and referral (these are not means-tested); services to help the elderly remain or be reintegrated within the community; and other supportive services that contribute to adequate social adjustment.

Because many of these services are relatively new, countries still show great variation in their availability. The following table, for example, shows the great disparity in the provision of home help assistance, and even the countries with the greatest provision, i.e. Sweden, Norway and the Netherlands, do not think they are meeting the total need.

Table 11.3: The Ratio of Home Help per 100,000 Population in Selected Countries, as Reported in May, 1973

Name of country	Total population (in millions)	Number of home helps	Ratio/100,000 population
Sweden	7,968	65,700	825
Norway	3,851	22,231	577
Netherlands	12,878	52,130	405
Great Britain	48,988	67,439	138
Finland	4,688	4,556	97
Belgium	9,581	4,018	42
Switzerland	6,150	2,060	33
Canada	21,377	5,000	23
West Germany	58,653	11,203	19
United States	203,166	30,000	15
France	49,756	7,144	14
Israel	2,879	273	9
Austria	7,373	355	5
Australia	12,296	30	0.2
Italy	53,708	50	0.1
Japan[a]	107,372	9,220	9

[a] Japanese figures supplied by Mr Mikio Mori.

Source: International Council on Home Help Services (reprinted from *Home Help Services for the Aging Around the World*, the International Federation of Ageing, Washington, DC, 1975.

Home help assistance for basic tasks such as cooking and cleaning is probably one of the most important of the supportive services for the elderly, because it can really make a significant difference in whether or not they can continue to remain in their homes. (A study conducted in Manitoba, Canada, found that home nursing and home help assistance together accounted for 77.1 per cent and 37.6 per cent respectively of all the community services used by clients enrolled in the province's home care programme.)[23]

Most home help aides are middle-aged or older housewives who find the occupation ideal because of the little formal training that is currently required and the part-time nature of the work. Increasingly though, formal training is being provided which covers, among other subjects, the special needs of the elderly. With more and more women entering the labour-force on a full-time basis, home help organisers everywhere are concerned about their future supply of personnel. It is hoped that by upgrading the quality of the training for home help aides, more women (as well as some men) will be attracted to this occupation.

In another attempt to upgrade the status of the occupation and to make better use of the knowledge acquired by the home help aides, some local authorities in the UK are experimenting with using the home help aide as a key liaison person with the health services; she, after all, probably knows more about the home conditions of the elderly person than anyone else, and her input can contribute much, for example, to the development of a coherent 'after care' plan following a hospital discharge.

The functions of a home help aide may differ from country to country. In some, she is empowered to perform tasks that elsewhere would fall within the jurisdiction of a practical nurse. In others, she does not perform any heavy cleaning; a separate service may be organised for this purpose. In rural areas or where home help services are still undeveloped, neighbours are sometimes paid a small stipend to provide meals or cleaning services to older people living alone. In one rural village in Yugoslavia, for example, four or five unrelated older persons share one house together, and housewives from the village take turns in cooking and cleaning for them.

Regardless of the functions performed by the home help aides, there is no question that it is an expensive service. Several countries, e.g. the US and Israel, still tend to impose means tests before making in-home services available. However, in the countries with the most developed services usually only a small fee based on ability to pay is imposed –

the underlying philosophy being that some help assistance should be universally accessible regardless of income level. The need for continuing assistance because of chronic health problems is seen as no respecter of income differences, and even those older persons with good incomes cannot necessarily be assured of obtaining needed services through private market forces. Some jurisdictions, e.g. several local authorities in the UK – had even abolished the small fee previously imposed for home help assistance because the administrative costs of collecting them were greater than the income actually obtained, although recent financial legislation is now reversing this trend.

Finland is taking a different approach to keeping costs under control. Some localities have found it more economical to bring the elderly once a week or every two weeks to a service centre where many of their personal care needs can be addressed at one time – including the provision of a sauna! Japan, similarly, has several hundred large multipurpose centres complete with bathing facilities in recognition of the inadequacies of much of the private housing. Group services also have the advantage of providing opportunities for socialisation. The policy debate over the merits of group services versus individualised in-home services will undoubtedly continue and perhaps intensify in the future as budget constraints become more important.

Expensive as in-home services are, the belief exists that in the long-run they are less costly than institutionalisation. Manitoba, Canada, is one of the few jurisdictions that may actually have proved this to be true. The preliminary findings of an important research study conducted there found that in the absence of Manitoba's home care programmes, 70 per cent of the clients recommended for home care would have been institutionalised at a much higher cost than was spent for home care.[24] Individuals are accepted into home care only if they are found to be at risk of institutionalisation by the assessment team; it is not an open-ended programme; and individuals will be recommended for institutionalisation at the point that home care becomes more expensive than institutional care.

Home care and institutional care can substitute for each other to some extent. In Manitoba, the waiting lists for entry into institutional care were greatly reduced as a result of the introduction of the home care programme. However, institutional care continues to be necessary even with the best of community programmes, and most countries are planning an increase in long-term care beds to accommodate the anticipated larger numbers of older persons needing intensive levels of care. Most countries, though, have not thought out, as carefully as

Manitoba has, at what point home care should no longer substitute for some form of institutional care. Clearly, there is a time when one's home can become a 'mini' institution, and an individual's needs might better be met in a group setting that also offers greater opportunities for socialisation.

Another important community service for many elderly persons is meals-on-wheels or congregate meal sites which provide nutritious meals at low-cost. Meal services exist in practically all developed countries, and often utilise many volunteers. In the Federal Republic of Germany, many of the organisations providing home-delivered meals are shifting to delivering frozen meals and providing a small home freezer to clients if necessary. Their advantage over hot meal delivery is that a number of meals can easily be provided at one time, thereby reducing transpota-tion costs. The human contact that accompanied hot meal delivery can then be replaced with more 'friendly visiting' by volunteers. About one per cent of Germany's elderly are receiving meals-on-wheels; an esti-mated five per cent of those over 65 are considered needy.[25]

In Stockholm, congregate meals are served in school cafeterias after the youngsters have finished eating. Pensioners can go to the school of their choice after reading each school's menu in the daily newspaper.

Most countries also have large networks of senior clubs or senior centres which, besides providing recreational opportunities, can offer a wide range of services, including various forms of occupational and physical therapy, hair-dressing and bathing facilities, employment bureaux, etc. If they do not provide many of these services themselves, they may provide information and referral to other agencies or serve as a co-ordinating body for the range of services offered by other community groups. In the US, such broadly-focused units are called 'multi-purpose senior centers'.

Senior centres by their very nature offer group services; given the higher costs of individualised service, it is likely that their role in service to the elderly will increase. In South Africa, a number of social workers specialising in service to the elderly are already working from senior centres; it seems probable that, in the future, individual casework will primarily be reserved for crisis intervention situations.

Finally, information and referral services with an outreach compon-ent are crucial if the elderly are to take advantage of existing benefits and services. Even in countries with good community services, ignor-ance about entitlements prevents many eligible persons from utilising services. If ignorance is not a problem, feelings of pride may equally deter eligible individuals from utilising services, which many older persons view negatively as a form of welfare or charity. The UK has found this sentiment to be still strong among the elderly despite the abolition of demeaning means tests. Public education and counselling then become important subsidiary goals of information and referral services.

11.5 Housing

Housing is of course a basic need for everyone, but countries still differ considerably in the extent to which the public sector has assumed responsibility for providing adequate housing to its population, and especially the elderly. Housing is especially important to the elderly because they spend considerably more time in their homes than do younger age groups, and because the adequacy of their housing will impact directly and indirectly on the quantity and effectiveness of health and social services required or available. Generally speaking, the poorer the quality of housing, the greater the need for community services and institutional care.

Despite the importance of housing for the elderly in most countries, the elderly tend to live in older and more dilapidated housing, or they must spend a larger part of their income on good quality housing. In rural areas of the US for example, the elderly live in 40 per cent of the country's substandard rural housing stock, and nationwide, 40 per cent of elderly households would have to spend more than 25 per cent of their income to obtain unflawed, uncrowded housing, compared with only 20 per cent of younger households who would fall into the same situation.[26] In France, about two million units of substandard housing are occupied by elderly households.[27] These usually do not have interior toilets, a bath or a shower. In the Netherlands, 22 per cent of the elderly sampled in one study do not have a bath or shower, and 66 per cent do not have central heating.[28]

At the same time, the elderly are disproportionately represented among home-owners who have finished paying off mortgages. Despite this wealth in assets, they still often find themselves facing an income squeeze because of high property taxes and the need for continuous maintenance and repairs. Many live in homes that are too large for them once their families have moved out, and at a time when others are facing a housing shortage.

Countries are practically unanimous in reporting that despite these problems, the overwhelming majority of the elderly wish to continue living in their own homes as long as possible. Many kinds of measures have been adopted to allow them to do so, not only in respect of the elderly's wishes, but also in the belief that encouraging continued residence in the community is less costly than alternative forms of institutionalisation, and promotes integration in the community.

11.5.1 Measures Facilitating Continued Living at Home

Many countries provide low-interest loans which permit individuals to modernise or adapt their homes. France, for example, has set as a policy goal the rehabilitation of 200,000 substandard housing units a year, of which 60,000 are estimated to be occupied by elderly households.[29] Applicants eligible for rehabilitation loans include the owner-occupant, landlord or tenant. To get around the problem of the displacement of low-income elderly tenants when the landlord passes on the costs or rehabilitation in the form of higher rents, the French government provides monthly housing subsidies to cover the difference between the rent and the tenants' ability to pay. Sweden deliberately favours low or no interest loans to the elderly over other age groups for home improvements or modernisation, in order to prolong older persons' independence.

Rent subsidies are another popular tool which permit many older persons to live in quality housing which they could not otherwise afford. These subsidies are quite common in France, the Scandinavian countries, and some use is made of them in the US as well. In all the socialist countries, rent is quite nominal for all. (There, the major problem is a housing shortage.)

For home-owners facing high property taxes, many States in the US have adopted circuit-breaker legislation which exempt older home-owners from paying the full tax rate if their income does not exceed a certain level.

A variety of home chore and repair services also exist, sometimes under the auspices of the voluntary sector – especially in the US – at other times under the authority of local government. A particularly innovative example of this kind of service is Maintenance Central in Detroit (US), where skilled, retired workmen and their young apprentices bring the dilapidated homes of low-income elderly up to acceptable standards at no out-of-pocket to the home-owner. Many of these elderly home-owners were threatened with dispossession because they could not afford to bring their housing up to code standards on their own. (Maintenance Central is a non-profit association, funded mainly by federal government monies.)

Protection against eviction can also be very important to the aged. In the US where much of the rented housing is being rapidly converted to unit ownership, older tenants in particular suffer greatly because of their inability to purchase their unit or property elsewhere. New York is one of the first States to enact legislation prohibiting the eviction of tenants 62 years or older when their apartments are being converted to condominiums or co-operatives. (To become eligible, tenants must have lived in their apartment for at least two years and have a annual income of less than $30,000). In Düsseldorf, Germany, a landlord who gives notice to old or sick tenants must suggest places to which they can move, and investigate the suitability of new locations from both a physical and financial viewpoint. And in Coburg, Germany, a court has ruled that elderly tenants cannot be evicted from their homes if it would cause great hardship.

The problem of elderly home-owners living in houses that are too large for them, especially in light of housing shortages for others, is being approached quite imaginatively in some countries – mainly by voluntary organisations. Shared housing or taking in boarders – young or old – is becoming popular again. In the US, a number of agencies have been established whose mission is to match elderly home-owners with compatible others with whom they can share their housing. This solution provides needed financial assistance, companionship and alleviates housing shortages. Some of the successful experiments match older people living near a university with students who can also help out around the house.

Help the Aged, a large voluntary organisation in the UK, has adopted 'gifted housing' as one of its programmes to deal with large, under-inhabitated homes and the need for additional housing. Through this scheme, older people owning large homes donate them to Help the Aged which, in turn, converts them into rental apartments for other elderly persons. In exchange, the donors receive renovated apartments themselves in which they and their spouses can live rent-free for the rest of their lives. It also frees them of the burden of property taxes and the costs of keeping up large homes, and provides them with companionship and emergency assistance.

Finally, a problem that many rural elderly face is how to survive harsh winters in isolated homes that have inadequate heating and sanitary facilities. One novel solution is the *Home du Cameroun* in the Vosges in France that serves as a winter residence for such people. This publicly subsidised facility charges its winter residents about 25FF (six dollars or £2.50 sterling) per day for food, lodging, physical therapy, chiropody, hairdressing and participation in crafts and other recreational activities.

11.5.2 Newly Constructed Housing

Most industrialised countries provide incentives for the construction of additional housing for the elderly, although the extent of public sector participation differs considerably – from socialist countries where practically all housing is constructed through public agencies, to the UK, where almost half of all housing for the elderly is owned by local authorities, to the US, where public housing for low-income elderly remains very inadequate.

Many Western European programmes make extensive use of low-interest loans and loan guarantees to stimulate the construction of low and moderate income housing for their populations. In France, about 50 per cent of new housing programmes receive low-interest government loans at the commencement, which means that rent can be kept relatively low. For-profit developers can also draw on low-interest loans if they agree to devote a portion of a large project to non-profit housing. France requires builders of projects with more than 300 units to allocate at least 20 per cent of these to the elderly in exchange for low-interest loans. About 40,000 new dwellings have thus far been set aside for the elderly.[30]

In Denmark, specially-equipped apartments for the disabled are built into new housing developments so that handicapped persons can remain integrated with other groups for as long as possible.

In the Netherlands, a quarter of new housing starts are made possible by 50-year loans at below market interest rates, mainly to non-profit associations.[31] In addition, the associations will be reimbursed the difference between rent receipts and increases in operating expenses attributable to inflation. Loan guarantees up to 100 per cent are the second major source of funding for low-income housing in the Netherlands.

The private sector has taken the initiative in the US in building retirement communities, often in the suburbs of a large metropolitan area. These usually provide attractive housing with ample recreational opportunities for middle- and upper-middle-class retired persons. Such housing is popular with older people who wish to live with their contemporaries, although problems have arisen when residents become too frail to continue living in these communities. Retirement communities rarely offer a full array of social and health services. While samples of retirement communities can be found in some other countries, as well, they are not as wide-spread as in the US. (Still, only a minority of the elderly in the US have chosen to live in a retirement community.)

11.5.3 Shelter with Services

Housing that includes services has become a very popular form of housing for the elderly in many countries. In some, it is called congregate housing, in others sheltered, warden or adapted housing. Whatever the terminology, the concept is the same – to provide certain services, such as communal meals, alarm systems, laundry and home help assistance, recreational opportunities, etc. along with shelter. Sheltered housing can range from the *béguinage* in France – i.e. one or two-storey houses, integrated into predominately single-family neighbourhoods – to pensioners' hotels in Sweden with several hundred dwelling units. Efforts are usually made to place sheltered housing in areas with good access to transportation.

All or only one of the services mentioned above may be provided through sheltered housing. For example, warden housing in the UK typically provides only an alarm system, some communal rooms and a resident warden to handle emergencies. As many of the residents of warden housing have become older and more infirm over time, the need for additional services has also become apparent. In the US the construction of sheltered housing has been slow because of separate funding sources for housing and social services. The Department of Housing and Urban Development (HUD) has only recently agreed to experiment with the provision of services in HUD-supported housing for the elderly.

Denmark may be in the forefront of providing services with shelter to all age groups through what it calls collective housing. A collective house provides services, such as restaurants, cleaning, baby-sitting, laundry, etc. – in short many of the services that a hotel might provide. Collective houses are considered suitable not only for the elderly, but for families with two working parents and single persons as well. Shelter, services and inter-generational contacts are all made possible through such living arrangements. Residents of sheltered housing elsewhere are usually older than those remaining in their own homes; they, for some reason, have experienced difficulty in living on their own. However, they do not yet require the full range of personal care and health services that might be available in homes for the aged or nursing homes. And some fit older people move into sheltered housing in anticipation that they will require services in the future.

To some extent, the availability of sheltered housing will reduce the need for future institutionalisation. The degree to which this will take place will depend perhaps on the extent that some medical services are also available on the premises. The UK has projected a relatively small number of elderly persons requiring long-term institutionalisation over the next few decades, i.e. two-and-a-half per cent to three per cent of those over 65, but this presumes a considerable expansion in sheltered housing and other community services.[32] Given recent cut-backs in social welfare expenditures, as well as the increasing number of people over age 75, this goal may not be realised.

Sweden and the Netherlands are two countries which have placed especially great emphasis on what they call pensioners' hotels and adapted housing respectively. Currently, 15 per cent of the Netherlands' older population live in adapted housing; the goal is to have 25 per cent in such housing by 1985.[33] In both the pensioners' hotels and adapted housing, older people have self-contained apartments with bathroom and kitchenette facilities, and access to communal dining facilities, recreational opportunities, home help assistance, and perhaps some medical care. In many cases, these activities are also open to the eldely in the community.

The size of sheltered housing units can vary greatly. France is concerned with distributing its *foyers-logements*, as its major sheltered housing programme is called, throughout the community in order to facilitate integration with other age groups; *foyers-logements* are rarely larger than about 80 units. In the UK, similar concerns limit warden housing to about 30 units. In Sweden, on the other hand, pensioners' hotels are usually quite large – sometimes with several hundred units, and sheltered housing units often form part of a large complex which includes long-term care provision, so that residents do not need to move far away if transfer to a more intense level of care becomes necessary.

While the common form of provision in sheltered housing has been efficiency apartments or bed-sitters for single people, the adequacy of this standard has been questioned lately both in the US and the UK. Both countries are now considering using one-bedroom units as the minimum standard. The reduction in space that many residents now experience when moving from a house to the sheltered housing unit is often very hard to adjust to, and may discourage entertaining or socialisation on the part of residents.

Sheltered housing is more expensive than ordinary housing. In Sweden, about half of the residents receive housing allowances in order to meet their payments. In France, tenants cover about two-thirds of the cost of the *foyers-logements*; local government subsidises the remainder.

The financing of sheltered housing is usually made possible through low-interest loans to non-profit associations, although in France a developer may earn limited profits on the *foyers-logements* and still be eligible for a low-interest loan if a non-profit operator runs the project. In the Netherlands, special housing for the elderly is constructed by a national corporation, the *Nederlandse Centrale voor Huisvesting van Bejaarden*, on behalf of non-profit organisations or local government. Usually the management of the housing project is turned over to the originating sponsor. Adapted housing is also entitled to a subsidy of f2,000 (about $1,000 or £418.40 sterling) per unit if various architectural barriers are removed and additional special safety features included.

It is interesting to note that countries with services for the elderly still in their initial stages are learning from the experience of the developed countries, and are beginning to include sheltered housing units for the elderly in their housing policies. Hong Kong, for example, plans to include hostels for the elderly in all new housing estates, and will set aside apartments for single older people and couples.

11.5.4 Housing as a Form of Family Support

While relatively few older persons live with adult children in the Western industrialised countries, even if they wished to do so, they might experience difficulty because housing today is not constructed to accommodate the extended family. This is beginning to be a problem in many of the developing countries too, even though the extended family is still the norm. In Singapore, regulations now permit families taking care of an older relative to knock down the wall of adjoining apartments in the new housing estates so they can expand their space. In Japan, where approximately 75 per cent of the elderly do still live with an adult child – an anomaly among industrialised countries – the government provides low-interest loans to people who wish to add a room to their home in order to accommodate an old parent.

Perhaps one of the more novel solutions to intergenerational living is the granny annex or granny housing as it has come to be called. Examples can be found in the UK and Australia. In the UK, granny annexes take the form of bungalows or flats built to adjoin family homes or apartments. They are constructed by local government as a form of public housing, and permit older persons to live independently, but still close enough to their families so that the two households can exchange services. The experience to date has been encouraging.[34] For those choosing this housing option, it permits a rich and supportive environment.

In Victoria, Australia, the housing authorities have developed prefabricated units which can be erected on the land of an established home and connected to the sewer, water and electrical supplies of the main house. When the granny housing is no longer needed, it can be dismantled and removed, which is not the case with the British version. They have proved very popular, and the demand continues to exceed the supply.

11.5.5 Homes for the Aged

Most countries, including the developing countries, run homes for the aged, usually under the auspices of voluntary, religious or governmental bodies. These differ from other long-term care institutions in that they provide some forms of personal care but little medical care. While an increasing number also provide some medical care, residents must usually move to long-term care institutions, such as a nursing home or long-term care hospital ward, if their physical or mental condition seriously deteriorates. Residents are usually quite old, i.e. over age 80. In an increasing number of countries, applicants for admission to homes for the aged must undergo careful screening to determine whether they really require this more intensive level of care.

The standard of provision can vary considerably, from providing everyone with their own efficiency apartment, which residents can furnish as they will, to a more dormitory-like facility offering little privacy or personal choice.

A number of countries, such as Sweden and the Netherlands, have made a policy decision to phase out homes for the aged in favour of more sheltered housing projects and community services. Dutch policy-makers claim that homes for the aged encourage social isolation and dependency, and do not have the necessary flexibility to deal with increased frailty among their residents. They also cite the greater costs of homes for the aged over community services, such as home help assistance. Thus, even though the demand for admission into Dutch homes for the aged remains large, no new homes are being constructed. (About ten per cent of Dutch elderly now live in homes for the aged.) According to observer James Rubenstein, however, the Dutch government has not carefully considered the proper mix of services required by the elderly –its cost comparison of homes for the aged with home help services overlooks what may be differing needs on the part of the two populations being served.[35]

Countries that have a pluralistic population, such as Israel, the US and Canada, have found that homogeneity in the cultural and class background of residents of homes is positively related to life satisfaction, even it it does foster what some may consider undesirable segregation. A central referral agency in Glasgow, in addition, tries to match the personality of the applicant for admission into a home with that of the matron in charge. For such a system to work well, the supply of places must exceed the demand, even if only slightly.

There is little agreement among countries on the number of places required in homes for the aged per a given population; each uses a different standard, which is related somewhat to the provision of other housing and community services. Sometimes there is little to distinguish a home for the aged from a nursing home or a long-term care ward, except that they are usually under different administrative and financial auspices. This can produce either jurisdictional disputes or co-operation with the health sector. For example, to the extent that medical services are provided in homes for the aged, they may be financed and staffed through the health care system. However, if the subsidy is smaller than that provided to medical institutions for similar services, enmity may result.

Transportation

Transportation is another essential service for the elderly if they are to remain integrated in the community. Many transportation systems provide discount fares or even free rides to the elderly, and almost all of the developed countries have become conscious of the need to create 'barrier-free' transportation facilities for the handicapped, many of whom are elderly. Most countries now have legislation or regulations requiring that all new public facilities, including the major modes of transportation, incorporate barrier-free features.Some are also modifying existing equipment and installations.

In many areas of the world, however, public transportation is inadequate or inaccessible for older people. The public response in a number of countries has been to experiment with alternative modes. In the US, where much of the experimentation is taking place, many jurisdictions have developed demand-responsive systems – essentially special transport services, such as vans, jitneys, taxis, etc. which can practically provide door-to-door service. An alternative response has been the provision of *user-side* subsidies, which permit consumers to purchase transportation, such as taxi rides, at a discount. The County of Stockholm in Sweden also provides extensive demand-responsive and user-side subsidies for the handicapped. In 1977, 26 per cent of the

County's pensioners were making use of these special transport services.[36]

Tension continues to exist between spokesmen for handicapped persons, who insist that full equality in access to public transportation requires that all existing modes be adapted to the needs of the handicapped – a very expensive solution – and decision-makers, who, for budgetary reasons, tend to favour special transport solutions.

11.7 Leisure Opportunities and New Retirement Roles

At the same time that societies are exerting strong efforts to assure the basic needs of the elderly, such as income, health care and shelter, both the public and the voluntary sectors have developed a range of activities whose goals are to provide older persons with a meaningful use for their leisure time and an opportunity to remain integrated in the community. It is also recognised that continued activity is probably very important as a preventive health measure, and might reduce the need for more costly interventions at a later time.

11.7.1 Centres and Clubs

Centres and clubs can be found in all developed countries and some of the developing ones as well. They range from the traditional *noinjong* (pavilions for the aged) in Korea, which are basically meeting places for the elderly where they can socialise and play games or musical instruments, to the multi-purpose senior centres in the US, which offer a large variety of recreational and educational programmes, as well as a number of health and social services. There are some 5,000 senior centres in the US, some 10,000 clubs for the elderly in France and over 90,000 clubs for those over 60 in Japan.[37]

Important factors to consider when examining their provision are the hours they are open, the number of days open per week and the kind of population served. There is general agreement that, optimally, they should be open five or six days a week, and for the full working day. Many cannot meet these criteria for financial reasons. Japan's numerous clubs, for example, are open only an average of one or two days a month.

Centres have also been criticised because many attract predominantly the relatively fit and persons of middle-class background, i.e, those naturally inclined to remaining active. As a result, some have undertaken active outreach programmes in the community, and the movement in the US is currently examining ways centres can better serve the frail.

Clubs and centres also differ in the extent to which the elderly themselves take responsibility for running the facility. France recognises a gradation among its clubs according to the extent of 'self-rule'. At one end are those which offer relatively simple recreational activities dictated completely by staff. At the other extreme are clubs that are completely run by the elderly themselves, and which have opened themselves up to the community by, for example, sponsoring joint activities with other age groups or taking strong positions on various community issues.

The number of older persons participating in centre or club activities varies greatly. In the US and Japan, figures of 25 per cent and 50 per cent have been reported respectively.[38]

11.7.9 Educational Opportunities

While centres and clubs are certainly one source of educational opportunities for the elderly, an increasing number of other activities organised under different auspices are now appearing too. There are now some 60 *universités du troisième âge* (universities of the third age), mostly in Europe, but some also in Latin America. They are loosely modelled on the first of its kind which was organised in Toulouse, France, as an extension of the University of Toulouse's regular programming. Many of them do not, however, have a formal university connection, but simply provide an array of courses for older persons. A few offer courses to all age groups in order to encourage intergenerational contacts. Courses do not usually have any eligibility requirements, and are not taught with the same rigour or demands as are formal university courses. Grades and examinations have largely been eliminated. Courses can cover a great variety of subjects – from current events, to preventive health measures, to gymnastics. Fees are usually nominal. A study of those attending a 'university of the third age' in Warsaw indicated that feelings of loneliness and depression decreased among regular participants.

In Scandinavia, folk high schools and study circles provide the greatest number of adult educational opportunities. Study circles in Sweden are organised by local educational associations and pensioners' organisations. Many are subsidised by the local and national government. Popular subjects are civics and foreign languages, sometimes organised in conjunction with group travel abroad. The experience of Sweden has been that unless the government undertakes active outreach, these forms of adult education widen the learning gap in the community. It is those who are already relatively well educated who participate in the greatest numbers in continuing education opportunities. As a result, the Swedish government has identified older persons with no more than a seventh grade education as a special target group for outreach efforts by study circles.

In the US, several hundred state colleges and universities now permit older persons to take any regularly scheduled course at no charge if space is available. The response here too has been somewhat disappointing in that only the relatively well-educated and economically advantaged elderly are availing themselves of these opportunities. How to reach low-income elderly with more limited educational backgrounds has not yet been satisfactorily dealt with. Some colleges and universities are responding to this dilemma by taking their courses to where many older people congregate, such as senior centres and retirement and nursing homes.

A relatively new educational opportunity for the elderly in the US is the *elderhostel*, which offers older people a week-long educational experience on a college or university campus. Most elderhostels are organised in the summer when schools are underutilised and when elders are most likely to combine a learning experience with a vacation. Some elders travel across the US by going from one elderhostel to another!

Like the 'universities of the third age' in Europe, elderhostels provide a variety of short courses that involve no grades or examinations or special educational background. Fees are kept as low as possible. However, like similar educational opportunities elsewhere, elderhostels, by and large, attract an educational élite – over 80 per cent of the participants have some college education. For these people, the elderhostel has been very popular, and consideration is now being given to organising some educational exchanges with older people from other countries.

Pre-retirement Education. The importance of pre-retirement education and planning is recognised by geronotologists almost everywhere, but with few exceptions remains in early stages of development in most countries. Only the US, the UK, Ireland and Norway have national organisations promoting pre-retirement planning, but the percentage of persons reached by most of them remains small. Only in Norway is pre-retirement education becoming as common as orientation for new employees. And only in Norway is the national organisation promoting pre-retirement education a semi-official public agency. France is also stimulating pre-retirement planning by permitting the 1.1 per cent tax on payroll, paid by employers to fund lifelong learning opportunities, to be used also for pre-retirement education. There is little doubt that pre-retirement education will greatly expand in the future under the impetus of what is already happening in the field, and promotion by organisations, such as the United Nations and the Council of Europe, which have already recommended policy guidelines in this area to their member nations.

It has been the experience of some countries that the closer one is to retirement age, the more reluctant one becomes to undertake pre-retirement planning – a reflection of psychological 'denial' about the impending change in one's life. Considerations such as these have led planners to recommend that pre-retirement education be started a number of years before the normal retirement age – perhaps five or ten. Many have even advocated that knowledge about ageing and retirement be built into the children's school curriculums at a very early age. *Pro Senectute*, the largest voluntary organisation serving Switzerland's elderly, has distributed material about ageing to school teachers throughout the country for use in their classrooms.

There is also general agreement that spouses should be included in pre-retirement courses, and that such courses can be offered through a wide variety of settings, e.g. work, institutions of continuing education, community centres, etc. There is lesser agreement on the content of pre-retirement training. Some courses stick to conveying factual information about pensions and programmes that will become available upon retirement. Others also include material relating to psychological adjustments in retirement and new roles or activities that can be assumed. The length of pre-retirement courses also varies – from one-day sessions to even several weeks stretched out over a number of years.

Pre-retirement planning has been criticised by some as a means of increasing acceptance for the *status quo* as far as existing provision for the elderly is concerned. Norway is dealing with this charge by encouraging participants to become involved in promoting change following their retirement and pointing to inequities in the current body politic.

At this point, little is known about the long-range effectiveness of pre-retirement planning; in the short-run, evidence suggests that people do seem to have more positive attitudes towards retirement at the end of their courses.

Besides sponsoring pre-retirement courses, a number of innovative companies, such as Gillette France (headquartered in Geneva), permit their workers, starting at age 59, progressively to increase their leisure time until by age 64-5, they may take as many as twelve weeks off a year. The intention is to provide individuals approaching retirement age with a feeling of what greater amounts of leisure will be like, and stimulate them to explore hobbies or other activities that they may wish to continue in retirement. For similar reasons, Norway has, since 1976, provided workers over age 60 with an additional week of vacation a year.

11.7.3 Exercise and Sports

Exercise and sports activities for the elderly have also increased tremendously over the last few years.

Faced with an increasingly large older population, a number of countries plan to expand the number and kinds of exercise programmes that are offered to the elderly, with prevention of illness certainly as a major goal.

In Switzerland, the Swiss Union for Gymnastics for the Elderly has over 50,000 active participants and the Union forms the largest organisation within the Swiss Association for Physical Exercise.[39] In the Federal Republic of Germany, the Red Cross has trained 1500 leaders to conduct gymnastic classes for the elderly at their request.[40] Similarly, 2,000 dance leaders have been trained for work in institutions and senior centres.[41]

In Grenoble, France, the Association Sportif du Troisième Age (ASTA) has trained over 2,000 persons between the ages of 65 and 80 to participate in such strenuous sports as skiing, tennis, cycling, etc.[42] The emphasis is on training older people in groups so that they can draw confidence from each other and improve their performance. ASTA also trains persons who work directly with the elderly in retirement homes and clubs. ASTA found it could dispense with the screening programmes it originally required to determine whether participants were suffering from some health problem that might be aggravated through physical activity. Experience showed these fears to be unjustified. Among the active elderly, there were almost no conditions which would be worsened by exercise – on the contrary, they could only benefit from regular physical exercise. ASTA does, of course, take careful precautions to avoid unusual dangers and hardships in the sports it selects.

In the US, the Senior Olympics, sponsored by Senior Sports International, have taken place across the country for ten years now. Competitive events in a wide variety of sports attract adults from their mid-20s to their 80s. A recent addition to competitive sports for seniors in the

US is the National Senior Sports Association, which will organise regional and national tournaments in golf, tennis, bowling, fishing and other sports.

Preventicare, another carefully conceived exercise programme for older persons, has now been offered to several thousand older Americans, and the results of a preliminary study of Preventicare's effectiveness indicates that a large majority of the participants experienced physical, social and psychological benefits.[43]

11.7.4 Vacations

In a number of countries vacations are so highly prized by all ages, that special efforts have beem made to provide vacation opportunities for the low-income and handicapped elderly. Many localities in France subsidise vacation residences within France or in neighbouring countries. The experience of the Paris Bureau of Social Services has been that two weeks are optimal, and that elders seek activity, not rest, on vacation.[44] Not all municipalities impose means tests to determine those eligible to participate, but will subsidise those with low incomes.

In the UK, many municipalities also arrange discount vacations for low-income elderly. Eligibility requirements vary; in a few places, as many as ten per cent of the elderly, are reached.[45] A charity in the UK has also put together *jumbulances*, specially adapted buses, so that the severely handicapped and terminally ill may take vacations on the Continent with the help of accompanying staff.

In the Netherlands, a travel organisation, *Het Buitenhof*, specialises in planning vacations for psychiatric patients, including those suffering from dementia. Another organisation, the 'National Foundation for Vacations for the Elderly', has been established in the Netherlands to help plan vacations within the country. It provides advice and seeks to improve the quality of transportation and accommodation that serve the elderly.

Pro Senectute, Switzerland's largest voluntary organisation service for the elderly, provides a seal of approval to establishments within the country that provide good service to the elderly and handicapped. And in another innovative step, it has arranged vacations for residents of retirement homes by having them exchange their accommodation with their peers in some other area of the country.

Most European countries also provide discounts for the elderly on the state-subsidised transportation systems, such as trains and airlines. These benefits are extended to older people from other countries as well.

11.7.5 New Roles

Finding meaningful roles to play in retirement has been one of the greatest challenges posed to the elderly. Many respond by remaining active in the community in a wide variety of volunteer roles. In the US, Action, an agency of the federal government, sponsors several programmes for older volunteers in which thousands participate. Foster Grandparents is one of the most popular, and one that has spread to other countries as well. Here, volunteers are assigned to work on a one-to-one basis with children living in institutions or in other difficult circumstances. In British Columbia, Canada, a variation on this theme provides families with no grandparent or none living close-by with an adopted grandparent. It has been especially popular with single-parent families who sometimes have no other relations in the community.

Many older volunteers are also active in the Peace Corps and the Executive Service Corps. Both of these American programmes have been designed to provide specific technical skills to developing countries. Canada offers similar opportunities.

The Canadian government provides small grants, up to $2,500, to groups of at least ten older persons who will use the monies for some activity of use to the community. New Horizons funds have been used in a variety of ways – from expanding the programming of senior centres to community oral history projects. In the UK the national voluntary organisation, Age Concern, England, administers a similar scheme called Operation Enterprise.

France, in its current five-year plan, also makes small grants available to groups of older people to undertake a survey of needs among the elderly in their community. The results are then considered in programmes planning for that jurisdiction.

In many of the countries of Eastern Europe, retired volunteers are used as outreach workers to older people in the community, as well as in direct service provision. The USSR, for example, makes extensive use of the skills of retired doctors in its geriatric clinics.

In the UK, Age Concern is developing a range of schemes using volunteers in bereavement counselling, victim support (for those who have suffered from crime), hospital discharge and in other ways.

11.7.6 Self-determination

Perhaps the most exciting new role undertaken by the elderly is that of advocates on their own behalf. In the US, organisations representing the elderly, such as the American Association of Retired Persons and the National Council of Senior Citizens, have been active for years as lobbying groups for the passage of stage and national legislation that would benefit seniors. Pensioner groups in Sweden have also been very successful in obtaining legislative measures that provide income security and needed health and social services to the elderly. The Gray Panthers have taken advocacy one step further by linking up with younger age groups to protest against adverse societal conditions which victimise everyone.

The case of Sweden may be instructive for the evolution of advocacy by the elderly elsewhere. Once pensioners' organisations in that country obtained most of the social measures they sought, they turned their attention to obtaining representation on councils of the elderly at the municipal, county and national levels. These councils are consulted by governmental bodies on policy matters that will directly impact on pensioners' lives.

A number of German cities have also established elected councils of the elderly in order to encourage the retired to help themselves. Unlike the case of Sweden, however, pressure for the establishment of these councils has come mainly from politicians and professionals, who hope that increased participation by the elderly in decisions that affect their lives may decrease the risk of dependancy as they age, as well as improve the effectiveness of social programming.

In the US, 'silver-haired legislatures' have been established in a number of States, in which older persons who have been elected by their peers meet for several days to draw up a legislative agenda for the real State legislature to consider. Many of the priorities that have been set by the silver-haired legislatures do become law.

Several countries, e.g. the Federal Republic of Germany, the Netherlands, and France, have also enacted legislation requiring that all retirement and nursing homes have elected councils of residents to advise their administrators. In the US and Canada, such councils are also common, but not required by legislation. In a small number of homes, residents also serve on the board of directors where their ability to influence policy is even greater. The evidence, at this point, on the effectiveness of residents councils is still skimpy.

11.8 The Continuum of Care

While many of the services described in the above sections, are essential to older persons' being able to remain in the community, relatively few communities have them all in place and accessible to the elderly.

Where they do, lack of co-ordination between the health and social services, which are usually funded through separate agencies, or between the voluntary and public sectors, which often divide or share responsibilities for the implementation of services, leads to a less than comprehensive response to individual needs. Where services are carried out through multiple agencies, they are less likely to reap the benefits of economies of scale, and more likely to lack co-ordination and expert management.

Both the US and the Federal Republic of Germany have relatively underdeveloped services for their elderly populations – in large part because of the fragmentation of service delivery among many different kinds of providers, i.e. public, voluntary and for profit groups, and the ideological predisposition of maximising the role of the private sector and minimising the role of government. It should be stressed that a strong role for the private sector in service delivery need not preclude effective co-ordination, but it does require greater planning and monitoring.

Many cities in Germany are now experimenting with *Sozialstationen* (literally social stations), which bring together public and private service providers in a central and easily accessible site, to which individuals with a variety of problems can come for services and advice. These stations serve all age groups. The Netherlands, whose voluntary sector also plays a strong role in service delivery, is establishing service centres throughout the country especially designed to cater to the medical, social, psychological and recreational needs of the elderly. Each is designed to serve about 400 older persons. Countries like Denmark and Sweden have for many years now had 'one-stop' service centres easily accessible to all age groups.

In the UK, personal social services are the responsibility of separate local governmental agencies. While 1974 legislation attempted to rationalise the delivery of health and social services, problems still remain in co-ordinating the two separate administrations in cases where people need both. Poland has tried to get around this problem by placing all its services to the elderly under one roof, i.e. the health ministry, but at the price of 'over-medicalising' services to the elderly.

What seems to be one of the more effective models in terms of co-ordination and comprehensiveness of services can be found in Manitoba, Canada, where all health and social services are funded from one ministry, the Department of Health and Community Services. A complete continuum of care for those at risk of institutionalisation is in place – from in-home services to several levels of institutional care.

Individuals are assessed by a diagnostic team and assigned to the most appropriate level of care. Because services are all funded from one source, it becomes easy to avoid setting up incentives which lead to the assignment of users to inappropriate levels of care – a common occurrence in many countries where multiple sources of funding lead to fragmentation of and inappropriate balances among services.

The minimum level of care that is required to obtain maximum user independence serves as an important operational guideline, and a built-in evaluation process assures changes in the formula of care with changing circumstances. While Manitoba's services are centrally administered, their implementation is decentralised, and a wide variety of service providers and community resources, including volunteers, can be tapped as needed. Manitoba's experience has been that the ages at which older people really begin to make serious demands on its welfare system are 79-80 for men and 84-5 for women.[46] Norway's experience is similar.[47] This is considerably higher than the age 75 used by policy-makers in other countries as the pivotal age for the start of high consumption of services.

11.9 Conclusion

While it is probably correct, as the Kanes have observed, that there is no 'single all-encompassing solution for the care of the elderly', the commonalities in approaches to their care by different countries certainly seem stronger than their differences.[48] There is general recognition, although it is not everywhere carried out in practice, that the need for chronic care by the elderly cuts across class lines and that services should be available to all without imposition of mean tests.

There is general agreement that a full continuum of care, incorporating many health and social services, is required if older people are to exercise the option of remaining in their own homes. And because health and social problems are often closely interrelated among the elderly, multidisciplinary assessments of older persons' needs become very important for the effective utilisation of services.

While the voluntary and private sectors can make valuable contributions to the care of the elderly, most countries have accepted the fact that significant public intervention is required in the areas of planning, standard setting and monitoring subsidies to the voluntary sector, and direct service delivery. This role is expected to increase as the population continues to age and as fewer informal supports –

especially in the form of caring daughters – become available.

Despite the great expenditure of money on services for the elderly, there has been surprisingly little research done on the impact, quality and effectiveness of health and social services, or client perception of and attitude towards these programmes. According to Kahn and Kamerman, 'the usual attitude is that most people know what services are good and needed, and that proof of service desirability or impact is not required'.[49] Stated another way by the Kanes, 'One senses an almost tacit assumption that if adequate resources are provided, good care will result.'[50] Curiously, the US has probably done the most research regarding services for the elderly, even though it has one of the more under-developed systems of health and social services in the industrialised world.

Not surprisingly, easy acceptance of programmes because they seem to work is being increasingly undermined by the economic constraints currently being experienced by practically all the industrialised nations. Questions regarding programme costs in relation to their effectiveness and alternatives are seriously being posed almost everywhere.

Both economic and demographic considerations will likely result in: expanded and more rigorous social geronotological research; greater emphasis on self-help by the elderly and in using them as service providers to their peers; more programmes to facilitate care of the elderly by the 'informal supports', i.e. family and friends; greater use of volunteers over the whole range of service provision, accompanied by closer links between the voluntary and statutory sectors; more rigorous assessment of older persons' needs; increased rationalisation of the whole service delivery system, including access, co-ordination and delivery of services; more sophisticated use of technology for the whole range of service-related functions; and finally, more options for the elderly to remain active in the community – particularly with regard to opportunities for flexible retirement. Hopefully, the combination of all these efforts will not only result in a more efficient use of resources by society, but will enhance the quality of life of the elderly and all those close to them.

Notes

1. A.J. Kahn and S.B. Kamerman, *Social Services in International Perspective* (US Department of Health, Education and Welfare, Washington, DC, 1978).
2. 'Utilization of Short-Stay Hospitals for the US – 1977, Annual Summary', *Vital and Health Statistics, Series 13-4*, (National Center for Health Statistics, Hyattsville, Maryland, USA, 1979); and Victor W. Sidel and Ruth Sidel, 'Medical Care in Sweden – Planned Pluralism', *Social Change in Sweden*, (Swedish

Information Service, New York, 1979).

3. *Social Protection and the Over-75s* (International Social Security Association, Geneva, 1979).

4. S.B. Kamerman, 'Community Services for the Aged: The View from Eight Countries', *The Geronotologst*, Vol. 16, December, 1976, p. 534.

5. E. Kreitler Kirkpatrick, 'The Retirement Test: An International Study', *Social Security Bulletin*, July, 1974, p. 3.

6. J. Schulz *et al.*, *Providing Adequate Retirement Income*, (Brandeis University Press, Hanover, 1974), p. 231.

7. S. Grad and K. Foster, 'Income of the Population Aged 55 and Older', *Social Security Bulletin*, July, 1979, p. 28.

8. M. Horlick and A.M. Skolnik, *Mandating Private Pensions: A Study of European Experience* (US Social Security Administration, Department of Health, Education and Welfare, Washington, DC, 1979).

9. S. Sternheimer, 'Retirement and Ageing in the Soviet Union: Who Works, Who Doesn't – And What Can be Done About It', unpublished paper presented at a meeting of the American Association for the Advancement of Slavic Studies, October 1979.

10. J.A. Califano, Jr, 'The Aging of America: Questions for the Four-Generation Society', *Annals* AAPSS, Vol. 438, July, 1978, p. 100.

11. *The Aged Today in Japan* (Japan Institute for Gerontological Research and Development, Tokyo, 1978). (The financial circumstances of the Japanese elderly are mitigated somewhat by the fact that most live with an adult child who earns considerably more.

12. M. Tracy, *Retirement Age Practices in Ten Industrial Societies* (International Social Security Administration, Geneva, 1979).

13. *The Wall St. Journal*, 5 November, 1979.

14. Sternheimer, 'Retirement and Ageing in the Soviet Union'.

15. Sidel and Sidel, 'Medical Care in Sweden – Planned Pluralism', *Social Change in Sweden* (Swedish Information Series, February, 1979).

16. *Organising Aftercare* (National Corporation for the Care of Old People, London, 1979).

17. *Profiles of the Elderly: Their Health and the Health Service* (Age Concern England, London, 1977), p. 4.

18. *Education and Training in Long-Term and Geriatric Care* (World Health Organization, Geneva, 1970), p. 3.

19. R.L. Kane and R.A. Kane, *Long-term Care in Six Countries: Implications for the US*, (Fogarty International Center for Advanced Study in the Health Sciences, US Department of Health, Education and Welfare, Washington, DC, 1976), p. 178.

20. *CIGS Newsletter*, November, 1979.

21. Kane and Kane, *Long-term Care in Six Countries*, p. 8.

22. S. Kamerman, 'Community Services for the Aged: The View from Eight Countries', unpublished paper presented at the US Western Gerontological Society's annual meeting, March, 1976.

23. E. Thompson and C. Motuz, 'The Manitoba/Canada Home Care Study: Some Preliminary Findings'; unpublished paper, presented at the Canadian Gerontological Association's annual meeting, November, 1979.

24. Ibid.

25. Kahn and Kamerman, *Social Services in International Perspective*, p. 296.

26. *Aging*, July/August, 1979.

27. J.M. Rubenstein, 'Housing the Elderly in France and the Netherlands', unpublished paper, presented at the US Geronotological Society's annual meeting, November, 1978.

28. J.M. Rubenstein, 'Housing Policy Issues in Three European Countries', unpublished paper, presented at the US Gerontological Society's annual meeting, November, 1979.

29. J.M. Rubenstein, 'Housing the Elderly in France and the Netherlands'.

30. Ibid.

31. Ibid.

32. S. Kamerman, 'Community Services for the Aged'.

33. J.M. Rubenstein, 'Housing the Elderly in France and the Netherlands'.

34. A. Tinker, *Housing the Elderly: How Successful Are Granny Annexes?* (Department of the Environment, London, 1976).

35. J.M. Rubenstein, 'Housing Policy Issues in Three European Countries'.

36. *Ageing International*, Spring, 1979.

37. US National Institute of Senior Centers (National Council on the Aging, Washington, DC); *Notre Temps*, October, 1976; Daisaku Maeda, 'Self-Defense of the Aged Through Old People's Clubs', *Defense of Ageing and Ageing, Mankind's World Problem*, (The International Federation on Ageing, Washington, DC, 1974).

38. US National Institute of Senior Centers; Maeda, 'Self-Defense of the Aged'.

39. *Zeitlupe*, June, 1975.

40. *Presse-und Informationsdienst der KDA*, October/November, 1977.

41. *Altenpflege*, November, 1977.

42. *Help Age International*, March, 1977.

43. F. Zeller and R. Knight, 'Preventicare's Impact: Preliminary Results of a Survey', unpublished paper, presented at the International Conference on Gerokinesiatrics (US), October, 1977.

44. *Années*, November, 1974.

45. *Age Concern Today*, Winter, 1973.

46. Thompson and Motuz, 'The Manitoba/Canada Home Care Study', unpublished paper presented at the Canadian Geronotological Society meeting, Halifax, Novia Scotia, 1-4 November, 1979.

47. E. Beverfelt, Norsk Geronotologisk Institutt.

48. Kane and Kane, *Long-term Care in Six Countries*, p. 170.

49. Kahn and Kamerman, *Social Services in International Perspective*, p. 18.

50. Kane and Kane, *Long-term Care in Six Countries*, p. 178.

References

Ageing International, Vols. 1-7 (The International Federation of Ageing, Washington, DC, 1974-80)

The Aging: Trends and Policies, United Nations, Dept. of Economic and Social Affairs, New York, 1975

Brocklehurst, J.C. (ed.), *Geriatric Care in Advanced Societies* (University Park Press, Baltimore, Maryland, USA, 1975)

Burgess, E.W. *Aging in Western Societies* (University of Chicago Press, Chicago, 1960)

Cowgill, D.O. and Holmes, L.D. (eds.), *Aging and Modernization* (Appleton-Century-Crofts, New York, 1972)

Doron, A. *Social Services for the Aged in Eight Countries* (Brookdale Institute of Geronotology and Adult Human Development, Jerusalem, Israel, 1979)

Exton-Smith, A.N. and Evans, J.G. *Care of the Elderly: Meeting the Challenge of Dependency* (Academic Press, London, 1977 and Grune and Stratton, New York, 1977)

Kahn, A.J. and Kamerman, S. *Social Services in International Perspective*, US

Department of Health, Education and Welfare, Social and Rehabilitation Service, Office of Planning, Research and Evaluation, Washington, DC, USA, 1976

Kane, R.L. and Kane, R.A. *Long-term Care in Six Countries: Implications for the United States*, Fogarty International Center for Advanced Study in Health Sciences, US Department of Health, Education, and Welfare, Public Health Service, National Institutes of Health, Rockville, Maryland, USA, 1976

McRae, R. *Elderly in the Environment – Northern Europe*, Florida Department of Health and Rehabilitative Services, Division of Aging, Tallahassee, 1975

New Directions in Social Policy – A Critical Examination of the Scandinavian Experience and its Lessons for the Region (International Council on Social Welfare, Regional Office for Europe, Paris, 1979)

Palmore, E. *The Honorable Elders: A Cross-cultural Analysis of Aging in Japan* (Duke University Press, Durham, North Carolina, USA, 1975)

Shanas, E. *et al. Old People in Three Industrial Societies* (Atherton Press, New York, 1968)

Teicher, Morton (ed.), *Reaching the Aged* (Sage Publication, Beverly Hills, California, USA, 1979)

Terris, M. 'The Three World Systems of Medical Care: Trends and Prospects', *American Journal of Public Health*, November, 1978

APPENDIX: THE INTERNATIONAL FEDERATION ON AGEING

In the last 40 years travel opportunities, exchange programmes and international conferences have all served to heighten interest in other countries and cultures, and the more practically-minded have also come to realise that there is much useful information that can be learned from other societies which has relevance to ones' own country. The field of aging is no exception. The *International Association of Gerontology* (IAG) was formed 30 years ago to further the exchange of knowledge in research on ageing among countries. It started with a very small membership and a heavy focus on bio-medical research. Over the years its membership has expanded greatly, and the social sciences have come more into their own. Not surprisingly, this interest in the social sciences has paralleled the growth of services to the elderly in all the developed countries of the world, and more recently in some of the developing nations as well.

Services for the elderly, including income, housing, health care, education, employment, the personal social services – such as home help assistance, meals-on-wheels, etc. are furnished by a combination of public and private providers in most countries; the balance between service providers and the extent of service provision, of course, varies from country to country. In some countries, this expansion in services was preceded by a strong pensioners' or senior citizens' movement which lobbied aggressively for increases or improvements in programmes; in other countries, movements of the elderly, paralleled or followed the introduction of services to the elderly, which served to crystallise client-consciousness among seniors as a distinct group for some purposes.

In 1973, delegates from 17 national voluntary organisations, which either represented or provided services to the elderly on four continents, met in London to discuss the formation of a new international organisation which would more specifically address their needs for some international representation and the exchange of practical information on developments in ageing around the world. The result was the *International Federation on Ageing* (IFA), which was legally incorporated as a private, non-profit organisation in December 1973; today it has 50 member organisations from 30 countries and every continent is represented in the IFA.

What links all these organisations in countries at very different stages of development is a common concern for the well-being of the elderly; a recognition that because they are at different stages of development, they probably can learn much from one another; an awareness that voluntary organisations representing or serving the elderly have a very important role to play in assuring the well-being of the aged; and the realisation that membership in an international organisation can enhance the effectiveness of such voluntary groups within their own countries. Full membership in the IFA is open to national voluntary organisations that either represent and/or serve the elderly; associate membership is open to regional and provincial organisations, gerontological societies, governmental groups, and other international organisations. The IFA obtains its revenues entirely from dues, sale of publications and member subsidies.

The Role of Voluntary Organisations in the Field of Ageing

A pattern commonly found in many countries of the world when a social need first arises is that a voluntary organisation, such as a religious or civic group, will take the first innovative step to meet that need. While charity is not looked upon with much favour today as a means of meeting the income needs of the elderly, at one time in the history of many of the developed countries, such private donations were the only resources available for destitute older persons. Eventually, alms evolved into non-means-tested social security programmes related to the recipient's age or work history. In the developing countries of Asia, Africa, and Latin America a similar pattern can be discerned today. Often the only service available to destitute older persons is an 'old age home' sponsored by some voluntary group – usually church-related. Once a service has been found to meet a real and growing need, government will often step in by first, for example, establishing standards for programmes under the auspices of the voluntary sector in exchange for financial benefits, and finally assuming major responsibility for the operation, as well as making the service more universally available. For example, the voluntary organisations that form the *Hong Kong Council of Social Service* provide the only personal social services available to the elderly there. At the same time, the Council's persistent advocacy has led to the adoption of the first five-year plan for the elderly by the government. In Uruguay, the *Agrupación Nacional de*

Entidades Privadas Pro Bienestar Social del Anciano, another federation of voluntary groups, is itself trying to develop standards for the many privately-run homes for the aged in that country, and to promote day centres as a preventive measure against premature institutionalisation. Many more examples could be cited.

Even in the developed countries, where government provision for the elderly is widespread, voluntary organisations continue to play strong roles as advocates, critics of public policy, innovators, and as partners with government in the provision of services. For example, the Netherlands expects that by 1985, as much as 25 per cent of its elderly population will live in congregate or 'adapted' housing, yet the government has purposely chosen voluntary non-profit agencies as its instrument in constructing and operating such housing by making available to them long-term, low-interest loans.

Sweden and Norway have both institutionalised an influential role for the elderly at the national, policy-making level on social security matters and other public issues that will directly affect this age group. Both countries have established committees composed of representatives of pensioner organisations and governmental agencies to be consulted before new departures or proposals for change in existing programmes serving the elderly are submitted to Parliament. In Sweden and in some German cities, such councils of the elderly also exist at the municipal level.

And even though the common conception is that the private sector is non-existent or weak in socialist countries, it is voluntary organisations such as the *Volksolidarität* in the German Democratic Republic and the *Institutul National de Gerontologie si Geriatrie* in Romania which provide the bulk of the services available to the elderly or serve as a guiding force for the improvement in the well-being of the elderly.

Programmes and Activities of the IFA

Information Exchange

From the start, IFA has vigorously pursued its educational role of keeping its membership, and others interested in the field, informed about developments in ageing around the world that have policy or programme implications. *Ageing International*, IFA's quarterly bulletin, serves as a major vehicle in this information exchange, and regularly features briefs, articles, summaries of research studies, etc. with an emphasis on those ideas, trends, policies, and programmes that might have relevance in more than one country. For example, the fact that organisations in Germany have been shifting towards the delivery of multiple frozen meals in the meals-on-wheels service may contain some lessons for nutrition-providers in other countries; the effectiveness of one-stop service centres in the Scandinavian countries and Germany at which individuals may apply for assistance for their many related needs is worthy of notice from the point of view of service utilisation, programme co-ordination, and cost effectiveness; the policy choices different countries reach with regard to how they deal with the greater numbers of 'old-old' persons projected in almost all developed nations should interest decision-makers everywhere; and what seems to be an emerging trend toward lower birth-rates and greater prosperity in the villages of the world has significant implications for policy towards the elderly in most developing countries. News for *Ageing International* is derived from IFA's membership, its world-wide network of correspondents, and publications from many countries which regularly cover ageing topics. *Ageing International* is available to the public on a subscription basis and is published in four language editions: English, French, German and Spanish.

In addition, IFA has published a number of monographs and special reports which examine a particular issue in greater depth and wherever possible, from a comparative viewpoint. These include: *Home Help Services for the Aging Around the World; The Voluntary Agency as an Instrument of Social Change*; *Effective Advocacy on Behalf of the Aging*; *Aging in a Changing Village Society; A Kenyan Experience*; *Social Services for the Aged, Dying and Bereaved in International Perspective*; *Planning for the Aging in Local Communities: An International Perspective*; *Mandatory Retirement: Blessing or Curse?*; *Crime Against the Elderly: Implications for Policy-Makers and Practitioners*; and two resource documents: *International Survey of Periodicals in Gerontology* and *Comparative Gerontology: A Selected Annotated Bibliography.*

Conferences

Over the years IFA has sponsored a number of symposia and workshops, usually in conjunction with an international conference on gerontology or social welfare. In the former case, the primary purpose is to acquaint researchers more thoroughly with the points of view of the practitioner and the elderly client; in the latter instance it is to raise the consciousness of social workers to the special problems of the ageing. Recent topics for symposia included mandatory retirement – an issue of much interest to policy-makers in other countries, and one in which the US has taken the lead in terms of national legislation; and in conjunction with the *Federazione Nazionale Pensionati* in Italy and the UN's *Social Defense Center* in Rome, an examination of crime against the elderly, with specific reference to the Italian situation.

Advocacy

A major reason for the IFA's formation was the need for service providers and representatives of the elderly to be better represented at the international level where organisations like the UN, the *World Health Organisation*, and the *International Labour Office* were becoming increasingly interested in the subject of ageing, and holding a number of meetings at which internationally-recognised non-governmental organisations (NGOs) concerned with ageing could have an opportunity to submit their views. The IFA now has consultative status as an NGO with the *Economic and Social Council of the UN*, the *International Labour Office*, the *World Health Organisation, the UN Fund for Population Activities* and the Council of Europe, which permits it to make its members' views known.

In addition, the IFA is an active member, along with other internationally recognised voluntary organisations, such as *CARITAS* and the *International Senior Citizens' Association*, of the *UN's NGO Committee on Aging*. This committee counsels the UN on all its activities related to ageing. Recently it has been most active in promoting a *World Assembly on the Elderly* to be held under UN auspices. It made its views known to the Economic and Social Council and the General Assembly, and the NGO's urged their own member organisations to lobby their national governments for a positive vote. Although voting on a *World Year on Aging* has been deferred, there will be a *World Assembly on the Elderly* in 1982. It is now the task of the NGO Committee to advise the UN as to its nature and structure.

Another aspect of the IFA's advocacy function is to raise the consciousness of other international organisations whose members' activities can impact greatly on the well-being of the ageing. Religious and social welfare groups, for example, have been found to be practically oblivious to the special problems and needs of older people, not as a result of insensitivity, but because of simple ignorance. The IFA has found that the process of education about ageing is a continuous one, and that efforts must constantly be made to reach out to groups whose traditional concerns have not been with the elderly.

Although the majority of IFA's members come from the developed countries, IFA also feels it has a special responsibility to the developing nations where ageing is only beginning to pose problems. There are signs of strain both in rural areas, from which the young have migrated, leaving the elderly to fend for themselves, and in urban areas where the traditional extended family is breaking down, resulting in many destitute older persons. Social security is too often still in its infancy stage, and if there is any service for the elderly, it is likely to be an old age home under the auspices of a church-related group.

Yet the elderly represent the fastest growing age group in most developing countries, and by the year 2000 the number of the elderly there will practically double. In recognition of the small likelihood that the governments of many of these developing nations will be devoting more resources to the elderly any time in the near future, the IFA has been working towards bringing together in a few selected countries representatives of voluntary and governmental agencies and several native anthropologists in order to raise their consciousness about the needs of their elderly, discuss ways in which the features of the extended family that provide continuing care and support to older persons may be kept intact despite the pressures of modernisation, and set up some model projects which might involve public and private sector co-operation.

Consultation

Finally, the IFA provides whatever assistance it can to associations wishing to start or expand services to the elderly and members of the general public desiring to learn more about ageing in other countries.

Note

Enquiries about the International Federation on Ageing should be directed to:

1909 K. Street NW, Washington DC 20049, United States of America

CONTRIBUTORS

Dr Mark Abrams is joint Head of the Age Concern Research Unit since retiring from the Directorship of the Survey Unit at the Social Science Research Council. A former Fellow of Brookings Institute, Washington, he has worked with the BBC, the London Press Exchange and was Chairman of Research Services Ltd.

Dr Robert Butler, a distinguished American psychiatrist and leading gerontologist, is Director of the National Institute on Aging in Washington. He is author of the Pullitzer prize-winning study *Why Survive – Being Old in America* and co-author of *Sex After Sixty* and *Aging and Mental Health*.

Michael Fogarty is Deputy Director, the Policy Studies Institute and United Kingdom team leader for a six country study on the future of Retirement Age. He is former Chairman of the Liberal Party Social Security Panel. Publications include *Pensions – Where Next?* and *40-60 How We Waste the Middle Aged*.

Derek Fox is Principal Lecturer in Housing Administration at Trent Polytechnic following appointments as Director of Housing for Hammersmith and Fulham and Advisor on Housing Management to the Secretary of State for the Environment.

Sally Greengross is an Assistant Director at Age Concern England where she is responsible for field work, training, research and information services. Previous appointments have been in research, teaching in the social sciences and in work with young offenders in psychiatric units.

David Hobman is Director, Age Concern England. He is a former President of the International Federation on Ageing. Lecturer and broadcaster, he edited *The Social Challenge of Ageing* and is author of *A Guide to Voluntary Service, Who Cares* and *All Our Futures*, among many other publications.

Bernard Isaacs is the first holder of the Charles Hayward Chair in Geriatric Medicine at the University of Birmingham following a period in charge of the Department of Geriatric Medicine at the Glasgow Royal Infirmary. Publications include *Survival of the Unfittest* and *Recent Advances in Geriatric Medicine*.

Alison Norman is Assistant Director of the Centre for Policy on Ageing and has experience in psychiatric social work and journalism. She is author of a recent publication *Rights and Risk in Old Age*.

Charlotte Nusberg is a senior member of the staff of the International Federation on Ageing where she is editor of the bulletin *Ageing International*.

William Oriol is Associate Director at the International Center for Social Gerontology in Washington. This follows twenty years work associated with the Senate of the United States of America, including a period as Director of the Senate Committee on Aging.

Cherry Rowlings, a former Child Care worker, is now Senior Research Fellow in the Department of Social Policy and Social Work at the University of Keele. She has recently completed a book on social work with elderly people and is co-author of *Social Service Teams, the Practitioner's View*.

Olive Stevenson is Professor of Social Policy and Social Work at the University of Keele following appointments at the Universities of Bristol and Oxford. She served on the Royal Commission on Compensation for Personal Injury and the Government Enquiry into the circumstances of the death of the child Maria Colwell. She is currently Chairman of Age Concern England.

INDEX